As rigging improved, a good helmsman could keep a sailing vessel on course to within a half or even a quarter of a point. The card was further subdivided to cater for it but, as steam replaced sail, greater precision became possible and steering orders came to be given in degrees (0–360) rather than points. Cards often showed both. This rose was drawn by Dr E. A. Wilson, Scott's companion on his last journey, to illustrate a South Polar Times *article on the history of the magnetic compass.*

COMPASS ROSE

SOUTH BY NORTHWEST

SOUTH BY NORTHWEST

The Magnetic Crusade and the Contest for Antarctica

Granville Allen Mawer

This edition published in 2006 by
Birlinn Limited
West Newington House
10 Newington Road
Edinburgh EH9 1QS

www.birlinn.co.uk

First published in 2006 by Wakefield Press, Australia

ISBN10: 1 84158 501 7
ISBN13: 978 1 84158 501 7

British Library Cataloguing-in-Publication Data
A catalogue record for this book is available from the British Library

For Sarah, Mick and Charlotte

CONTENTS

PART TWO
The Second Crusade 1898–1914

List of Illustrations and Maps

Chapter 3

Chapter 4

Chapter 5

Chapter 6

Chapter 7

Chapter 8

I am but mad north-northwest: when the wind is southerly I know a
hawk from a handsaw.

Introduction

Before the men of Douglas Mawson's Australasian Antarctic Expedition left their winter quarters in 1912 – to head for the magnetic pole and other points south – they entertained themselves with a homemade burlesque. *The Washerwoman's Secret* told the story of Jemima, otherwise Princess of The Other End of Nowhere. As the title implied, all was not what it seemed.

They were not the first and would not be the last Antarctic explorers to feel that sometimes their activities were scripted by Lewis Carroll to plots written by W. S. Gilbert. In such a topsy-turvy land, where water came in the form of white rocks, where a night and a day lasted a year and where ground and sky often conspired to appear as one, an ordinary mortal seemed out of place. On such a bewildering stage, built to such a superhuman scale, it was to be expected that achievements would be dwarfed, with vanities and pretensions exposed.

The early explorers aspired to heroic epic, but few could altogether avoid comedy and tragedy. Not many reputations emerged altogether unscathed from an encounter with the Antarctic and, famously, lives were lost. For many, Antarctic history begins and ends with the race between Robert Falcon Scott and Roald Amundsen for the geographic South Pole. It has great emblematic value for the Western historical imagination – appalling conditions, noble ambition, hardihood, manly competition, self-sacrifice, and the triumph over adversity or, failing that, a tragic end.

And yet, seventy years before that Homeric age, there had been another race to the Antarctic. It also is a tale of ambition and achievement, and if it has failed to resonate in our own day it is not for want of epic quality, which it has in abundance. It lacked tragedy, at least during the event, but a far greater handicap was the absence of a winner. The result of the 1840–41 race between French, American and British expeditions for the South Magnetic Pole might still be in dispute to this day were it not for the balm of the Antarctic Treaty, which in 1959 suspended all territorial claims. And pessimists would argue that Jemima only sleeps until the treaty regime fails and snow-dusted claims of discovery and priority are again put forward in contention for her hand.

Even that great self-publicist Ernest Shackleton found it difficult to gain public attention in competition with the Amundsen and Scott stories. The minor characters of the heroic age had little chance. Australians, for whom Mawson is a national hero, might have heard of his solo trek to survival in 1913, but few would know that he and another Australian, Edgeworth David, with a lone Briton, were the first men to reach the vicinity of the South Magnetic Pole, and that they did it by the longest unsupported manhaul of the era of discovery. Still fewer would know that it was two Australians and a New Zealander, at Mawson's direction, who made the second attempt, from the opposite direction, four years later.

The story I will tell, of the quest for the South Magnetic Pole, is not only that of the origin of systematic Antarctic exploration, but of the pole's subsequent relevance to the progressive unveiling and claiming of the last continent. It will be seen that many men from many nations went in pursuit of a scientific phenomenon, only to find something rather more substantial in their way. Geographical discoveries along the Antarctic littoral became a consolation prize for early expeditions that failed to reach the South Magnetic Pole. The stories wind about each other in a double helix, the ladder links of which are the explorers and their armchair supporters. Claims, counter-claims and criticisms have echoed down the years, most virulently when information is scantiest. Although it may be foolhardy to say so if past commentaries are any guide, knowledge of the coastal topography and magnetic characteristics of Greater Antarctica (the continental mass which fronts the Indian and Southern Oceans) is now sufficiently extensive to resolve some of the controversies over Antarctic discovery which have festered for the past 160 years. And that also is part of the ambition of this book.

Some of the specialised vocabulary employed by nineteenth century seamen and polar explorers has fallen into disuse, but to disregard it would be a disservice, denying modern readers an opportunity to share the explorers' experiences in their own terms – to taste the salt and feel the pinch of hunger and cold. Even where the terms are distinctly archaic (for example, pulley-hauley), context will usually suggest meaning (it was slang for manhaul). Where it does not, reference should be made to the glossary.

Prologue

A Great and Dark Power

The calendar alleges that it is the first day of summer, but here, in the Canadian Arctic, the ice is still thick about the shoreline. A more inhospitable place than this limestone beach on the west coast of the Boothia Peninsula would be difficult to imagine, although three abandoned igloos testify that the Inuit call it home. The sky is a blanket of unrelieved overcast, and the landscape is empty save for a number of black dots pricked into the grey where the southern horizon should be. As the dots slowly grow, they resolve themselves into six men hauling a sled. These cannot be the Inuit unless the natives have taken to wearing the blue box cloth of the Royal Navy. At 8 am the party halts near the igloos. An officer unpacks a small box with a vertical tube on top of it. The box contains a magnetised needle that is free to move horizontally, suspended by a few fibres of floss silk from the top of the tube. There is no movement in the needle, irrespective of the direction in which it is pointed. Suspension by a single fibre, and then by one of flax, produces the same result: the needle cannot find north.

The officer unpacks another instrument: the dipping circle has its needle pivoted to swing vertically rather than horizontally. In action like a divining rod, it points downwards to the source of the earth's magnetic attraction. Less than a minute and a half from the vertical, he announces. He decides that camp will be made down by the shore. There it will not interfere with the magnetic observations he proposes to make from the igloos.

In the course of that day – 1 June 1831 – the officer, James Clark Ross, made six sets of magnetic observations, the middle pair of which gave him a mean dip of little more than half a minute from the vertical.[1] Whereas most of his readings were on the same side of vertical, which could have been instrument bias, one set was on the other side. He was experiencing the diurnal wandering of the pole. If this was not the North Magnetic Pole, it was as close to it as any geographical place could be for more than a few minutes at a time. The party raised a silk flag, solemnly took possession by naming the pole for King William IV, and built a cairn.

> Had it been a pyramid as large as that of Cheops, I am not quite sure that it would have done more than satisfy our ambition, under the feelings of that exciting day. The latitude of this spot is 70°5'17", and its longitude 96°46'45" west.[2]

Ross knew that he had not fixed a precise place for the pole and, indeed, that such precision might be beyond the capability of the instruments he had. He was conscious of the incongruity of piling rocks at a place that the pole might have merely touched in passing, but exploration had its conventions. The cairn would be of some significance should British title subsequently be disputed, and there was public opinion to be considered.

> . . . if popular conversation gives to this voyage the credit of having raised its flag on the very point, on the summit of that mysterious pole which it perhaps views as a visible and tangible reality, it can now correct itself as it may please; but in such a case . . . the very nonsense of the belief gives an interest to the subject which the sober truth could not have done.[3]

The magnetic pole might be intangible, but the expedition that had reached it was highly visible, and just the kind of enterprise to appeal to a public avid for tales of extreme exploration. Not the least part of Ross's achievement was to bring to public attention what would become known as the Magnetic Crusade. The movement was then regarded as something new – a modern scientific adventure – but in fact it was as old as the religious crusades and, like them, had a devotional object: in the humanist tradition of the West few artefacts are as revered as the magnetic compass. It is regarded as an invention that made it possible to spread the influence of Western civilisation across the face of the globe. The Age of Discovery would have been possible, but scarcely imaginable, without it. More important, the desire to understand magnetism as a natural phenomenon – the better to exploit it – was a powerful stimulus to the development of Western scientific method.

Knowledge of the attractive force of magnetite, known as lodestone, and of its capacity to impart that virtue to iron appears to have been widespread from an early date. Realisation that the force was also directive was more limited, confined to those who could suspend iron freely enough for the directive force to act. Whether Europe owes the concept of the magnetic compass to China and/or the Arabs, or came by it independently, is beside the point; it was the Europeans who refined it into a sophisticated instrument that was also robust enough to withstand the rigours of an ocean voyage. It brought greater precision to course steering than could be achieved by relying on the sun, the stars or the direction of the prevailing wind, and there was reassurance in the knowledge that the face of the compass, unlike that of the heavens, could not be obscured by cloud.

Yet even among the Europeans, something as useful for maritime conquest and commerce was long regarded as a trade secret – which is why its early history is far from clear. Suffice to say that it was in widespread use by the end of the Middle Ages and already at such a level of sophistication that Flemish and other makers felt compelled to make allowance, on the cards printed with the points of the compass to which they attached their magnetised needles, for its declination of a few degrees from the earth's axis of rotation. The cards then indicated true north, but the allowances were local and rendered a compass unreliable when taken far east or west of its point of manufacture.

Although Portuguese navigators sailing to the Azores and Africa were aware that the declination, or variation as mariners called it, was not constant, it was Christopher Columbus who first advertised the fact. Three degrees west of Flores in the Azores, on 13 September 1492, he found that there was no longer the easterly variation observable in Europe. Beyond this line of no variation his compasses pointed ever more west of true north. He could not correctly explain the phenomenon but, astute seaman that he was, saw that it might have potential for solving the navigator's most intractable problem, that of establishing longitude at sea. If the compass variation between known meridians of longitude were to be charted, a seaman could find his east-west position by observing the angle between the compass needle and true north.

Another secret of the magnetised needle was revealed in 1581. Robert Norman, a London compass maker, published an account of his accidental discovery of its dip, or inclination.

Havyng made many and divers compasses, and using alwaies to finish and ende them before I touched the needle, I found continually, that after I had touched the Irons with the Stone, that presently the north poinct thereof would bende or Decline downwards under the Horizon in some quantitie: in so much that to the Flye [card] of the Compasse, whiche before was made equall, I was stil constrained to put some small peece of Ware in the South part thereof, to counterpoise this Declining, and to make it equal againe.[4]

Norman had given no special thought to this until he was asked to make a particularly long needle – six inches of steel wire. He carefully cut it to length and centred it on its pivot. After magnetisation with the lodestone it dipped so far that he felt it necessary to cut away some part of the end to rebalance it, but he cut too much and spoiled the needle. 'Hereby beyng stroken into some choller, I applied my self to seeke further into this effect . . . Whereupon I made diligent proofs . . .'. For this purpose he invented the inclinometer, more commonly known as the dip needle, by mounting a magnetised needle vertically.

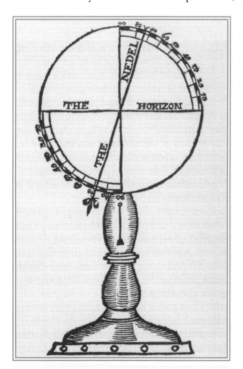

Norman invented the inclinometer to measure the dip of the magnetic needle.

Norman believed that directive force, both vertical and horizontal, was inherent in the magnetised needle. William Gilbert, physician to Queen Elizabeth, thought differently. He made a globe of lodestone and, after observing the effect on needles placed on it, concluded that the earth itself was a single huge magnet. Its North Pole attracted the south end of magnetised needles, and vice versa. At the Equator the forces cancelled out and there was no dip, neither north nor south, but at the poles the needles stood vertically. Like Columbus with the variation, Gilbert believed that his explanation of the dip would be of practical use in navigation: in this case the angle of inclination could be used to calculate latitude. There was now a valid theory by which the main magnetic phenomena could be explained, but it was incomplete. Gilbert himself believed that Columbus's line of no variation was where the magnetic attraction of the European and American continents cancelled out. On the lodestone globe the geographic and magnetic poles coincided. In the real world, clearly they did not (nor did the geographic and magnetic equators). There were many unanswered questions. Were the magnetic meridians regular arcs, like lines of longitude, as both Columbus and Gilbert assumed? Even if they were regular, were the magnetic poles antipodal?

In 1635 Henry Gellibrand, an Oxford mathematician, revealed an additional complication. He showed that the variation at London had reduced by more than seven degrees over the previous 54 years. Allowance had therefore to be made for movement over time – secular variation – in addition to movement in space. In the two hundred years that followed Gellibrand's demonstration of this variation of the variation, strenuous efforts were devoted to obtaining a sufficiently large body of observations worldwide for mariners to know how much variation there was at any particular point on the earth's surface and the rate at which it changed over time.

Henry Bond, writing shortly after Gellibrand, speculated that the magnetic poles slowly rotated around the geographic poles, and urged any navigator searching for a north-west passage into the Pacific to make magnetic observations for his own fame and for the honour of the kingdom. Although observations from the extreme north were few, there were none at all from the higher latitudes of the Southern Hemisphere, and into this void sailed Edmond Halley. Between 1683 and 1692 he had developed a theory on the variation which attributed it to the influence of four magnetic poles, two fixed on the earth's surface and two others revolving on an inner nucleus of the planet over a period of about seven hundred years. In 1698 King William III gave him a small vessel, the *Paramour*, to see if the theory could be refined sufficiently to determine longitude. Halley published his observations in the first map to show isolines, a type of presentation most familiar today in the weather charts that show isobars. Halley's map showed isogonic lines, lines of equal variation for the whole Atlantic and, although they were only valid for the date of his observations, they were a great advance in promoting understanding of the phenomenon. In particular, they dispelled the notion that the magnetic meridians might be regular arcs.

Additional confusion, however, was created by George Graham, a London clockmaker, who in 1722 was able to make a declinometer sensitive enough to show that magnetic needles were constantly in motion during the course of a day. Some elements of this variation were repeated day after day while others seemed random. Anders Celsius confirmed Graham's results by making similar observations at Uppsala in Sweden. Collaboration between the two also disclosed

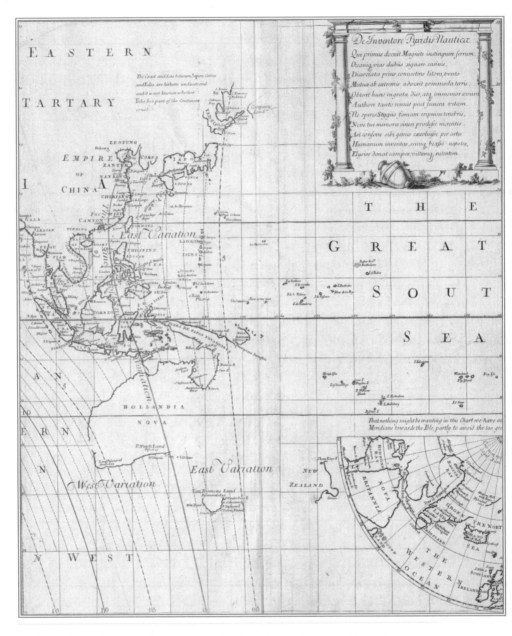

Edmond Halley's magnetic chart was the first in print to show isolines, but he 'durst not presume to describe the like curves in the South Seas, wanting accounts thereof'.

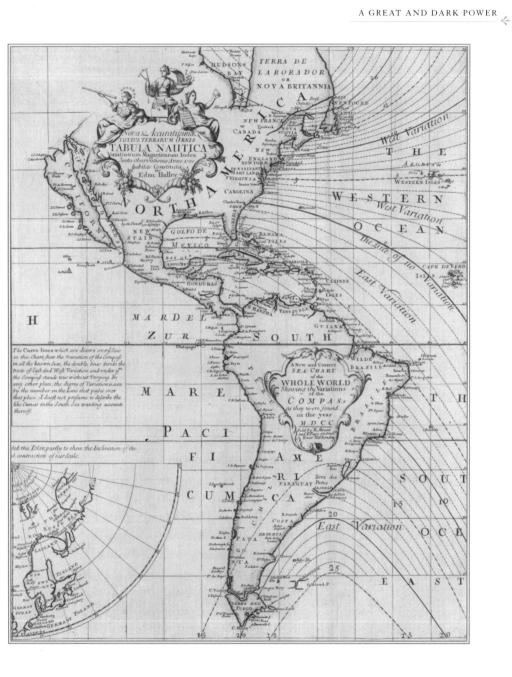

that the cycle of regular diurnal changes ran to local time in both places, but the irregular variations occurred simultaneously. Graham was also the first to realise that the time it took a dip needle set in the magnetic meridian to come to rest was indicative of, and could be used to measure, the differing strength (intensity) of the magnetic force at different locations.

Not until the circumnavigations of James Cook were there substantial numbers of observations from high southern latitudes in the Pacific and Indian oceans. The French also studied magnetic phenomena on their voyages of discovery, being particularly interested in Graham's intensity experiments. During the ill-fated voyage of La Perouse, the physicist Jean-Honoré de Lamanon used a dip magnetometer with its needle suspended instead of pivoted, thus reducing friction and allowing free oscillation. He made good observations of intensity in the horizontal plane, and from Macao wrote to inform the Academy of Sciences that the number of oscillations of the dip needle increased with latitude. Although he was killed in Samoa in 1787, Lamanon's observations were not forgotten.

Eleven years later a young Prussian inspector of mines named Alexander von Humboldt arrived in Paris intending to go on a private expedition up the Nile. His interest in magnetism was, unusually, not related to navigational matters: his lifelong study was the unity of nature and he sought to understand the relationship of magnetism to other natural forces. He met a boyhood hero, Bougainville, and learned that the great navigator was preparing to circumnavigate the globe and reach the South Pole. When Napoleon's invasion of Egypt precluded Humboldt's Nile project, Bougainville invited the young man to join his expedition. The Bureau des Longitudes encouraged him to accept. It saw in the expedition, and the Humboldt's expertise, the best prospect since Lamanon's death of obtaining reliable observations of magnetic intensity in both hemispheres at different latitudes. If all went well in the Antarctic, Humboldt would also be able to fix the position of the South Magnetic Pole. In the event Bougainville's expedition also had to be postponed because of the financial demands of Napoleon's Egyptian adventure but, undaunted, Humboldt took himself off to the Americas, and for six years, amid the pursuit of countless other scientific interests, he counted oscillations at 104 separate locations until he was satisfied that magnetic intensity did indeed vary, increasing from the Equator to the magnetic poles.

Humboldt's announcement of his intensity findings, and the nature of his own interest in the subject, signalled a shift in magnetic research. John Harrison's perfection of the marine chronometer in the 1760s had made finding longitude a relatively straightforward matter, if expensive, and although the pursuit of cheaper and simpler alternatives continued, it had become an issue of secondary importance. Humboldt might still urge the practicality of studying inclination as a means of determining latitude, as Gilbert had two hundred years earlier, but latitude had always been easier to find than longitude. And magnetic intensity was of little relevance to navigation.

Humboldt's own work seemed to indicate that the future of research into terrestrial magnetism lay in the realm of disinterested inquiry rather than as applied science. The mystery was not so much in the separate magnetic phenomena – declination (variation), inclination (dip) and intensity (strength) – as in their relationship to one other and to other natural forces, electricity in particular. Learned men all over Europe began collaborating but, while Humboldt kept on towards the goal of comprehensive terrestrial observation, many were tempted back into the laboratory by Hans Oersted's discovery in 1820 that the conducting wire of an electric circuit strongly attracted compass needles. The methodology of hypothesis and experiment increasingly drew electromagneticians away from their geomagnetic brethren, who continued for the time being to rely on observation and the inductive method.

As early as 1807, Humboldt, following Graham and Celsius, had advocated simultaneous observations at a number of locations in order to track changes in the geomagnetic field over time, particularly the irregular effects he called 'magnetic storms'. He also actively recruited colleagues to the magnetic cause and it was probably at Humboldt's urging that, in 1810, the Bureau des Longitudes asked its former secretary, François Arago, to take charge of the Paris Observatory. While there, Arago revived systematic magnetic observation. The Napoleonic Wars had precluded international collaboration on the scale sought by Humboldt, but in 1828 he arranged for simultaneous observations to be made at two sites in Germany – at Berlin and down a mine at Freiburg. By then Humboldt's international standing was so great that, in the following year, he was able to persuade France and Russia to establish collaborating stations in Paris and Kazan, each making observations on the common specified days nominated by Humboldt. So enthusiastically did the Russians embrace the cause that by 1835 they had eleven stations in operation, from Archangel and St Petersburg to Sitka (Alaska) and Peking. It was no small commitment; on the six so-called term days of each year observations were made simultaneously every five minutes of the 24 hours.

A conversion of even greater moment had taken place in 1828. Carl Friedrich Gauss, who in his day was regarded as another Archimedes or

Newton, had spent a number of weeks as Humboldt's guest at his garden observatory in Berlin. The instruments were explained to him and from that time the great mathematician's interest in magnetism was rekindled. In the 1790s he had studied it theoretically but had abandoned the subject for lack of empirical data, a deficiency that Humboldt's network of observatories promised to make good. Within four years Gauss had arrived at a method for measuring intensity absolutely, in units of mass, distance and time, rather than by comparison between the number of oscillations of the same needle in different locations. The observational technique devised with his collaborator, Wilhelm Weber, involved counting oscillations, as before, and then using the dipping needle to deflect a compass needle.

In 1834 Gauss and Weber opened their own observatory in Gottingen which, in the following year, became responsible for coordinating term days and collecting and publishing observations. Humboldt called their network the Magnetic Union, and at about this time its activities began to be referred to as the Magnetic Crusade. By the mid-1830s Humboldt had ambitions to see the union extended across the world. On 23 April 1836 he wrote to the Duke of Sussex, then President of the Royal Society, suggesting that the time had come for magnetic observatories to be established throughout the Empire on which the sun never set.

Unfortunately, the Admiralty, the only British institution capable of such a task, had little professional interest in magnetic research by the mid-1830s. As they saw it, the last practical problem presented by magnetism had been solved in-house. Matthew Flinders, during his epic circumnavigation of Australia in the early years of the century, had observed that a change in his ship's heading could produce significant variation in the compasses, and he correctly attributed this to iron aboard the ship. In a last contribution to his profession before his untimely death, aged forty, he demonstrated that these effects could be measured and taken into account if ships were swung at anchor through the 32 points of the compass and the change in variation noted in each direction. For the time being, until iron-hulled vessels appeared, this expedient sufficed and the Admiralty felt no compulsion to use expensive men and ships to pursue magnetic research in distant parts. It was the good fortune of British scientists, however, to be able to hitch their magnetic re-searches to a very active hobby-horse: after the defeat of Napoleon, Sir Joseph Banks, with the active support of the Admiralty's Second Secretary, John Barrow, had persuaded the government to resume the 300-year search for a north-west passage to Asia.

From 1818 onwards the British Admiralty sent a procession of futile and costly expeditions to the Arctic. Today they seem quixotic. It was obvious, from as early as the second attempt, that even if a north-west passage did exist it would not be a commercially viable route for sail-powered vessels. The most charitable explanation for Admiralty persistence is that the search was prompted by concern over the extent of Russian ambition in North America and how it might be forestalled. Be that as it may, for nigh on forty years gentlemen magneticians had unequalled opportunity to make observations in the highest northern latitudes attained to that time.

Many, including James Clark Ross, were young naval officers keen to seize any opportunity for distinction that peacetime service might offer. Their doyen, however, was a soldier, an artilleryman with a strong scientific bent. Edward Sabine used his status as a Fellow of the Royal Society to obtain the post of astronomer on the 1818 expedition. He and Ross first sailed to the Arctic in the *Isabella* under the command of the latter's uncle John. Sabine's main task was to conduct pendulum experiments which, by measuring gravitational force worldwide, would indicate the earth's shape more precisely. The voyage ended in acrimony when Captain John Ross turned back from Lancaster Sound, believing that its western end was closed. William Parry, his second-in-command, and Sabine were convinced that the unexplored sound was the long sought sea road to the Orient.

Sabine's enthusiasm extended to magnetism and, with the younger Ross, he made many of the observations during Parry's first Arctic command, which in 1819 was sent to correct John Ross's oversight. In the *Hecla* they penetrated through Lancaster Sound and Barrow Strait as far as Melville Island, passing on the way between the geographic and magnetic North Poles, thus becoming the first to see, insofar as the compass could be said to be working at all in the absence of much horizontal force, the north-designating end of the needle pointing to the south.

The observations made on this voyage consistently indicated that the North Magnetic Pole would be found somewhere in the maze of icy inlets, promontories and islands of the eastern Canadian Arctic but, as the pole was not near any of what were then thought to be possible north-west passages, no attempt was made to locate it. Sabine moved on, vibrating the pendulum and dipping the needle in more congenial climates until the army realised it was unlikely to get him back to service and allowed him leave of absence to become one of the secretaries of the Royal Society. Although far removed from the practical realities of regimental service, he rose to the heights and is thought to be one of the inspirations for Gilbert's Modern Major-General, whose only ignorance was of his profession.

> When I have learnt what progress has been made in modern gunnery,
> When I know more of tactics than a novice in a nunnery . . .[5]

When Sabine published his magnetic observations in 1825 he pointed out their incompatibility with the hypothesis of a single magnetic axis. The lines of equal dip (deviation from the horizontal) and equal force (intensity) were so different that the latter could not be computed as a function of the former. This he found coincided with views published by the Norwegian scientist Christopher Hansteen in 1819. In his *Magnetismus der Erde*, following Halley, Hansteen had postulated two magnetic axes or, strictly, four principal points of convergence in the direction of the magnetic needle, none of which was stationary. The northerly points he placed in the Canadian Arctic and Siberia. For the far south, his most recent observations were those made by Cook in 1773–74, which placed the points south of New Holland and Tierra del Fuego. If there were multiple axes, they were two in number, one between the stronger points, the other between the weaker. Three of the points appeared to be moving eastwards and the fourth westwards; beyond that little was known. Sabine concluded, as had Humboldt and Arago, that what was needed were more and better observations in the south.[6]

While Sabine was crusading in the learned societies, James Clark Ross had been pursuing his career in the ice. Three times he had sailed with Parry in search of the north-west passage, and with him had also attempted to reach the geographic North Pole. This expedition had dragged boats north across the ice to test a persistent notion that the pole was surrounded by open water through which the Pacific could be reached. All four expeditions had been failures, the most spectacular involving the shipwreck of the *Fury* in 1825. The Board of Admiralty was discouraged. Ross had sufficiently distinguished himself to advance from midshipman to commander, but the winter of 1827–28 found him, for the first time in a decade, without an Arctic expedition or the prospect of one.

Uncle John again took him up. John Ross had been knighted for his 1818 voyage but had not been further employed. He had smarted for a decade at the ridicule heaped upon him because he had turned back from Lancaster Sound after declaring it blocked by what he called the Croker Mountains. He had never forgiven his then second-in-command, Parry, for asserting that the sound was open, nor for subsequently demonstrating that it was. Now that there was no prospect of a further Admiralty expedition, Ross saw the field clear for a private attempt to salvage his reputation. He persuaded a gin manufacturer, Felix Booth, to provide funds and the Rosses, uncle and nephew, made ready to sail for Lancaster Sound with the intention of seeking a passage through its main southern lead, Prince Regent Inlet.

John Ross planned that the *Victory*, a tiny paddle steamer, would push its way through ice that had repeatedly resisted the sail power of much larger naval vessels. The visitors who came to farewell the expedition from London, among them Louis Philippe, Duke of Orleans, were unimpressed. The *Victory* proved incapable of more than four knots, sail-assisted, even when the engine could be made to work, which was not very often. There was a mutiny on the expedition's tender in Scotland and the season was already far advanced when, on 26 July 1829, the expedition sailed west from Holsteinborg in Greenland, not to be heard of again for more than four years.

John Ross found that his ship could not overcome the ice. In August 1829 the expedition was trapped in Prince Regent Inlet. His nephew was not one to remain inactive. He took to the land and, with the assistance of six Greenland huskies, made a number of unprecedented sledging explorations, some of which took him away from the security of the ship for a month at a time. He travelled far enough south to satisfy himself that information gleaned from the Inuit wintering near the ship was correct: in that direction Prince Regent Inlet was indeed a dead end. He crossed the Boothia Peninsula from east to west to discover Peel Sound, although he was unsure about what was land and what was sea.

> Those unacquainted with frozen climates . . . must recollect that when all is ice, and all one dazzling mass of white, when the surface of the sea itself is tossed up and fixed into rocks, while the land is on the contrary, very often flat . . . or when both are equally undiscriminated, as well by shape as by colour, it is not always so easy . . . to determine [which is which].[7]

Young Ross later followed the coast of Boothia south and west towards Point Turnagain, which John Franklin had reached overland from the south a few years earlier. He travelled light, and the only magnetic instrument he had on this journey was a compass. It pointed north-west, although without conviction because of the lack of directive force. From observations he had made coming south from Lancaster Sound, Ross was convinced that the North

Magnetic Pole, a secondary object of the expedition, was within reach. He was keen to make an attempt, but the summer of 1830 was spent in futile attempts to free the *Victory*. It was only when winter again shut them in that an excursion to the pole became a serious project.

With three seamen and the ship's mates, Thomas Blanky and Thomas Abernathy, Ross left the *Victory* in mid-May 1831 and proceeded west to Peel Sound. The season was hostile, and it was not until 28 May that they reached the sea. The dip was 89°41' and the horizontal needle pointed N57°W. Fortunately the coast appeared to trend in that direction and, if it continued to do so for another 35 miles, they could expect to find the pole on land. Four days march took them to the limestone beach. Its igloos caused Ross to reflect that it was as well that they were empty, as it would have been hard to account to their builders for his delight. They were, however, disappointing as markers.

> . . . I could even have pardoned any one among us who had been so romantic or absurd as to expect that the magnetic pole was an object as conspicuous and mysterious as the fabled mountain of Sinbad, that it even was a mountain of iron, or a magnet as large as Mont Blanc. But Nature had here erected no monument to denote the spot which she had chosen as the centre of one of her great and dark powers; and where we could do little ourselves towards this end, it was our business to submit, and to be content in noting by mathematical numbers and signs . . . what we could but ill distinguish in any other manner.[8]

For two-and-a-half years the achievement remained their secret. In 1832, after a second summer's effort to extricate *Victory* from the ice had failed, the expedition abandoned ship and began to walk home. Another winter trapped them at the beach on which James had been wrecked in the *Fury* seven years earlier. Without the *Fury*'s abandoned stores and boats they all would have perished. As it was, they had sunk to a deplorable condition before Lancaster Sound opened sufficiently to release them in the following year. When John Ross hailed a whale ship at the entrance to the sound and announced who he was, he was solemnly informed that he had been dead for two years. The astonishment of the whaler's mate at this resurrection was no greater than that of Ross when he was told the name of the ship; it was the *Isabella*, the whaler in which he and his nephew had sailed to the very spot fifteen years earlier.

On returning to London James Clark Ross was particularly pleased to find that, during his four years absence, Peter Barlow of the Woolwich Military Academy had collected all of the recent observations of compass variation in the Northern Hemisphere and charted the curves towards their point of convergence.

Ross's observations agreed with Barlow's implied point of convergence to within a few degrees, but in spite of this, and Ross's own disclaimer about precision, there was criticism in scientific circles. In an anonymous review of the voyage, Sir David Brewster queried whether observations made on the spot were better than those made at a distance, and whether polarity was definite or diffused, but he reserved his most scathing comments for the naming of the pole, pointing out that, were a Russian or French navigator to find it next year a degree to the east or west of the cairn, he would be equally entitled to give the new place the name of the Magnetic Pole of Nicholas, or of Louis Philippe.

> The magnetic pole belongs to science and not to courts . . . Our revered sovereign . . . is destined to be carried around the Arctic zone, pointed at by all the needles of all the world for nearly 2000 years, till he returns to Boothia Felix in AD 3725, unless he may have suffered dethronement in passing through the territories of other candidates for polar fame.[9]

Brewster's satire was misdirected. The French were still interested in magnetic exploration, but not in the Arctic. After the Napoleonic Wars their attention was focused on the tropics and the Southern Hemisphere. Magnetic research featured prominently in the instructions given to their captains. The Freycinet expedition (1817–20) was able to confirm that diurnal variation in the tropics was very small. Louis-Claude Freycinet made meticulous observations of the dip, but their lack of coherence prompted a committee of the French Academy of Sciences, with Humboldt in the chair and François Arago as secretary, to complain that his isolines formed 'such singular forms upon the globe, that it is scarcely possible to determine any points on them by interpolation'.[10]

There were not enough observations, and so Louis-Isidore Duperrey, Freycinet's subordinate, was sent back to make some more. He circumnavigated the globe in the *Coquille* (1822–25) and came back with the news that the magnetic equator crossed the geographical at only two points, which was reassuring news for those who craved symmetry in the natural world, but that the points were not antipodal, which was less welcome. Duperrey extrapolated his lines of variation to their convergence at the South Magnetic Pole, which he placed in 76°S and about 135–6°E. His associate and second-in-command, Jules Sébastien César Dumont d'Urville, was already well known as a scientific explorer in the Mediterranean. Dumont d'Urville's interests were botanical

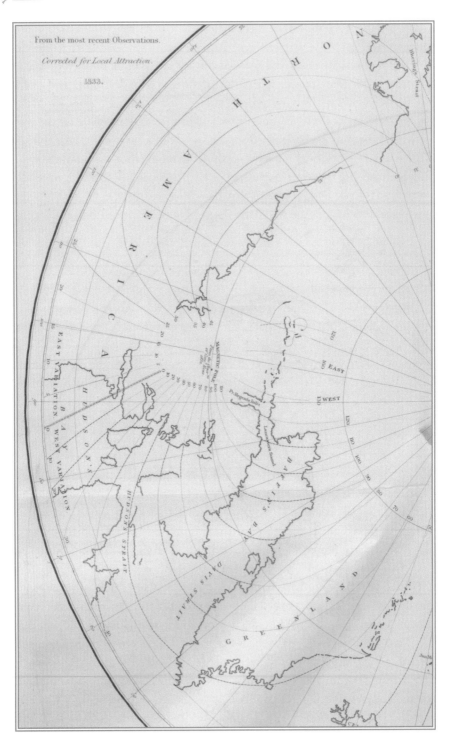

rather than magnetic, but his work was sufficiently impressive to earn him an expedition of his own. In 1826 he was given command of the *Coquille*, renamed the *Astrolabe*, and again despatched to the Pacific. Dip and intensity were conscientiously observed, but the popular fame achieved by the expedition derived not so much from its scientific work as from the relics it recovered from the wreck of La Perouse's ships at Vanikoro in the Santa Cruz Islands. Arago in fact thought that, by wasting time to satisfy popular interest in La Perouse, d'Urville had thrown away the opportunity to make a major scientific contribution. There was also public discontent that French navigators seldom matched the British in the significance of their discoveries.

In the context of British polar exploration, the achievement of James Clark Ross had been a welcome if meagre result from an otherwise disappointing search for the north-west passage. For scientists, his observations had definitely, if temporarily, located one end of the earth's magnetic axis. Their attention now turned towards the other Jerusalem of the Magnetic Crusade – the South Magnetic Pole. Across the Channel, the elevation of Louis Philippe from Duke to King as a result of the 1830 revolution had an unexpected consequence: French exploration would also be taking a new direction.

Opposite page: Barlow extrapolated isogonic lines towards the North Magnetic Pole to indicate a position that was later found to agree well with the observations of James Clark Ross.

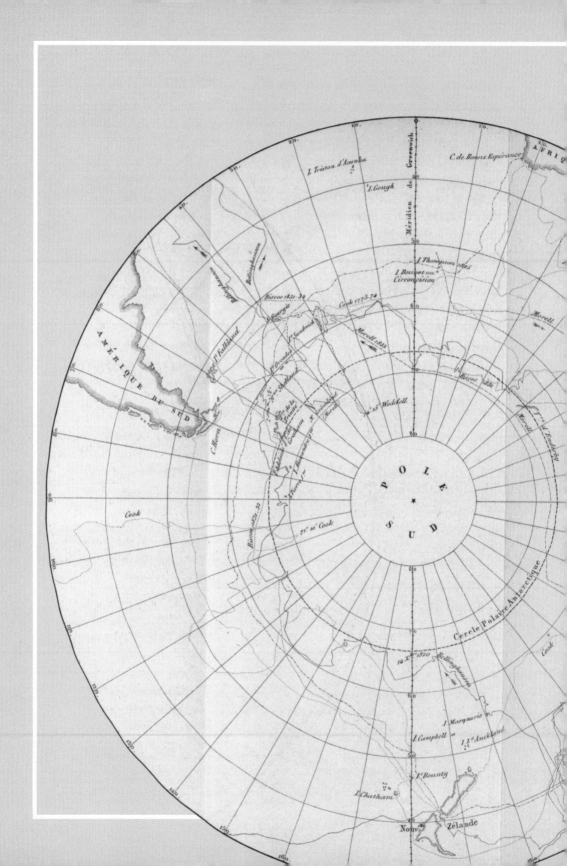

PART ONE

THE ANTARCTIC CRUSADERS 1837–43

Left: Antarctic exploration before the Magnetic Crusade.

PART ONE THE ANTARCTIC CRUSADERS 1837–43

	Jules Sébastien César Dumont d'Urville (France)	Charles Wilkes (United States)	James Clark Ross (Great Britain)
1837	To Southern Hemisphere		
1838	To Antarctic Peninsula	To Southern Hemisphere	
1839	In Pacific	Off Antarctic Peninsula	To Southern Hemisphere
1840	Discovers Adelie Land	Discovers Antarctic Continent	At Kerguelen Island
1841	*Voyage* publication begins		Discovers Victoria Land
1842	Dies in railway accident	Court martialled	To Falkland Islands
1843			To Weddell Sea
1844		*Narrative* publication begins	
1845		*Narrative* publication complete	
1846	*Voyage* publication complete		
1847			*Voyage* published

CHAPTER 1

Le Roi S'Amuse

The Norman family into which Dumont d'Urville was born in 1790 was sufficiently old and noble to have a very good opinion of itself, so much so that when the young naval officer married beneath him his mother neither forgave him nor acknowledged his wife. It was characteristic of the man that he regarded the matter as unimportant.

He failed to be accepted for the Ecole Polytechnique and, despite there being no seafaring tradition in the family, opted for a career in the navy. It was a strange choice for a young man to make after the humiliation of Trafalgar and at a time when Napoleon's army was at the peak of its glory, but in the views he expressed during the idleness imposed by the British blockade there is a hint of his motivation.

> I found that nothing was nobler or worthier of an expansive mind than to devote one's life to the advancement of knowledge. There was a feeling that my interests were pushing me towards the navy of discovery rather than the fighting navy.
> I was not afraid of battle, but a republican spirit could not see real glory in risking oneself and killing others for differences of opinions over things and words.[1]

Naturally uncouth, socially inept and contemptuous of the distractions pursued by fellow officers, he devoted his time to private study and, in the course of time, became a more than passable botanist. When Napoleon went into exile on Elba, d'Urville was an ensign in the ship that reunited Louis Phillipe, Duke of Orleans, with his family in Sicily. In 1817, when preparations were being made for the Freycinet expedition, he was disappointed not to be selected, but two years later he was assigned to the *Chevrette* on her survey of the Mediterranean islands. This was the start of his scientific voyaging and thereafter he was seldom at home until the return of his *Astrolabe* expedition in 1829.

It might be wondered how this private and disdainful man was afforded, in the absence of patronage, first, almost equal status with Duperrey on the *Coquille* expedition and, subsequently, command of the 1826–29 *Astrolabe* expedition. Ability had much to do with it, and the virtues of his vices. Even his enemies, and they were legion, had to concede that his coldness, his meticulousness and his inflexibility led to a single-mindedness that overrode all obstacles. The same, no doubt, could have been said of many French naval officers, but d'Urville also had the attribute that Napoleon valued above all others in military leaders – he was lucky.

In 1819 the *Chevrette* had anchored off Melos and d'Urville had gone ashore on one of his botanising excursions. He encountered a Greek peasant who had something to show him. He was led into a hole in a field where there was a niche of dressed stone in which stood the bottom half of a female statue. Where was the other half? The peasant took him to a cowshed.

> [The] two pieces seemed to me to be beautifully wrought. The statue . . . represented a naked woman, whose raised left arm was holding an apple and the right arm was skillfully holding a draped sash which fell casually from her hips to her feet . . . All these attributes would seem to fit the Venus of the Judgment of Paris . . .[2]

The peasant would have sold the statue to d'Urville on the spot but his captain decided that the ship had no suitable storage for the Venus of Melos and they sailed for Constantinople without it. There the matter would have rested but for d'Urville's sketches and the story he told to the French ambassador, who promptly sent his secretary and a naval vessel back to the island where they found the statue in the hands of a priest who had a Turkish buyer in prospect. A higher bid ensured that the statue was theirs, but a skirmish with Greek brigands on the way to the ship cost Venus her arms, which were never recovered. For his role in securing for the Louvre what was regarded in the nineteenth century as the most beautiful of all classical female nudes,

Dumont d'Urville, France's Captain Cook.

d'Urville was awarded the Legion of Honour and promoted to lieutenant. More importantly, he became known, although this was a mixed blessing for someone as prickly and ready to take offence as he.

After returning from the Pacific in 1829 he caused widespread offence by accusing the naval authorities of neglecting the claims of his expedition for reward and recognition, particularly promotion. Even after escorting Charles X, the last of the Bourbons, into exile in 1830, d'Urville found himself in no better favour with the new regime than the old, and in the absence of sea duty he had ample leisure to prepare his account of the *Astrolabe* voyage for publication. It was a productive estrangement. The thirteen volumes and four atlases were five years in the making, and were published by the government to such a lavish standard that they became the envy of scientific voyagers everywhere, in spite of the absence of significant discoveries.

For eighteen months after the completion of the great work, d'Urville was stranded in Toulon, underemployed on port duties and tormented by gout. He dreamed, literally, of returning to Oceania to make a third voyage of discovery like his hero Cook, but it was a disturbing experience.

> What was strange in these dreams was that they were always taking me nearer to the Pole and invariably ended by my ship running aground in narrow channels, on reefs, or even in ravines on dry land, where I would still be trying to sail her. However, while admiring the courageous efforts of Cook, Ross and Parry through the ice, I had never aspired to the honour of following in their wakes; on the contrary, I had always declared that I would prefer three years of navigation under burning equatorial skies to two months in polar climes.[3]

In January 1837 d'Urville wrote to the Minister of the Navy proposing a third expedition to Oceania under his command. The response was more than he bargained for. The Minister had consulted the King, Louis Philippe, who had added a proviso: the expedition should begin with an attempt to reach the South Pole. It seemed that His Majesty had been impressed by the claims of the sealers Weddell and Morrell to have approached as near to it as 74°S. Their accounts had also reached d'Urville. In 1823 James Weddell had confounded conventional wisdom about the impenetrability of Antarctic seas. Not only did he claim to have sailed three degrees further south than any other navigator, but he also claimed that his return was dictated by the state of his stores rather than the state of the ice. On the day he turned back, he said, the southern horizon had been clear with only a few ice islands in sight. Might it be possible to sail as far as the pole itself by following Weddell's track? Benjamin Morrell said that he had been nearly as far south as Weddell during the same season, but doubts created by his highly coloured account had discounted Weddell's claim as well as his own, the more so as no one had been able to emulate their success. Dumont d'Urville had reservations about Weddell, and distrusted Morrell as far as to decline the latter's offer of his services. There was much to consider. What if his ships were damaged on this excursion into the ice, aborting his own research program? But would he have a research program at all if he refused to attempt the pole?

I finally recognised that an attempt to get to the South Pole would have the character of novelty, of greatness and even of wonder in the eyes of the public, and which could not fail to focus its attention. 'People like to be astonished', Napoleon is supposed to have said, and never perhaps was there a truer axiom.[4]

Not all shared the King's enthusiasm. François Arago of the Paris Observatory, amongst whose wardrobe of hats was that of a deputy in the National Assembly, queried the utility of the expedition and its cost. He did so without reflecting on d'Urville, although earlier he had been critical of the meagre results from the previous expedition. Typically however, d'Urville chose to react as though it were a personal attack. In June and July 1837 there was an unseemly exchange of correspondence in the national press from which d'Urville emerged somewhat the worse for wear. The only weapon he knew how to use was the cutlass, and when he hacked about with it he left himself exposed to Arago's poignard: the unkindest prick was an observation that, while sailors considered d'Urville to be a botanist, botanists thought of him as a sailor. Fortunately for d'Urville, the King took little notice of the views of left-wing deputies.

Once he had decided to accept the expedition, d'Urville was no longer troubled by polar nightmares. They were replaced by more immediate concerns, such as a lack of essential reference works and charts. In April and May he visited London to make inquiries about the most recent discoveries in the Antarctic regions. He was received cordially by Francis Beaufort, hydrographer of the Royal Navy, and John Washington, secretary of the Royal Geographical Society, but felt that they regarded him as an interloper in a British field of endeavour. This is hardly surprising given that, even as they met, Captain Washington was urging a similar expedition on the British Government. During a dinner at the Raleigh Club d'Urville was assured that Weddell was 'a true gentleman' whose account could be relied upon. Beyond that, the British could tell him nothing more recent than Biscoe's discoveries in 1831–32, of which he already knew.

John Biscoe was a sealer and whaler employed by the Enderbys, a whaling firm which encouraged its captains to search for unexploited grounds in the far south. In a truly remarkable circumnavigation Biscoe had first taken the *Tula* and *Lively* south of Africa where, after flirting with the ice edge for many days, he sighted bare hills beyond and, proceeding east, discovered a coast which he named Enderby Land. From this coast, which he saw in 66°S and 47–49°E, he was forced north by bad weather and put into Hobart to refresh where, in one of those implausible encounters that are a recurrent feature of Antarctic exploration, he met and was assisted by Weddell. Resuming his southern campaign, he continued east in high latitudes until he reached the Antarctic Peninsula. This he named Graham Land. Biscoe was awarded the Royal Premium of the Royal Geographical Society, which saw in his discoveries the renewed possibility of an icebound southern continent, suspected by Cook but called into question by the open sea reported by Weddell.[5]

On his return to Toulon d'Urville found that work on his ships did not have priority, the only concern of the dockyard being to have them just ready enough to sail in time for the Antarctic season. Saws were fitted to their cut-waters but no attempt was made to harden *Astrolabe* and her consort, *Zélée*, for the ice. When they sailed on 7 September the ships were overloaded and the stores were in confusion, but the crews were up to strength and of reasonable quality, attracted by the promise of one hundred francs per man if they reached 75°S, and five francs more for each degree higher. On13 December they reached the Straits of Magellan and, to impress his men, d'Urville entered at night. He was rewarded by their consternation, which had the intended effect of establishing his credit as a navigator. With the excellent charts made by Phillip Parker King of the Royal Navy it was less risky than it appeared, but the crews did not know that. The ships were at Port Famine, within the Straits, for the better part of a month and left word in the sailors' post box announcing that they would be attempting the South Pole.

By 20 January 1838 they were 62°S, practically on Weddell's track and moving freely through drift ice. On the following day, however, they encountered a continuous barrier of pack ice extending from south-west to north-north-east. Dumont d'Urville called this barrier *la banquise*, using the cod fisher's term for compact, immobile ice fields. For three days the ships sailed east, hoping to outflank the pack but, unsuccessful, retreated north towards the South Orkney Islands. Bad weather pursued them until 2 February when d'Urville was again able to turn south, only again to encounter the ice barrier in 62°20'S. This time d'Urville looked for a weakness in the barrier and, finding an opening, pushed into it. It was a mistake. The ships found themselves in an enclosed basin, cut off by the wind from their point of entry. That night the ice hemmed in the ships and closed the only exit. On 5 February the expedition began efforts to break out to the north. Sailing when they could, cutting and hauling when they could not, the crews worked the ships through the ice. On the following day they cut only one mile in ten hours and scouts reported that, to the north, the pack was extending faster than the ships were able to work through it. A breeze from the east-south-east saved them; as it pushed the ice north the margin of the pack broke up.

Astrolabe and *Zélée* being freed from the ice near the Antarctic Peninsula, 1838.

To this point there had been no result for Louis Phillipe, and d'Urville felt that his own scepticism about Weddell had been justified. How could a barrier of the kind that they had just encountered ever be penetrated by ships? He bore away again to the South Orkneys and then to the South Shetlands. These had been discovered by sealers twenty years earlier, as had a vaguely known coast further south. By steering towards that coast from the east, d'Urville discovered the tip of the Antarctic Peninsula, although he mistook this land mass for islands. The first he named for his king, the second largest for the King's sailor son Joinville, and then, in early March, with winter looming and scurvy threatening, he turned the ships for Chile. As far as the pole was concerned, d'Urville had to concede that the campaign had been a complete failure. At Talcahuano the squadron encountered the British frigate *President*. The officer she sent across to offer the usual courtesies was quizzed by d'Urville for news of a proposed American Antarctic expedition which should by then have sailed. The British had no news of it.

D'Urville's instructions provided for the return of the *Zélée* to France at

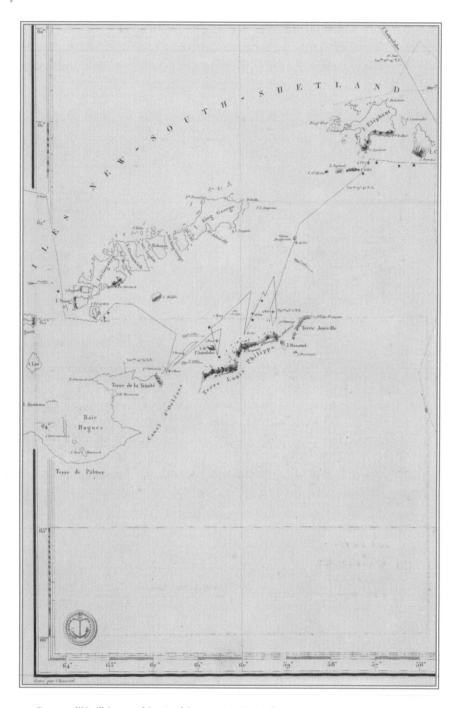

Dumont d'Urville's map of the tip of the Antarctic Peninsula.

the conclusion of the polar campaign, but gave him the option of retaining her services if he had use for them. He decided that he did, and for the next twenty months the two ships surveyed and researched among the islands of the Pacific and the East Indies. It seemed that the Antarctic had seen the last of them.

CHAPTER 2

America Ventures Abroad

In the 1820s the United States of America was the awkward adolescent of the family of nations. Conscious at once of cultural immaturity and enormous economic potential, and desperately anxious to be accepted as the equal of the European nations which had been its progenitors, the country fairly seethed with half-baked schemes for national glory. Few were more bizarre than the proposals of John Symmes, 'the Newton of the West', who was able to persuade a large number of otherwise rational people that the earth was open at the poles, and that it would be possible to descend to the globes within globes of which the earth's habitable interior consisted. This notion has echoes of Halley's floating magnetic core, but there is no evidence to suggest that he was Symmes's inspiration.

One of Symmes's acolytes, motivated more by opportunism than conviction, was Jeremiah Reynolds, an Ohio lawyer and newspaper editor obsessed with Antarctic exploration. He saw Symmes's followers as a lobby that would persuade Congress to authorise an exploring expedition. He and Symmes soon parted company, not least because Symmes was looking to the North Pole rather than to the south, but not before the idea of an expedition had taken root in Washington. Reynolds skilfully put together a coalition of interests. The

search for an open polar sea appealed to those hoping to improve interconti-
nental communication; sealers were attracted by the prospect of finding the
winter refuges of the fur seal; and Pacific whalers and traders were keen to
have the protection of the American flag. One of the arguments that Reynolds
put to the Secretary of the Navy was that 'nations as well as children must
have play things, and the exploring expedition will do for our country as well
as anything else'.

When it came to the point, however, Congress would not authorise the
construction of a purpose-built vessel. Not to be thwarted, the Secretary of the
Navy, Samuel Southard, plundered his repair budget to build a sloop of war
expressly designed for exploring service. In terms of funding appropriation, the
construction was accounted as a rebuild, although little other than the name
passed from the old *Peacock* to the new. A scientifically inclined lieutenant
named Charles Wilkes sought appointment as the expedition's astronomer.
Southard denied him the post but told him that he could go in another
capacity, a promise he schemed to translate into second-in-command. In the
meantime he began gathering the scientific instruments that the expedition
would need, but all to no purpose. Southerners inimical to federal activities,
especially those requiring expenditure, scuttled the enterprise in the Senate.

Reynolds was not deterred. He enlisted the help of Edmund Fanning, the
most eminent of American sealers, and assembled a 'South Sea Fur Company
and Exploring Expedition'. In October 1829 the expedition set out in the brigs
Seraph and *Annawan* and the schooner *Penguin*. Fanning believed in both the
open polar sea and an Antarctic continent, but his expedition found neither,
nor the seals which were supposed to finance the project. Reynolds left the
expedition before it returned to the United States and wandered in Chile for
two years. There would have been few to argue with Benjamin Pendleton,
captain of the *Seraph*, that polar exploration was beyond private means, but
there appeared to be no place for a public expedition, given the anti-government
and anti-intellectual rhetoric of Andrew Jackson's administration.

In this, as in other things, the Jacksonians were not quite as they represented themselves to their backwoods constituents. Back home again, Reynolds
was encouraged by a reference to 'diffusion of knowledge' in the president's
second inaugural address. He began regathering support and, as ever, skilfully
cut his cloth to the prevailing fashion. The administration had already been
urged by shippers and traders to send ships, including the *Peacock*, to the
Pacific to support American commercial enterprise. Reynolds prompted the
East India Marine Society at Salem to memorialise, or petition, Congress

about the natural and human hazards of navigation in the Pacific, particularly among the Fiji Islands. The memorial's tales of shipwreck and cannibalism captured the attention of congressmen and public alike, and if a surveying and protective expedition were to be sent, surely a few scientific men might be added to it at very little expense?

The cause prospered, and Reynolds was invited to speak in the hall of the House of Representatives on 3 April 1836. There he set forth his vision. National dignity and honour required America 'to throw back on Europe, with interest and gratitude, the rays of light we have received from her' and a demonstration of the country's capabilities would silence the taunts so long directed against the republic. The errors of former navigators would be corrected and 'there should be science enough to bear on every thing that may present itself for investigation'. One other thing: it should be possible to reach the South Pole by sea. One would not send an expedition solely for the purpose, but should it find itself in the vicinity why not make the attempt?[1] Land and sea became one when his imagination turned to contemplate the place itself.

> . . . to circle the globe within the Antarctic circle, and attain the Pole itself; – yea, to cast anchor on that point where all the meridians terminate, where our eagle and star spangled banner may be unfurled and planted, and left to wave on the axis of the earth itself! – where, amid the novelty, grandeur and sublimity of the scene, the vessels, instead of sweeping a vast circuit by the diurnal movements of the earth, would simply turn round once in twenty-four hours![2]

It was heady stuff, and Congress responded. Southard, now Senator for New Jersey, ushered an act through the Senate which authorised an 'Exploring Expedition (forever afterwards referred to as the Ex Ex) to the Pacific Ocean and the South Seas'. President Jackson was supportive, but in his Secretary of the Navy, Mahlon Dickerson, the expedition found an implacable enemy. Dickerson's opposition was partly ideological (he was a minimalist), partly temperamental (he was naturally indolent) and wholly political – Southard had long been his opponent in New Jersey politics and Reynolds had pushed a memorial through the New Jersey legislature against his wishes. If there were an obstacle that could be placed in the way of the expedition, Dickerson would find it. When the expedition's designated commander, Commodore Thomas ap Catesby Jones, suggested that he would need a frigate, two brigs, two schooners and a storeship, Dickerson referred Jackson to d'Urville's *Voyage of the Astrolabe.* See, he said, how much a small expedition can achieve: why so many ships for Jones? With impeccable logic, Jackson replied that with more ships the achievement would be greater. And if his old naval comrade from the Battle of New Orleans thought that more ships were needed, he should have them. Dickerson, an amateur botanist, also had no time for scientists with pretensions to professionalism; he would look to find whatever experts the expedition might need among the officers on the Navy List.

Construction of two brigs and a schooner to Jones's specifications commenced. They were to be strong enough for ice work, but buoyancy and speed should not be compromised by the additional weight of timber. Edmund Fanning saw the brigs on the stocks at Boston and predicted that they would easily be dismasted. A shakedown cruise to Mexico proved the point at the cost of jib booms and masts. Jones had the rigs altered and declared himself satisfied but there was a public perception of mismanagement. A year had gone by, there was no sign of the expedition sailing, and now news came that the French king had Antarctic ambitions.

Jones had control over the ships, but on personnel matters he was confounded by Dickerson at every turn. The Secretary refused to appoint the officers selected by the commodore, according to naval seniority, for command of the other ships. Appointment by seniority was not what Dickerson had in mind. He intended one ship for Charles Wilkes, brother-in-law to his friend Professor James Renwick, America's foremost magnetician. Another command had been dangled in front of Alexander Slidell, a popular author as well as a naval lieutenant, who Dickerson hoped would then also accept the post of historiographer and so squeeze Reynolds out of the expedition, in spite of Jackson's direction that Reynolds should be included and the public's expectation that he would be. Dickerson outmanoeuvered his chief by offering Reynolds the post of captain's clerk, which he knew would be refused. It was.

In June 1837, after Jackson had been succeeded by Martin Van Buren, Dickerson again queried the size of the expedition and the suitability of the Jones ships for 'high southern latitudes'. By emphasising the polar mission, which Reynolds had downplayed for fear of further Congressional attack by those who saw merit in island surveys but in little else, Dickerson was calling into question the very constitutionality of the expedition, which had been authorised under the commerce head of power. Even supporters were worried about the prominence given to 'a minor object of the voyage'.[3]

But it was just this lure of the unknown south that piqued the interest of others. As editor of the *Southern Literary Messenger*, Edgar Allan Poe soberly supported Reynolds's voyage of survey and observation on the grounds of its public utility, even though he doubted its prospects for discovery. Poe's other self, the feverishly imaginative storyteller, dashed off *The Narrative of Arthur Gordon Pym*, which – shipwreck, mutiny and cannibalism apart – owed much of its inspiration to Symmes and Reynolds. It purported to be the journal of a whaleman wrecked among white natives near the South Pole in 1827–28. Many readers refused to believe that it was fiction. The journal was tantalisingly incomplete, as 'two or three final chapters' had been lost. The entries ceased abruptly, leaving Pym and his companion in a boat that was being swept towards the South Pole.

> [It] is the more deeply to be regretted, as, it cannot be doubted, they contained matter relative to the Pole itself, or at least to regions in its very near proximity; and as, too, the statements of the author [Pym] in relation to these regions may shortly be verified or contradicted by means of the governmental expedition now preparing for the Southern Ocean.[4]

To counter the Secretary of the Navy's subversion, Reynolds ('A Citizen') went public and, in a correspondence with Dickerson ('A Friend to the Navy') that scorched the columns of the *New York Times*, destroyed whatever hope remained of his own participation. He upbraided Dickerson for allowing the French to steal a march through the personal interest of their king.

> Now, sir, does this account of the 'enthusiasm' of his majesty arouse no spirit of rivalry in your breast? Does it not suggest an occasion for the American minister of marine to do one act in his official career that shall save the pages of his biography from being assigned to the trunkmakers' and pastrycooks' shops.[5]

On the list of the Dickerson's crimes was his attempt to reduce the size of the expedition to that of the *Astrolabe*. Reynolds accused Dickerson of refusing to look further than the pretty pictures in the *Astrolabe* volumes, reminding him that, as far as Arago was concerned, d'Urville had voyaged for three years with his eyes and ears shut.[6] And why was this? Reynolds's answer was that d'Urville personally had to undertake too much – botany, entomology, meteorology, geography, historiography – and failed; 'and so will this expedition fail if you are permitted to cut it down and reduce its naval and scientific corps'. Dickerson was unkind enough to suggest that Reynolds saw the pole as a huge flagstaff, but rejoiced that at least this repudiated Symmes's theory that it was a hole sixteen degrees wide.[7]

For seventeen months Commodore Jones had laboured in the face of interference and obstruction. The climax came in November 1837, when he finally received the sailing instructions he had been seeking for months. There he read that a Navy chaplain was to be historiographer. There was no post for Reynolds, who had done all of the groundwork to recruit credible scientists, and with whom the commodore had been associated since the aborted expedition of 1828. It was too much. Jones resigned. Two days later news was received that the French expedition had sailed in time to attempt the South Pole that summer season, which was already too far advanced for an American effort.

Having crippled the expedition, Dickerson feared that he might be held accountable. If the acclaim with which officers of the expedition had been greeted when they attended the theatre in New York were any indication, there would be political damage in further delay. But Dickerson had been too successful in representing exploring service as degrading to naval officers. He offered command of the expedition to three other captains; all refused. By now Van Buren was nervous. He asked his Secretary of War, Joel Poinsett, to assist. Poinsett ordered a lieutenant to the command and had him promoted to captain only to have the man withdraw because, implausibly, his wife had met the news with a flood of tears. Those better informed believed that he was more likely to have been unhappy about being expected to dispense with the services of most of the scientists. Poinsett then offered the command to Captain Joseph Smith, who consented, subject to the appointment of Charles Wilkes to one of the other vessels.

Wilkes was in an interesting position. Jones's insistence on seniority for command had thwarted Dickerson, who initially had only been able to offer Wilkes the post of astronomer. Wilkes had refused, seeing in it

Lieutenant Charles Wilkes promoted himself to captain during the Exploring Expedition. Here he wears the uniform of a commander, the less exalted rank to which he was officially promoted a year after his return.

no chance for professional distinction, especially as all the other scientists were to be civilians, but again he accepted the role of instrument collector that he had performed in 1827. He reached London in mid-1836 and, like d'Urville nine months later, was received with the mixture of kindness and condescension reserved for foreigners who aspired to emulate British navigators. Gentlemen naturalists with priority on the order books of instrument makers were happy to yield to the American, and he obtained most of what he sought. The unfortunate exception was Mr Fox's dipping circle, which for sea use was the latest word in precision and durability. While in London Wilkes met most of the men prominent in navigation and physics, including James Clark Ross, who spent several days instructing the American in the use of magnetic instruments. Ross confided his own ambitions and plans for a south polar voyage to complete the chart of magnetic observations.[8] Wilkes was also honoured at a Royal Astronomical Society dinner meeting. The truth was that many of those who feted him hoped that the prospect of an American expedition could be used to shame the government into funding a British one.[9]

On his return to the United States in January 1837 Wilkes found that a professor from the Franklin Institute had been appointed to the expedition to direct the physical sciences. Wilkes was assigned to a survey of American coastal waters. In what can only be regarded as an act of spite, he diverted many of the purchased instruments to his own work and that of the magnetician Renwick, and when confronted with the reasonable request to restore them for their intended purpose, professed himself mortified. With this background, and still sore about the role of civilian scientists in what he believed should be as far as possible a naval enterprise, Wilkes refused Captain Smith's offer of a command and even denied the captain's request to be shown how to use the pendulum. Having so greatly exposed himself to humiliation, Smith withdrew, but Poinsett had been impressed by Renwick's recommendation of Wilkes's talents. Renwick assured him that not only was Wilkes pre-eminent in the navy for his hydrography and geodesy, but that in magnetism he had now surpassed his teacher, Renwick himself.

The recommendation was good enough for Poinsett, who was in danger of seeing his own reputation follow that of Dickerson. Inspired, desperate, or both, he offered Wilkes command of the whole expedition. Although Wilkes was forty years of age there was only one lieutenant on the Navy List with less sea service. It would be difficult to find lieutenants junior to him with sufficient experience to command the other ships. Wilkes's own enthusiasm for the expedition had evaporated as the muddle had grown. It was clearly a poisoned chalice that was being offered to him and he hesitated. Could the command be offered to more senior lieutenants first? Poinsett demurred – it was yes or no. Wilkes swallowed.

> I told him . . . I should not decline provided my views were to be carried out and the organisation placed entirely in my hands and under my control, that I would require of him a full explanatory statement of the reasons I had offered, and particularly those relating to my brother officers, and that I had made no influence to forward or interest to secure to myself the Command.[10]

The reply revealed the man: confident of his ability and with an inflated notion of his own importance, prickly and demanding. Poinsett was sufficiently anxious to overlook the presumption and Wilkes was given a free hand. He dismissed many of the civilian scientists; naval officers would perform all tasks related to the physical sciences, including astronomy, magnetism and meteorology. The frigate was dispensed with and two sloops of war, *Vincennes* and *Peacock*, substituted. Wilkes's former command, the *Porpoise*, replaced Jones's brigs. Two New York pilot schooners were acquired as tenders which, with the store ship *Relief*, made the squadron as large as the one Dickerson had objected to. Few of the vessels were in good condition for the arduous duty they faced, especially the by now decaying *Peacock*, but Wilkes was determined to get away from Washington, with its delays and backbiting, as soon as possible. Once under way they would make repairs as best they could.

Wilkes asked for a lieutenant senior to him, William Hudson, to be given the *Peacock* and made second-in-command of the expedition. Hudson agreed, subject to a formal declaration by Poinsett that the expedition was not military in nature, and to which therefore the normal rules of naval seniority need not apply. That did not save them from the wrath of the Navy's traditionalists, some of whom so far swallowed their distaste for the expedition as now to volunteer for command of it rather than see seniority violated. Poinsett stood by his man, and in five months the squadron was ready to sail. Wilkes drafted instructions for the expedition based on those prepared for Jones by the Department of the Navy and found them practically unaltered when they were formally issued to him. The constitutionality of polar exploration was glossed over in a neat ambiguity: Congress, the instructions said, had authorised the expedition 'in view of the important interests of our commerce in the whale-fisheries, and other adventures in the great Southern Ocean'.[11] 'Other adventures' could be read as a reference to non-whaling interests, for example sandalwood and *bêche-de-mer*, or to non-commercial adventures like those pursued by exploring expeditions. Was the 'great Southern Ocean' just another name for the South Seas or the Pacific, or was it the Antarctic ocean, where there were no longer any commercial interests since the seals, formerly the object of 'adventures' in the area, had been exterminated?

In only one matter did Poinsett disappoint Wilkes. The Secretary decided that to promote him to acting captain would be too inflammatory, and took refuge in a lawyer's opinion that long-term acting appointments were illegal. In one last incongruous reminder of the confusion and ill will that had so far dogged the expedition, six vessels of the United States Navy, ostensibly a commodore's command, sailed on 18 August 1838 in the charge of a junior lieutenant. A few days before their departure a New Haven whaler brought word from the Port Famine post box that the French had sailed for the Antarctic. The news was eight months old.

The Antarctic tasks that Wilkes had set himself in his instructions were few in number and precise. He was to get as far south as possible by following Weddell's track to the east of Palmer's Land (as the Americans called the tip of the Antarctic Peninsula) and, on the western side, by exploring in the direction of Cook's *Ne Plus Ultra*, the most southerly point reached by that explorer. That done, he should make an attempt to penetrate the Antarctic to the south of Van Diemen's Land (Tasmania) and as far west as 45°E, which was Enderby Land.[12] The attraction of Cook's mark of 71°10'S was not that it was a record – Weddell had bettered it – but the provocative hint left by that great navigator.

> That there may be a continent, or large tract of land, near the pole, I will not deny; on the contrary, I am of opinion there is; and it is probable we have seen a part of it.[13]

As the expedition sailed south through the Atlantic Wilkes found that there was real enthusiasm among his officers, glad to be off at last, and that even the handful of civilian scientists seemed to be settling in. It was a fund of goodwill that he wasted little time in dissipating. An early sign of what was to come was an edict frowning on officers' moustaches, which gave 'a notoriety and appearance of a want of attention to neatness, &c'. There was to be no unmilitary laxity on this non-military duty. His own appearance soon gave offence to some of his officers: one day, without warning, a commodore's broad pennant was hoisted to the masthead of the *Vincennes*, and Wilkes and Hudson paraded on their respective quarterdecks wearing the epaulettes and buttons of a captain. No one was to know that Wilkes himself had presumed to promote both of them in defiance of Poinsett's decision, because in this, as in almost everything else to do with the command of the expedition, Wilkes kept his instructions to himself. The government, anxious to prevent premature disclosure of discoveries, had sworn the expedition to secrecy, but the precaution meant little to Wilkes's officers; most of the time they did not even know their next port of call, much less the overall plan of campaign.

Wilkes had no experience of ice navigation and believed that late in the season he would be able take fullest advantage of the summer melt before new ice began forming. However, so much time had been expended on a mandatory search for Atlantic shoals that the expedition did not reach Orange Harbour in Tierra del Fuego until 19 February 1839. Wilkes was still trying to weld the expedition into a unit and, finding lack of harmony in the time-recording practices of his subordinates, directed that all logs etc. would be dated in civil time, midnight to midnight, rather than according to the nautical day, noon to noon. Conscious by then that time was short as well as out of joint, Wilkes divided his ships. He would try to follow Palmer's Land to the south-east. At the same time Hudson would sail south-west towards Cook's furthest point. Hudson was instructed to return, if possible, by sailing east and north to circumnavigate Palmer's Land, which Wilkes conceived to be an island or archipelago.

Wilkes's own cruise was a complete failure. His vessels entered Bransfield Strait, between the South Shetland Islands and Palmer's Land, and sailed for the eastern extremity of the latter. There the coast could be seen extending south-west for 25 to 30 miles but there was no open water between land and ice as he had been led to expect. The icebergs were already too thick for the liking of the *Porpoise*, let alone the schooner *Sea Gull*, and a gale on 5 March convinced Wilkes that the season was over. The ships turned north.

Hudson began with no better weather and *Peacock* was soon parted from Lieutenant William Walker in the schooner *Flying Fish*, which began making the rounds of the four rendezvous points pre-arranged against the possibility of separation. On 18 March, having visited all of them without finding Hudson, Walker decided that he was free to attempt Cook's *Ne Plus Ultra* alone and turned south. Within a few hours he was confronted by a wall of ice fifteen to twenty feet high which extended from east to west as far as the eye could see. From the masthead the ice field was seen as a jumble stretching away into the southern distance. Much of the ice was 'a dingy white (if I might say so)' and had the appearance of being not long detached from land. Walker worked his schooner westwards, looking for an opportunity to get further south. On 21 March the ice islands opened out and the *Flying Fish* dodged through them. That evening, when they hove to at about 70°S, Walker had hopes of getting further south than Cook by the following noon, but a rising gale began to concentrate the ice islands and by 4 pm it was difficult to find a passage between them. Walker adopted the tactic of getting to windward of an ice island, drifting down in its wake until it forced an opening in the ice, when he would push the schooner past it, relying on 'our own resources, flat sails and a pilot-boat's bottom'. The weather grew thicker and colder, but Walker believed they were heading into clear sea. He was below

Near Cook's furthest south, *Flying Fish* uses icebergs as icebreakers.

warming his toes when the lookout called that the fog had lifted but that they were surrounded by ice.

> I did not know at first how I should proceed; but, after a careful look round, I ran over to the weather shore of the pond, and stood along it in search of a passage, that I could not find; but, observing at intervals 'sutures' in the ice, where it did not appear firmly formed, I resolved to take advantage of this, and if possible, force a passage . . . Having the wind free, I gave her the mainsheet, and manned it well, and having got about six knots way on her, kept close to the ice, and when at the proper distance, put the helm down, hauled the main-sheet forcibly to windward, and let fly the head sheets; this brought her around suddenly, before she had passed through sufficient water to deaden her way; the ice cracked, we slipped over, or brushed through, and before eight o'clock I had got into a tolerably clear sea.[14]

Undaunted, Walker again worked south and east and was rewarded in the afternoon of 23 March by appearances of land that persisted for three hours. He was now in 69°17'S and 100°30'W, but on the following day again had to break out of the ice and, fearing that his vessel was 'ill-constructed for such rough contusions', decided that the *Flying Fish* had done all that could be expected of her and turned north. On 25 March, quite by chance, they fell in with the *Peacock*, which had reached nowhere near as far south, Hudson having been defeated by her 'miserable condition for a winter's campaign'. His only consolation was that, as ice froze on the hull, the 'Antarctic caulker' had temporarily stopped her leaking. Walker reported the puzzling 'deep earthy stain' seen in the ice. 'I cannot pretend to account for it', he wrote.[15]

The ships of the expedition sailed for Valparaiso to prepare for a Pacific cruise. Even if there was little to show for their first season in the ice, there was satisfaction that it had concluded safely, particularly for the fragile coast-bred schooners. When the untimely blow fell therefore, it was doubly felt. Somewhere off Cape Horn, on the way from Orange Harbour, the *Sea Gull* ran into the kind of weather all Cape Horners dreaded. She disappeared with all hands.

CHAPTER 3

Science Conspires

Wilkes had been in London in late 1836 and d'Urville a few months later, both to drink at the fount of geographical knowledge. Neither had made any secret of their respective nations' interest in polar exploration, an arena in which the British regarded themselves as supreme, yet there was no public clamour for a British expedition to match these rivals, the one emerging and the other traditional. Interest was confined to the elite and, unusually, it was primarily driven by scientific curiosity rather than by the pursuit of glory or profit. It was also international in scope, building upon Anglo-French cooperation in the 1820s to establish the exact difference in longitude between Paris and London, a program of work that had brought Edward Sabine into contact with François Arago and John Herschel.

John, the brilliant son of Sir William Herschel, private astronomer to George III, had ambitions to reform the Royal Society, but in 1830 he had failed narrowly to defeat the Duke of Sussex, a son of the King, for the presidency. As the Royal Society seemed to prefer society to science, Herschel involved himself in the creation of the British Association for the Advancement of Science, founded to redress what was seen as the elitism and amateurism of the older institution. By contrast with the society's frequent London meetings but random contributions, the association offered annual conferences held in different locations, with sections and speakers focused on the various disciplines of a rapidly expanding and sub-dividing scientific universe. One of the association's earliest concerns was magnetism and, in an act that exemplified the scientific spirit of the times, it appealed for some of its members to conduct a survey of magnetic dip and intensity in the British Isles. What today would be the work of universities or agencies of the state was carried out by Edward Sabine with the part-time assistance of Professor Humphrey Lloyd of Dublin Observatory and James Clark Ross.

The association invited Arago to attend its 1834 meeting in Edinburgh, knowing that he was looking for areas of science in which France and Britain might collaborate. Magnetism was an obvious choice and it was agreed that the association and the Institute of France would cooperate to set up magnetic observatories throughout the British Empire, with a view to coordinating British and French programs of measurement. Representations made to the British Government for the construction of observatories were met with indifference, as was a similar approach the following year which urged in addition:

> ... the importance of sending an expedition into the Antarctic regions ... with
> a view to determining precisely the place of the Southern Magnetic Pole or
> Poles, and the direction and intensity of the magnetic force in those regions.[1]

Even hints that Britain would otherwise fall behind the French in the observatory race failed to move the government. Then Humboldt's considerable weight was thrown into the fray. His letter to the Duke of Sussex might have been the brainchild of Sabine or Arago, but it had the desired effect of opening a second front through the Royal Society. The society appointed a committee which included Sabine, but still the crusade languished for want of government interest. For the association's 1837 meeting Sabine prepared a paper on magnetic intensity observations around the globe. He was able to draw on 753 'distinct determinations' made over more than forty years at 670 stations widely distributed. He also had the results of Hansteen's later work in Siberia, which had confirmed the existence there of a second focus of intensity that did not coincide with the highest dip. But there was still a gap in the data. Earlier observations of terrestrial magnetism had been made without reference to theory, Sabine said. As facts had accumulated, general conclusions had been drawn, leading to an hypothesis of four magnetic poles. Experiments to verify or disprove it had followed. In the Northern Hemisphere the verification was complete, proving the value of experiment directed by theory. Similar verification in the Southern Hemisphere was still needed and the observations necessary for that purpose would also supply those 'elements of calculation' whereby the hypothesis could be fitted to the facts.[2]

Sabine wished to share with the meeting a most flattering letter he had received from M. Hansteen urging Britain to follow the example of the latter's own nation. Had not tiny Norway funded an expedition that had taken observations from 40° to 75°N, from the meridian of Greenwich to that of Okhotsk? Surely, Hansteen wrote, it was not asking too much of England, 'so great, so rich, so powerful', with a greater interest in science and navigation, to fill in the southern part of the chart? To ensure that no one missed the point, Sabine gave it a patriotic flourish. Was it not an Englishman, Halley, who first discerned that there were four 'governing centres'?

There were sceptics: William Whewell, Cambridge polymath and later Master of Trinity College, pointed out that, in the previous century, Leonhard Euler had shown that the Halleian lines were largely compatible with the supposition of two magnetic poles, not four. He had been able to indicate locations for these two poles which were quite compatible with the observed direction of magnetic variation at that time. Whewell could not, however, quite bring himself to dismiss Hansteen's Siberian observations: 'this curious collection of facts awaits the hand of future theorists, when the ripeness of time shall invite them to the task'.[3] Sabine was not prepared to wait.

> As the research would require to be prosecuted in the high latitudes, a familiarity with the navigation of such latitudes would be important in the person who should undertake this service; and a strong individual interest in the subject itself would be of course a most valuable qualification. I need scarcely say that the country possesses a naval officer in whom these qualifications unite in a remarkable degree with all others that are requisite; and if fitting instruments make fitting times, none surely can be better than the present.[4]

And James Clark Ross was available. To his uncle's chagrin, most of the limelight cast by the *Victory* expedition had fallen on the younger man. It was he who had been to the North Magnetic Pole and, in the public tussle for credit which had followed John Ross's assertion of his claims as leader, the uncle had been at a distinct disadvantage. He presented as an elderly choleric Scot; his nephew was young, dashing, intelligent and, according to a partial witness, Lady Jane Franklin, 'the handsomest man in the Royal Navy'. The navy had bent its rules to promote him to captain, but his only sea duty since his return from the Arctic in 1833 had been on an unnecessary mission in HMS *Cove* to rescue some Hull whaleships. That apart, he had devoted his time to Sabine's survey, and to Anne Coulman.

James had met Anne, who was distantly related to him by marriage, in 1834. She was then 17, half his age, but it was as much the hazards of Ross's

James Clark Ross, first direct observer of the North Magnetic Pole, with dip circle.

vocation as the discrepancy in years that prejudiced her family against him. For years the couple carried on a clandestine romance by correspondence. In one letter Ross sentimentally recalled some of their earliest shared moments.

> Those [dip observations] we made together at Wadworth are included [in the survey] altho' they manifest a considerable degree of perturbation. Your major problem dearest is not difficult to solve. In September 1834 the intensity was found to be immense; that which is immense is immeasurable. That which is immeasurable may vary but because it is immeasurable these variations are imperceptible; that which is imperceptible we call infinitely small; therefore equals 0.[5]

Ross the lover confidently added 'QED' to the end of this theorem, but Ross the scientist was less certain and crossed it out. Anne's 'problem' was the intensity of her parents' opposition; James could equate that to nothing, but unfortunately nothing was also the content of his purse. He had found it necessary to decline the offer of a knighthood after the *Cove* mission because he could not afford the fees involved. An Antarctic expedition offered the prospect of a long period on full pay, the possibility of royalties on a book, and honours. Only through such a long separation could he hope to become more financially independent. He toyed with the idea of marrying Anne before sailing, as she was by then of age, but realised that it would be unfair to leave her to face her family alone.

But for the moment these were castles in the air, for the government remained unmoved, and it was not until the return of John Herschel, who had been studying the southern stars in South Africa from 1834 to 1838, that the cause was re-energised. Herschel's prime interest was astronomy rather than magnetism. At Capetown he had established a system of hourly meteorological observations on certain days of the year, much like that instituted by Professor Lloyd at the Dublin Observatory for the British magnetic survey. There was no reason why meteorological and magnetical observations could not be made from associated observatories and so Herschel and the magneticians made common cause. Unlike most of the crusaders, Herschel, now a baronet, had access to influential people both in government and at court. He visited Germany to present Gauss with the Copley Medal of the Royal Society and took the opportunity to sound him out about possible cooperation between Gauss's Magnetic Union and the proposed British observatories. Lloyd successfully appealed to Herschel to present the magneticians' case at the 1838 meeting of the British Association.[6]

Herschel had no difficulty in persuading the association and he accepted responsibility for lobbying the government on its behalf, but progress was slow until the Earl of Minto, First Lord of the Admiralty, suggested that Royal Society involvement might assist. Whewell had the matter referred to a committee of the society and Herschel drew up its report which, not surprisingly, recommended the same program of observatories and expedition as that proposed by the British Association. On 6 January 1839 the Prime Minister, Lord Melbourne, met with a deputation from the society which included Herschel, Sabine and Whewell and gave approval in principle to the expedition and the observatories. Sabine took this as his cue to write to Humboldt, Arago and the Duke of Sussex 'as nothing is done without agitation with such a ministry as the present'.[7]

With Herschel and Sabine mobilising the international and domestic scientific communities, and Ross and Beaufort working the corridors of the Admiralty, government resistance was eroded from without and within. Importantly, there were no nay-sayers. Herschel had persuaded George Airy, the Astronomer Royal, who had reservations, to keep them to himself. Even John Barrow stood back, although he viewed the Antarctic as a distraction from the north-west passage and was, as President of the Royal Geographical Society and Second Secretary of the Admiralty, in a position to make difficulties.

On 11 March Minto told Herschel that the Antarctic expedition had been approved, and in April Ross was appointed its commander. Minto had no doubts about Ross's qualifications and zeal but allowed himself a little scepticism about his motives, writing that Ross's thinking 'runs quite as much upon the discovery of a Southern Continent as on the professed object of the expedition'.[8] There was, moreover, no decision on the fixed magnetic observatories and without them the expedition would lose much of its purpose. As the months passed and Ross made ready to sail, Sabine began to fear that his appeals to national pride and international rivalry had been too successful, obscuring the scientific objectives. There were also difficulties abroad. In August the Royal Society sent Sabine and Lloyd to the Continent to coordinate with Humboldt, Gauss and Kupffer, the director of the Russian network. The last was an enthusiastic collaborator, but none of the German observatories was prepared to adopt the British system of observations. Arago was unwilling even to have the Paris Observatory participate, which might seem surprising given his enthusiasm in 1834, but at that time there was no prospect of a French expedition, whereas by 1839 d'Urville had already been two years at sea. And perhaps Sabine's noisy chauvinism had carried as far as Paris.

Humboldt was concerned about the 'English Sunday', which precluded observations on one day in every seven no matter how important that day might be. Gauss believed that the British observations were too intensive (every two hours on normal days, every two-and-a-half minutes on term days, of which there would be twelve in a year) and, besides, he had now published his *Allgemeine Theorie des Erdmagnetismus*, which attached no greater importance to a magnetic pole than to any other point of observation. From his viewpoint there was no need for an expedition at all. This was a scientific thunderbolt and, had there been active opposition from someone like Airy, the expedition might well have been brought into question.

Gauss's 'beautiful' theory, as Whewell described it, started with a simple hypothesis of heroic ambit (that magnetism is distributed throughout the earth) and a collection of facts (magnetic observations). Gauss had undertaken to find the order behind the apparent confusion of the facts, and for that purpose had invented what became known as spherical harmonic analysis.

> By using the most refined mathematical artifices for deducing the values of [the three elements of magnetic force] he is able to derive . . . coefficients . . . from the observed magnetic elements at certain places, and hence, to calculate them for all places. The comparison of the calculation with the observed results is, of course, the test of the truth of the theory.[9]

Such was the power of these 'artifices' that values for intensity, variation and dip derived from complete observations at just eight places could be sufficient, Gauss believed, to calculate the magnetic elements anywhere. From the best isomagnetic charts of variation (Barlow 1833), dip (Horner 1836), and intensity (Sabine 1837) he had taken twelve points, thirty degrees of longitude apart, along each of seven parallels of latitude. Spherical harmonic analysis met Sabine's demand for 'elements of calculation' whereby Hansteen's hypothesis could be fitted to the facts. Unfortunately for Sabine, Gauss's calculations had disproved Hansteen's Siberian pole. To accept that there could be two poles with the same polarity in the same hemisphere would, in Gauss's opinion, require a third, intermediate point between them with some of the characteristics of each. There could be no such place. The Royal Society agreed, on the commonsense ground that if the dip needle was vertical at each of these poles, as it had to be, where would it point when between the two?[10] The Siberian phenomenon appeared to be something more mysterious than a pole, an area upon which north-pointing needles appeared to converge, but where, if sought, the convergence would be found not to come to a point.

Gauss noted that the position he had computed for the North Magnetic Pole was 3°35' further north than Ross's observation had placed it. He expected a greater displacement of the South Magnetic Pole because the observed dip at Hobart, the closest station, was 3°38' less than it should have been according to calculation. If the Hobart observation was correct, it seemed probable to Gauss that the pole would be considerably to the north of the position given by his calculation, and that it could be sought in about 66°S latitude, and 146°E longitude.[11]

In spite of the disappointing reception by Gauss and Humboldt, Sabine's coalition of interest had reached critical mass. The East India Company promised to establish four observatories and Indian princes another two. The Russians volunteered eleven. Observatories in Prague, Milan, Philadelphia, Cambridge (USA), Algiers, Breslau, Munich, Cadiz, Brussels and Cairo signed up. Sabine had even wheedled and bullied his own corps, the Royal Artillery, into providing manpower for three of the six proposed Imperial observatories, at Toronto, St Helena and Capetown. The Admiralty gave in: Ross would set up observatories at St Helena, Capetown and Hobart on his way south.

The Royal Society was asked to advise on all matters relevant to the science of the voyage and produced a document which later became the basis of the Admiralty Manual of Scientific Enquiry. It directed Ross's attention to Gauss's predicted position for the South Magnetic Pole, which it believed would be accessible, and recommended that if it was not to be found there it would have to be sought, if necessary 'by circumnavigating the antarctic pole compass in hand'. There was, however, a note of caution.

> It is not to be supposed that Captain Ross, having already signalized himself by attaining the northern magnetic pole, should require any exhortation to induce him to use his endeavours to reach the southern. On the contrary, it might better become us to suggest for his consideration, that no scientific datum of this description, nor any attempt to attain very high southern latitudes, can be deemed important enough to be made a ground for exposing to *extraordinary* risk the lives of brave and valuable men.[12]

The society also wanted him to locate Sabine's two foci of maximum total intensity. The Admiralty was particularly concerned to have the best possible instruments for Gaussian observations and asked Lloyd to supervise their construction. The models were Gauss's own – those for which he had received the Copley Medal. Variation was to be measured by an instrument of the type Ross had used at the North Magnetic Pole: the unifilar magnetometer was a magnet bar suspended by fibres of untwisted silk enclosed in a tube to shield it from air currents. Horizontal force would be measured by Gauss's bifilar magnetometer. Its magnet bar was suspended from the ends of a looped wire, the top of which could be turned to hold the bar at right angles to the magnetic meridian by torsion. The horizontal force of the magnetic field was expressed in terms of its power to overcome the resistance of the suspension. The third instrument, the vertical force magnetometer, measured dip and vertical intensity. Its dip needle had a knife-edge axis resting on agate planes and could be weighted to hold a horizontal position. By reference to the mean inclination at the point of observation and the oscillations of the needle vertically and horizontally, changes in the vertical force could be inferred. Among the more robust instruments provided for use at sea was Fox's dip circle, the axis of which was pivoted rather than rested. It could also be used to measure intensity by the old method.

Gauss and his theory were all-important in the magnetic arrangements, but the Royal Society could not resist chiding him obliquely for the position he had adopted. The best test of 'a' magnetic theory, they argued:

> . . . would be, not servilely to calculate its results for given localities, however numerous, and thereby load its apparent errors with the real errors, both of observation and of local magnetism; but to compare the totality of the lines in our charts with the corresponding lines, as they result from the formulae to be tested . . .[13]

Only by such testing could the truth of theory be demonstrated and the need for any modifications indicated.

Ross was given the *Erebus* and the *Terror* for his command. They were former bomb vessels, built to withstand the shock and stress of firing shells from large mortars. Trial and error had shown that they were better suited to ice service than any other ships in the Royal Navy inventory and the *Terror* was already an Arctic veteran. Ross showed a similar preference when it came to his crews. For his second in command he asked for Francis Crozier, an old shipmate who had been his first lieutenant on the *Cove*. Thomas Abernathy, who had been with him at the North Magnetic Pole, was gunner, the usual post held by an icemaster. All the magnetic work would be done by uniformed personnel: soldiers at two of the land observatories, sailors at the third and at sea. A young botanist, inspired by Charles Darwin's example, sought appointment as a civilian naturalist. He was told by Ross that there was no such position but that, if he could acquire the qualification for appointment as assistant surgeon, a place might be found. Joseph Dalton Hooker did so, to find himself subordinated to yet another Arctic veteran, Surgeon Robert McCormick. McCormick had sailed in the *Beagle* with Fitzroy and Darwin until displaced as naturalist by the latter.

A few days before the expedition was due to sail, the whaleship owner Charles Enderby came to see Ross, bringing information. His sealing schooner *Eliza Scott*, whose master was John Balleny, had just returned from the Pacific. Balleny had been instructed to penetrate as far south as he could and, in January at Campbell Island, he had come across John Biscoe, also sealing. Although Biscoe had long since parted from the Enderbys, Balleny had not hesitated to pump him for information. Biscoe was in the difficult position of trying to assist a fellow navigator without giving away commercial secrets to a competitor. He said that in 1831 he had been told that a Hobart whaler, the *Venus*, had been as far south as 72°. It was rumoured that there was land south of Macquarie Island. In a good season it might be possible to get through the ice to it, or at least close enough to confirm its existence. As for seals, who could say?[14]

Balleny had needed no further encouragement. He had sailed south along the meridian of 170°E until brought up by pack ice in 68°S. He then steered north and west along the ice towards the meridian of Macquarie Island. A few degrees short of his objective he had come across a chain of islands straddling the Antarctic Circle. They were volcanic and inhospitable in the extreme, but a landing was effected at the only accessible spot, a shingle beach drowned by each succeeding wave. There was no seal rookery; Enderby would have to be content with a few rocks. After running west before a south-easterly in about 64°S amid worsening weather, the schooner and her tender, the cutter *Sabrina*, had been able briefly to get a degree or so further south, and on 2 March had seen the appearance of land a mile to windward. There had been no prospect of closing with it and Balleny turned north. The Antarctic was reluctant to let them go. One night in a gale of wind the *Eliza Scott* was knocked down and took an eternity to right herself. A blue distress light was seen burning on the *Sabrina* a mile astern but Balleny was unable to assist. Morning found the *Eliza Scott* alone on a desolate sea. The islands were named after Balleny and the supposed land for the lost cutter. They were the first Antarctic lands reported between Enderby Land and Peter I Island south of South America, a sector traversing fully 220 degrees of longitude.

A Rock In A Hard Place

When Balleny reached London there was great interest in the rocks he brought from the Antarctic, but one penetrating mind was even more interested in a rock that had not been obtained. Charles Darwin was told that a boulder had been seen lodged in an iceberg. Charles Enderby arranged an interview for him with the second mate of the *Eliza Scott*, John McNab, who had made a sketch.

Charles Darwin's erratic boulder.

On 13 March 1839, in 61°S and 103°40'E, McNab had seen a black spot on a distant iceberg. Inspection from a quarter of a mile revealed it to be an angular piece of rock lodged at least 20 feet above sea level in a 250–300 foot high berg. About 12 feet of the rock protruded. What appeared to be its greater part, to judge from the discolouration of its surrounds, was beneath the surface of the ice. The schooner was then 1400 miles from the nearest known land and 450 from Sabrina Land ('if such land exists', noted Darwin). It seemed to the naturalist 'exceedingly improbable' that there was land within 100 miles of the spot.

The fragment of rock must, therefore, have travelled at least thus far from its parent source; and, from being deeply embedded, it probably sailed many miles farther on before it was dropped from the iceberg in the depths of the sea, or was stranded on some distant shore.

Darwin saw in this immense transporting power of ice an explanation for the 'erratic boulders' of Europe, which had long puzzled geologists by their presence amongst dissimilar rock. 'If . . . but one iceberg in a thousand, or in ten thousand, transports its fragment, the bottom of the Antarctic sea and the shores of its islands must already be scattered with masses of foreign rock'. Just as the glacial sheets of the Ice Ages must have scattered them across the face of Europe.[15]

Although he would have unaware of it, Darwin had also accounted for those 'earthy stains' in the ice that had so puzzled Lieutenant Walker of the USS *Flying Fish*. Cook had been right. There was land further south.

This report was a mixed bag for Ross. That there was open sea south of the Antarctic Circle was promising for a maritime expedition, but land in those parts was less welcome. Ross had done enough walking and sledging in the Arctic; he was hoping to sail to the South Magnetic Pole. On 14 September 1839 he received his final instructions from the Admiralty. They set out a detailed itinerary but, acknowledging that in such an enterprise much had to be left to the 'discretion, temper and judgment' of the commanding officer, placed their confidence in Ross's 'combined energy and prudence'. Their Lordships repeated the Royal Society's injunction about safety, warned against being iced in over winter, and cautioned against allowing the ships to separate. Eleven days later the ships slipped their moorings and proceeded down the Thames. They reached Madeira on 20 October. A party ascended the island's highest peak to ascertain its altitude. On its summit their guides indicated a cairn that had been erected by the Wilkes expedition. The Americans were a year ahead of them. Ross wrote to Anne that he might be away from her for some time. If it was to take him two seasons to attain the South Magnetic Pole, so be it. He did not intend to disappoint those who had sent him off with such high hopes.[16]

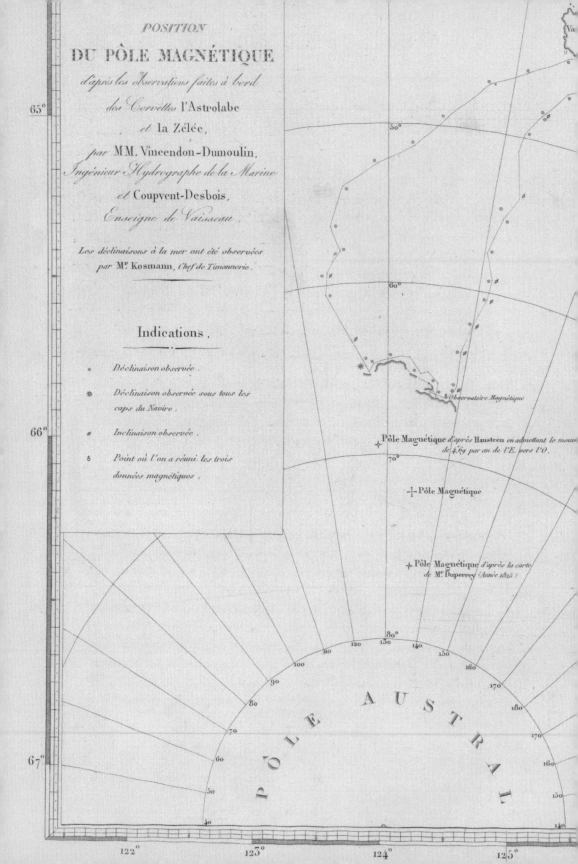

POSITION

DU PÔLE MAGNÉTIQUE

d'après les observations faites à bord

des Corvettes l'Astrolabe

et la Zélée,

par MM. Vincendon-Dumoulin,

Ingénieur Hydrographe de la Marine

et Coupvent-Desbois,

Enseigne de Vaisseau.

Les déclinaisons à la mer ont été observées
par Mr. Kosmann, Chef de Timonnerie.

Indications.

- ° *Déclinaison observée.*
- ✳ *Déclinaison observée sous tous les*
  caps du Navire.
- ⌐ *Inclinaison observée.*
- ⌐ *Point où l'on a réuni les trois*
  données magnétiques.

Observatoire Magnétique

Pôle Magnétique *d'après Hansteen en admettant le mouv.*
de 4,69 par an de l'E. vers l'O.

Pôle Magnétique

Pôle Magnétique *d'après la carte*
de Mr. Duperrey (Année 1825.)

PÔLE AUSTRAL

CHAPTER 4

Terre Adélie

In accordance with his instructions, Dumont d'Urville arrived at Hobart on 12 December 1839. Contrary to his instructions, he still had both *Astrolabe* and *Zélée* with him. Although given discretion to retain the *Zélée* after the Antarctic Peninsula cruise, that concession had expired in Java, whence his orders required him to detach her for return to France. The difficulty facing d'Urville was that whatever the success of his Pacific campaign, it was on his so-far trifling Antarctic results that his voyage would be judged by those who sent him. He had resolved to make a last quick attempt on the geographic South Pole before visiting New Zealand, as his instructions stipulated, prior to returning to France by way of the Cape of Good Hope.

The health of his crews, however, had deteriorated badly between Java and Hobart. Scurvy, to a greater or lesser degree, had dogged them across the Pacific, but it was dysentery caused by bad Javanese water that had ravaged the weakened crews on the two months' voyage to Tasmania. Between them the ships had lost sixteen officers and men. A hospital had to be established ashore in Hobart for the many sick. So many were incapacitated that d'Urville feared he could man only the *Astrolabe* for the cruise south, but the urgent

Opposite: One discovery precludes another: Adelie Land blocked d'Urville's way to the South Magnetic Pole.

representations of Charles-Hector Jacquinot, commander of the *Zélée*, and the unstinted help of the Hobart authorities persuaded him otherwise. He was also concerned about the safety of single ship operations in the ice and the adverse effect it might have on morale.

The Lieutenant-Governor of Tasmania at this juncture was none other than Sir John Franklin, naval officer and Arctic explorer. By nature the kindest of men, he had an abiding interest in both exploration and science. Convicts were made available to carry magnetic instruments to the top of Mount Wellington for observations. Franklin visited the magnetic observatory set up by the expedition's hydrographer, Vincendon-Dumoulin in the hospital garden, and the pair spent an hour discussing the construction and use of the instruments. Nothing was too much trouble for the Governor, but he was unable to give d'Urville the news he craved most, the outcome of the American expedition's Antarctic cruise earlier that year. Not until Christmas Day was there a hint.

> The 24th was a holiday for the whole colony; we still had not changed dates since we left France, so that the English, who had brought time from the west[1], were one day ahead of us . . . I spent my day with Sir John Pedder[2]; he informed me that the American expedition commanded by Captain Wilkes . . . was busy in Sydney making preparations to go back to the ice . . . 'Extreme reserve has been imposed on the men', he told me; 'the officers are instructed to remain absolutely silent, so that nothing has transpired about the discoveries and work of that expedition'.[3]

But how had Sir John been able to learn even this much? From a merchant captain trading between Sydney and Hobart, his host replied; would d'Urville like to meet him? On the following day the merchant captain visited the *Astrolabe*. It was John Biscoe. He had met Wilkes in Sydney, he said, and they had talked for a long time. He had been told nothing about American discoveries but, on the other hand, he had some other information that might be of interest. Only recently he had tried to penetrate south on the meridian of New Zealand but had been stopped by ice in 63°S. Some colonial sailors believed that there was land further west, to the south of Macquarie Island.

It was clear to d'Urville that the Americans intended to operate in the same sector of the Antarctic as he did. The French ships were ready to sail within a week of his meeting with Biscoe and, after enjoying Hobart's New Year's Day at a ball held in their honour, the French spent their own 1 January 1840 at sea. On the last day in port d'Urville wrote to the Minister of Marine in Paris to explain that his original purpose in making the forthcoming cruise – to add an 'honourable supplement' to the work already accomplished – had been overtaken.

> . . . what I have heard here has converted a venture into an obligation. The American expedition, which is now in Sydney, and the James Ross expedition, which is expected here at any moment, are ardently in pursuit of the same objective, and each thinks only to penetrate as far as possible into the Antarctic regions. In the same spirit, it would be regrettable if a French expedition was obliged to hold itself back. It remains to be seen how far fortune will favour us in this new venture.[4]

Despite the trials of two years earlier, spirits were high and all accepted that honour required another attempt.[5] Dumont d'Urville planned no extended campaign, no continuous exploration of the ice barrier. He intended only to sail south of Tasmania as far as it was possible to go before being stopped by the ice.

> An important discovery remained to be made; the position of the magnetic pole . . . From the start I intended to follow the most direct route to take us towards this goal. I knew also that the most useful observations of this nature would be made on a magnetic meridian, so I tried to keep our corvettes on this direction, and to do this, I gave the order always to hold to the compass route south whenever the winds allowed.[6]

The plan bore little relation to the ambitions of Louis Philippe. It was just possible, if unlikely in the light of Biscoe's information, that the venture might yield a new furthest south, at least in this sector. As for the South Magnetic Pole, in the King's eyes it would be a poor substitute for the real thing. Even these humbler ambitions, however, were soon threatened by reappearance of the scourge that had left so many of the men dead, dying or convalescing in Hobart. After only four days at sea, nine of the crew of the *Astrolabe* were reported sick, and nearly as many on the *Zélée*. Magnetic observations were taken several times each day. Gambey's dip circle performed reliably on the *Astrolabe*, but the magnetic observers were frustrated in their attempts to get an instrument by a different manufacturer to work, and d'Urville fumed about the folly of having different instruments when simultaneous and comparable observations – the most useful kind from ships travelling together – were required.

On 16 January they encountered scattered icebergs in 60°S. Two seasons earlier ice had first been seen in 59°S and they had been stopped in 65°S, but this ice was different. It seemed too massive to have formed in the open sea and d'Urville speculated that it had detached from land in the vicinity. The observations also indicated that they were very near the Magnetic Pole. By 18 January they were in 64°S and in hopes of reaching the 70th parallel, but at midnight the ships found themselves surrounded by table-topped bergs. They reminded d'Urville of those seen near the South Orkneys and reinforced his view that land must be near, which would put an end to his hopes of penetrating to a high latitude.[7]

On the following day, at 9 am, a large, stationary black mass was seen west-south-west of the ship. It bore the appearance of an island of some height. At 10 am the sun broke through the foggy sky and the island disappeared. Towards 3 pm the officer of the watch, Gervaise, reported a greyish appearance of land, this time to the east. With no great expectations, Vincendon-Dumoulin climbed to the mizzen top for a better view. He told Gervaise that his land was a cloud – he could see its base above the horizon – but added that straight ahead, much closer and clearer, was the distinct appearance of land. Was it really land, he was asked? The magnetician was non-commital; he had been fooled before.

The wind dropped, arresting their progress, but the sun shone. The sick list had been cleared and the sailors sought permission to hold a ceremony to mark the crossing of the Antarctic Circle, like those customary on crossing the Equator. Conscious of the need for some light relief, d'Urville agreed with a single proviso: there was to be no water on the deck and no ducking. A shower of beans and rice from the masthead heralded the arrival of a messenger mounted on a seal. He announced that Father Antarctica would be visiting the following day whether they had crossed the circle or not. At 10.50 pm the sun set behind the supposed land, the horizon contour of which stood out with great clarity.

Father Antarctica arrived as promised and held court for most of the 20th, with mummers, a sermon, a feast, singing and dancing. The land was his best jest; it teased, just out of reach.

> . . . before us rose the land: details could be distinguished. It was very uniform in appearance. Entirely covered in snow, it stretched from east to west and seemed to slope gently down towards the sea. Amid its uniformly grey colour we did not see a single peak, not even one black spot. So there remained more than one unbeliever.[8]

Father Antarctica visits the *Astrolabe*.

What convinced the doubters was the arrival of a boat from the *Zélée*. Its officers declared that all aboard had been sure since the night before. The rejoicing was general; whatever else happened, they could report the discovery of a new land. Early the next day a light breeze from the south-south-east enabled them slowly to work towards the land, but the clustering ice islands became a continuous wall through which narrow winding passageways beckoned the ships. The sheer walls of the icebergs, much higher than the masts, gave d'Urville the impression of wandering the narrow streets of a city of giants. If cut off from the wind by these cliffs, the ships could have been drawn to destruction by the powerful eddies that swirled about their bases. For an hour the ships wended their way through an otherwise silent icescape which repeated, unbidden, the officers' orders. They emerged into a vast basin, the ice islands behind, the land ahead. By noon it appeared no more than three or four miles distant but it was entirely covered in snow. There was not the slightest patch of earth showing to confirm that they were looking at land.[9]

They coasted westward, looking for any sign of bare earth or any break in the ice cliff. The magneticians were anxious to get ashore or, failing that, to land on an iceberg where they could take more accurate observations than from a moving ship. At about 6 pm an iceberg with a sloping side presented an opportunity, and Dumoulin was rowed across. The ships hove to so as not to move too far from the icy observatory. It was a fortuitous halt. Earlier in the afternoon there had been a sighting of a black patch at the sea's edge but it had disappeared when the ship changed position; now the officer of the watch, Duroch, was able to keep a number of similar patches under continuous observation. In the interval before they were again obscured by a passing ice island, he satisfied himself that they were, in fact, rocks.

The hour was late, but the sun would linger in the Antarctic summer sky. The danger in sending a boat to investigate was that an onshore wind might spring up, in which event the ships would have to abandon it and escape from the lee shore. Duroch was given the cutter and six men, with the naturalist and the artist for company. The rocks had also been seen from the *Zélée* and they also had lowered a boat. Duroch was not about to be denied the reward of his keenness and the reconnaissance became a race.

> My men who are full of enthusiasm get the boat moving at incredible speed. Go to it men! *Zélée*'s yawl is close behind us. We must get there first! But there is no need to stand over them; responding to their powerful arms, the boat devours the distance . . . There can be no further doubts that this is land; the sailors redouble their efforts and we enter into a labyrinth of icebergs we must get through to reach our goal . . . Surrounded by this sublime spectacle, our boats, the tricolour on the prow, glide in. We are quite silent and enraptured but our hearts are beating wildly and then suddenly a long shout of '*Vive le Roi*' announces our landing. And indeed that's it! There it is![10]

In two-and-a-half hours they had covered seven miles. There was no place to haul the boats up so they jumped onto the rocky western shore of the highest islet, one of a group standing five or six hundred metres offshore. They could see a headland and several bare peaks on the mainland but the intervening space was choked with ice. Dubouzet, First Lieutenant of the *Zélée*, ordered that the tricolour be planted on the islet.

> Following the ancient and carefully preserved English custom, we took possession of it in the name of France, as well as of the adjacent coast which the ice prevented us from approaching. Our enthusiasm and joy were boundless then because we felt we had just added a province to France by this peaceful conquest. If the abuse that has followed such acts of possession has often caused them to be derided as worthless and faintly ridiculous, in this case we believed ourselves to have sufficient lawful right to keep up the ancient usage for our

The French claim a land 'that will never start a war against our country'.

country. For we did not dispossess anyone, our title was incontestable, and as a result we regarded ourselves as being on French territory. There will be at least one advantage; it will never start a war against our country.

And, in keeping with a far older and most authentically Gallic tradition, they emptied a bottle of Bordeaux. 'Then we all set to work to collect everything of interest for natural history that this inhospitable land had to offer'.[11] It was not a lot – there were penguins and there were rocks. Half an hour exhausted the possibilities. An easterly breeze allowed them to sail back to the ships but by then the Bordeaux had worn off and the temperature was falling. The boats were covered in a crust of ice but otherwise unscathed and d'Urville at last felt confident enough to give the discovery a name – *Terre Adélie*, after his wife. A cape seen in the morning was named *Découverte* (Discovery) and the headland near which the boats had collected their samples became *Point Géologie*. Vincendon-Dumoulin had returned from his iceberg at 9 pm. He had made his magnetic observations as planned, but reference to a point on the distant shore disclosed that his station was not aground, as he had hoped. Now he learnt that he had missed his chance to set up on land, although it is doubtful whether he could have accomplished much in half an hour. There would not be another opportunity.

On the following day d'Urville took advantage of the continuing east wind to follow the coast of his discovery westwards but the ships encountered an ice barrier which ran north from the land and hooked east. They were obliged to tack east to escape from the cul-de-sac but d'Urville was hoping to resume a westerly course after rounding its northern extremity. Instead the wind strengthened, it began to snow and by 1 am on the 23rd visibility was down to three cables. In this murk they were dodging icebergs which were being driven by the wind onto the ice barrier, and d'Urville signalled Jacquinot to forget about keeping station with *Astrolabe* and steer as the safety of his ship required.

The message was not seen, for at that moment the ships lost contact in a whirlwind of snow. As much sail was crowded on to the *Astrolabe* as she would carry – at considerable risk to her masts and causing her to heel so far that the sea all but covered the lee gunports – but still the corvette lost ground towards the ice barrier. The forepart of the ship was soon covered with ice, snow froze on the ropes and fog made it scarcely possible to see from one mast to the next. To cap it all, at a time when precise direction was at a premium the compasses became quite inaccurate.[12] Their only point of navigational reference was wind direction. If it shifted, undetected, they might sail straight into the ice barrier.

Not until 10 am the following day did the storm begin to abate and by 6 pm *Zélée* was able to rejoin the *Astrolabe*. Over the next few days Vincendon-Dumoulin made observations of variation with the ship's head pointing in all directions, in effect swinging the ship while on the move. He also calculated their route during the storm and found that the northern part of the pack had been blown three miles to the westward. Had it not, *Astrolabe* might not have been able to keep off. They beat towards the land, where they again encountered the ice islands they had passed through six days earlier. The east wind persisted and by the 28th d'Urville had decided that there was no prospect of regaining Adelie Land. He turned south-west in search of the magnetic pole. The course was suggested by Vincendon-Dumoulin as the one most likely to cross the line of no variation while approaching as close to the pole itself as wind and ice would permit.

At midday the corvettes were running before the breeze under full sail in about 64°48'S. At 4 pm ice was seen extending across their bows from south-east to north-west. So that they might track northwards along this line of ice, the order was given to bring the ships closer to the wind. Before this evolution could be completed, and while the *Astrolabe*'s mainsail was still clewed up, the watch reported a brig coming fast out of the fog to windward. No sooner had she emerged than the stars and stripes was hoisted at her mainmast. In the sign-and-motion language of the sea the message was unmistakable: 'I am an American man of war and I wish to speak'. *Astrolabe* hoisted the tricolour and d'Urville's broad pennant in acknowledgment. Custom then required that, being to leeward, *Astrolabe* should maintain course and speed while the windward vessel ran across her stern and rounded up under the lee quarter.

In this unfrequented place d'Urville knew that his visitor must be one of Wilkes's ships. For a short time he kept *Astrolabe*'s mainsail idle but then, when the brig was almost within speaking distance and the American commander already had his speaking trumpet in hand, d'Urville gave order for the maintack to be boarded. *Astrolabe* began gathering way. The American immediately struck his ensign and bore away to the south. The Frenchman was later to insist that he had been prepared to speak and had only made sail out of concern that the American was coming on too fast and might have overshot. But more than one of his crew suspected that he was unwilling to share their discoveries.[13]

Morning on the 29th found the corvettes running east. The horizon was clearer and, when a massive ice barrier was seen to the south, d'Urville had no hesitation in hauling his wind to investigate. By 10 am they were only three or four miles off, but no wiser. They were looking at an ice cliff, uniformly 30 to 45 metres in height, which appeared to be calving ice islands larger than any they had previously encountered. It had capes and inlets, but in the 60–75 nautical miles they coasted along it not a single peak could be seen above the rim. At 6 pm they rounded a projecting headland to find that the line of ice cliff trended to the south-west. No end to it could be seen. In the lee of the headland d'Urville paused to sound for depth of water and to consult with Jacquinot. There was no bottom at 200 fathoms.

> As to the nature of this enormous wall, opinions were once more divided . . . some holding that this was a mass of compact ice independent of all land, and others, of which I am one, maintained that this formidable belt was at least an envelope, a crust, covering a solid base, either of land, of rock, or even of scattered shoals round a vast land. This view I base on the principle that no ice of great extent can be formed in the open sea, and that it must always have a solid point of support to allow of it being formed while stationary.[14]

On the strength of this hypothesis he named the ice barrier *Côte Clarie*, after Jacquinot's wife, and decided to end their geographical exploration. There was still, however, the matter of the magnetic pole. The corvettes bore south-west but lost contact with the ice barrier during the night. On the following day, 30 January, they steered south in an attempt to rejoin it but were frustrated by a chain of ice islands. The longitude was 128°E and the variation of the compasses had changed from north-east to north-west. They had crossed the line of no variation in about 65°20'S. Vincendon-Dumoulin and his assistant Coupvent believed that they now had sufficient data to determine the position of the magnetic pole to within a degree. They had been taking daily dip observations since 12 January and had been gratified by the regularity with which it had increased from 74° to 86°, regularly enough to serve as an independent check against lines of variation extrapolated to their point of convergence. To make sure, they again wished to have the ship swung and, if possible, to make observations from an iceberg. Two days were spent trying to find one suitable for landing but all were either unapproachable by boat or too small to be steady even if the boat were to be risked. The magneticians had to be content with simultaneously measuring the variation fore and aft as the *Astrolabe* was turned in her own length. To their chagrin, the results, described by d'Urville as 'strange', showed differences of nearly twelve degrees between fore and aft on the same heading. Such discrepancies would make it all but impossible to plot convergence with any confidence. In the evening of 31 January d'Urville decided that the men, among whom sickness was again appearing, had done enough.

> Of course it would not have been impossible to push on further west, and trace out a greater extent of the ice pack, or perhaps even find land again. For I believe that the greater part of the polar circle is surrounded by land, and that in the end it will be found by some navigator sufficiently fortunate and bold to break through the masses of accumulated ice which ordinarily surround it . . .[15]

He also confessed to being a little tired. The ships were in 65°20'S and 130°20'E when he gave the order to set course to the north. Contrary to his original plan, which provided for *Zélée* to pick up the sick men in Hobart and follow *Astrolabe* to New Zealand, the commodore now felt the need to promulgate personally the news of his discoveries. It would not do to allow others, like the captain of a certain American brig, to pre-empt them. The corvettes arrived at Hobart on 17 February, expedition time.

CHAPTER 5

An Antarctic Continent?

After leaving the coast of South America the American squadron had surveyed its way through the islands of the Pacific. The *Relief* was sent ahead to land her stores in Sydney before returning to the United States, Wilkes having decided that she was such a dull sailer that the squadron was better off without her. He also took the opportunity to offload those officers he considered the least efficient, but this did not prevent a steady deterioration in relations with those who remained. The plain fact was that the man was a martinet by nature, and while such a character was far from unique among the captains of his day, the navy had not seen fit to give him the rank that might have legitimised it. As a result, Wilkes was guilty of trying far too hard: every query about the propriety or appropriateness of a decision was interpreted as opposition; every order not immediately and meticulously obeyed was open to the suspicion of sabotage. The atmosphere on the *Vincennes* became poisonous. Officers schemed to achieve transfer to the less authoritarian regime of Hudson's *Peacock*.

The lead ships of the squadron approached Sydney Heads on the night of 29 November 1839. It was too late for a local pilot but Wilkes decided to take the *Vincennes* and *Peacock* in regardless, and there was consternation the next morning when the town awoke to find foreign warships in the harbour.

Wilkes was later full of praise for his own skill and daring, neglecting to mention the services of Benjamin Vanderford, the expedition's Pacific pilot, a former whaling captain who more than once had taken ships into Sydney.

The Australians greeted the squadron with enthusiasm. Governor Gipps, who had been in Washington at the time the expedition was being proposed, handed Wilkes the key to Sydney's threadbare defences, Fort Macquarie, for his observations. Wilkes and his officers had the run of the town, including the Australian Club. Its president, the gentleman naturalist Alexander McLeay, was pleased to extend hospitality on behalf of the members. Biscoe came forward and, although he did not at that time know the outcome of Balleny's voyage, no doubt told Wilkes of the land rumoured to lie south of Macquarie Island.

Peacock was found to be in a bad state. Her carpenter reported that the planking was rotten in many places, as were the stanchions that supported the spar deck bulwark and the boats. Repairs would take two months. Wilkes had already decided to leave his scientists behind and considered doing the same with the *Peacock*, but in the end he and Hudson agreed that it would not look good in Washington. All the vessels therefore were prepared as well as could be for the ordeal ahead. The locals had heard of the extensive strengthening and special ice equipment with which Ross's ships had been prepared and were most unimpressed with the American outfits.

> They inquired, whether we had compartments in our ships to prevent us from sinking? How we intended to keep ourselves warm? What kind of antiscorbutic we were to use? and where were our great ice saws? To all of these questions I was obliged to answer, to their great apparent surprise, that we had none, and to agree with them that we were unwise to attempt such service in ordinary cruising vessels; but that we had been ordered to go, and that was enough! and go we should. This want of preparation certainly did not add to the character for wisdom of our government, with this community; but they saw us all cheerful, young, and healthy, and gave us the character, that I found our countrymen generally bear, of recklessness of life and limb.[1]

One gentleman went so far as to tell Wilkes that most of the visitors to his ships considered the whole expedition 'doomed to be frozen to death'. Wilkes was prepared to admit to himself that it was a real possibility should they be iced in for a winter. Even if crammed to the beams, the ships could carry less than twelve months' rations, and short allowance at that. The fuel would last only seven months and the ships were ill-equipped for battening down into winter quarters. Nevertheless, on 26 December, the day appointed in Wilkes's orders of more than a year earlier, the squadron sailed for the Antarctic. For the first few days, sailing line abreast, the ships completed their preparations. The gunports were tightened and caulked, then seamed with tarred canvas which was nailed down under sheet lead. Casings were built around all the hatchways and fitted with self-closing doors operated by a system of weights and pulleys. The regular drying stoves were supplemented by others bought in Sydney.

On 31 December Wilkes issued orders for the cruise. He emphasised the dangers of separation and appointed three successive rendezvous points in the Antarctic seas. The object of the cruise was to attain as high a southern latitude as possible while making observations in transit, particularly of dip and intensity. The orders anticipated that the ships' southward progress would eventually be arrested by ice, along which they should then sail west, from 160°E to 105°E, looking for openings to the south until 1 March 1840, by which time the lateness of the season would preclude further exploration. Should a commander be so fortunate as to penetrate the ice into an open sea, he should 'steer to the westward, bearing in mind that the only prospect of again clearing it is on the route you first followed, or that supposed to have been taken by Weddell, between the longitude of 35° and 49°W'. To put it another way: if a ship should find itself unable to get out by the opening through which it entered, it should continue half way around the world to look for the open sea reported by Weddell in 1823, hoping to find it still clear – always assuming that Weddell had not invented it.

As the New Year dawned, the Americans were a day's sail to the south of the French, who had not then left Hobart, and three degrees further east. The tracks of the two expeditions diverged further when the *Flying Fish* lost contact with the other American ships in a rising sea on 2 January and all made for the first appointed rendezvous, Macquarie Island. Speculation in the squadron was that the schooner had gone the way of the *Sea Gull*, lost off Cape Horn. *Peacock* was next to part, on 3 January, and neither had rejoined by the time *Vincennes* and *Porpoise* came up against the floe ice in 64°11'S on 11 January. By then, more than twenty degrees of longitude separated the Americans from the French, who were following a magnetic meridian almost due south. Wilkes was surprised by a change in the colour of the water to olive green:

... and some faint appearances resembling distant land; but as it was twilight, and I did not believe the thing credible, I put no faith in these indications, although some of the officers were confident they were not occasioned by icebergs.[2]

On the following morning a thick fog separated *Vincennes* and *Porpoise*. All four of the squadron's vessels were now operating independently but under common instructions to work westwards along the edge of the ice. On 13 January Lieutenant Ringgold, commanding the *Porpoise*, believed that he could see distant mountains to the south-east. In the late hours of the 15th, when the *Vincennes* was in 66°15'30"S and 158°E, the departure of accompanying birds at 8 pm suggested to Wilkes that land was not far distant to the south and south-east. At 11.30 he was called up on deck to find the ship embayed in field ice from which it took five hours to escape. When he went below again at 4.30 am on the 16th, he sketched what he thought he had seen beyond the ice. He labelled it 'supposed land'.

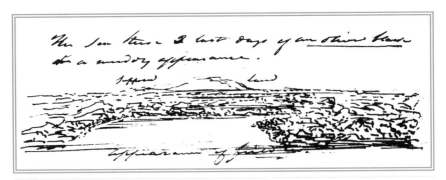

The 'supposed land' as sketched in Wilkes's journal, ostensibly in the early hours of 16 January 1840.

On the 17th *Vincennes*, *Peacock* and *Porpoise* met again, coming within sight of each other at the edge of the ice in 157°E. But still there was no sign of the *Flying Fish*. Contact was made with the *Peacock* by semaphore telegraph. Hudson reported his furthest south (66°15'), the greatest dip recorded (85°) and all well on board. There was no mention of land. The brevity of semaphore had left much unsaid; two of his midshipmen, Eld and Reynolds, had spent many hours aloft on the 16th and had reported mountains stretching to the south-west as far as could be seen, with two distinct conical peaks and others whose summits were obscured by light cloud. These peaks they estimated to be one to two thousand feet high. Had the *Porpoise* been able to make contact with Wilkes, Lieutenant Ringgold could have told a similar story of the 16th. He had seen a 'large, dark and rounding' object that resembled a mountain in the distance. He thought that it was an island surrounded by immense fields of ice, bearing south by east.

Even had these sightings been reported at the time, Wilkes would have been entitled to treat them with caution. On that same day, *Vincennes* had seen a ship, presumed to be the *Peacock*, within a mile of her. There was no response to signal or gun and the ship was lost to sight shortly afterwards. When the *Vincennes* caught up with the *Peacock* on the following day the officers of the latter were bewildered, and adamant that it could not have been their ship. Wilkes wrote:

> . . . I should be disposed to believe that the cause of her image appearing so close to us in the morning was produced by refraction above a low fog-bank; but the usual accompaniment of such phenomena, a difference of temperature below and aloft, did not exist.[3]

In his keenness to find a way through the ice, Wilkes then did a most dangerous thing. He told Hudson that their chances would be increased by separation, although his own instructions for the cruise had specifically warned against it. Now, as Wilkes saw it, keeping company would not add to safety, whereas separation would excite rivalry. There were those among his officers who suspected that Wilkes was determined to find his own way through the ice, that he doubted their commitment to the task, and did not wish to share the glory of finding land. A more likely explanation is that Wilkes was reacting to criticism from his officers: in the Pacific some had privately remarked that sailing in company wasted a great deal of time that could be better spent on separate surveys, a view which may have owed more to a desire to escape Wilkes's heavy-handed supervision than to any concern for economical exploration. Nevertheless, what was an acceptable risk in the Pacific was extremely hazardous in the Antarctic. The ships went their separate ways to mixed fortune. On 19 January *Vincennes* and *Peacock* found themselves in an extensive bay in the ice.

> Land was now certainly visible from the *Vincennes*, both to south-southeast and southwest, in the former direction most distinctly. Both appeared high. It was between eight and nine in the morning when I [Wilkes] was fully satisfied that it was certainly land, and my own opinion was confirmed by that of some

of the oldest and most experienced seamen on board. The officer of the morning watch, Lieutenant Alden, sent twice, and called my attention to it.[4]

The winds were light and the *Vincennes* sagged towards the line of ice. Wilkes had the boats tow her off and left the bay for *Peacock* to explore. This was not the action of a man keen to reach land he said he could clearly see. The 'experienced seamen' he had consulted was Gunner John Williamson. The reason that Williamson had been singled out for this condescension by his captain, who had a deserved reputation for aloofness, was that when Lieutenant Alden had sent his news Wilkes had disregarded it. When Wilkes subsequently came up to see for himself, he could not bring himself to admit to Alden that he might have been right. Williamson was certain that it was land but Wilkes must have remained unconvinced at the time, for in his journal he initially recorded only 'appearances of land to the SSE'. More positive is the entry on the previous, otherwise empty, facing page of his journal, which appears to have been written as an afterthought.

> I wish I could speak [to] the *Peacock* to be confirmed in my own opinion relative to this land I feel confident of existing to the southeastward and southwestward. There is no one on board my own ship that I can communicate with. I fully believe that they would be as sorry to find land here because [illegible] it may add some degree of *éclat* to the Expedition and myself. It is provoking that we can't get through this interminable barrier and get on to the land that I am confident exists now but I feel that every opportunity will be taken by me whatever may be the risk (if I know myself) to get to it and if I do not succeed it is because I cannot and an all wise Providence has otherwise ordained so I must be patient, altho' I cannot help feeling how disgusting it is to be with such a lot of officers (one or two I must exempt) who are endeavouring to do all in their power to make my exertions go for nothing. We shall however see how we will all come out of this scrape. I keep to my old motto *Nil Desperandum* . . .[5]

Alden's journal contains no entry for 19 January, so he seems to have set little store by what he reported. *Peacock* had been in sight until early afternoon and contact could have been made for consultation with Hudson. It is an open question as to how long it took for Wilkes's doubt on one page of his journal to become confidence on the previous page: the journal's format made it hard to rewrite history, but there was space for a retrospective addendum. Years later, a court martial would labour inconclusively over this very point.

The *Vincennes* abandoned the bay to *Peacock* and proceeded west. Hudson persevered and in the afternoon was rewarded by the appearance of an 'immense mass' towering above and beyond an ice island which he judged to be 150–200 feet high. The land, for that was what he and most of his crew supposed it to be, bore south-west from the ship. It was 2000 feet high in the shape of an amphitheatre, grey and dark under the shadows of the clouds, with two distinct snow-covered ridges running its entire length.

Cape Hudson as seen from the *Peacock* on 19 January 1840.

Lieutenant George Emmons, second officer of the *Peacock*, was at first sceptical, then dismissive.

> Discovery stock ran high – spy glasses were in great requisition – and many officers confirmed their opinions by a survey from the mast heads. A name was fixed upon not only for the land but for some of its capes etc . . . At midnight it was sufficiently light to discover that our supposed (not my supposed land, for I was among a few that thought otherwise, not withstanding the favourable appearances) land was apparently nothing more or less than a large ice island . . . that had been considerably magnified by refraction and although much nearer now than when we first saw it, it did not appear so high.[6]

As there was no prospect of a closer approach within the bay, Hudson quitted it with a view to trying again on the other side of its western arm. His journal entry for 19 January refers to 'supposed land'. His opinion seems to have firmed overnight, as the entry for the 20th opens with '. . . we have seen mountains of snow and ice, at least some of which we verily believe to be land covered with snow – and most aboard are still of the same opinion'. In an afterthought to this afterthought he associated himself with the majority by interpolating 'myself among the number' after 'most aboard'. A cautious man, he had restrained the enthusiasm of midshipmen Eld and Reynolds on the 16th by telling them that if they had seen land they could look forward to less ambiguous signs in a day or two. On the 19th the two had been equally certain, but Hudson had still been non-committal; indeed, when the officer of the deck had recorded the sighting of land on the log slate, Hudson had cautioned him to be very certain before making a positive report. The entry had been erased. Now, after the event, he was prepared to join the ranks of the believers.

It was four days on and three degrees further west before the *Peacock* was able to edge herself into another bay in the ice. At its head, in 66°52'S and 150°24'45"E, the water was much discoloured – 'a dark dirty green'. Hudson sent two boats to the ice, one for water and the other, under Eld, to make magnetic observations. In the meantime he sounded and found bottom at 320 fathoms. The lead brought up slate-coloured mud and a small stone, and was itself 'bruised' on a lower corner as though it had struck rock. Eld came back with a large penguin, probably an Emperor, which was found to have 32 small stones in its craw. The midshipman had also been able to take three sets of observations using both Robinson's and Lloyd's needles which gave a mean dip of 86°16.5'. There were strong appearances of land to the south and south-east. Proximity to the magnetic pole played havoc with the compasses. Unless the card was shaken with some force, the needle would move with the ship whatever its heading.[7]

The following day, 24 January, found the *Peacock* picking her way through floe ice with little room for manoeuvre. In trying to box off from a floe ahead, the ship gathered sternway and rammed another floe behind. The collision jammed the rudder. Sails had to be used to control the ship while the carpenter surveyed the damage. He advised that it would be necessary to unship the rudder. An ice anchor was taken out to a floe ahead, but before it could be secured it was carried away and the ship again backed into the ice. This broke off two of the pintles and the upper brace, almost wrenching the head off the rudder, which, with great difficulty, was brought amidships by the use of quarter tackles. The wind was rising and the floes began to compact. Of even more concern was an ice island to leeward, 7–8 miles long and 100–150 feet high. When the ice anchors again failed, the *Peacock* was driven, still sternmost, into this immense block. The spanker boom was carried away, the stern boat was smashed and the whole of the spar deck bulwark as far forward as the gangway was jarred out of position. A huge overhang of ice high on the island threatened to finish what wind and sea had begun.

Peacock, ice anchors parted, in collision with a tabular iceberg, with an avalanche about to descend on the ship.

Fortunately the ship rebounded, for she had barely moved half a length before the avalanche descended, a mass of ice large enough to have overwhelmed her. By judicious use of the fore and aft sails, Hudson was able to slip along the side of the island until it receded to the south and west. All useful sail was now set to force a way through the few narrowing passages to the open sea, but by 3.40 pm the ship was hard and fast, with snow obscuring the way out and the wind dead ahead. There was no option but to wait for a shift in the wind and to hope that it would come before the ship was driven back into the ice barrier. Along with other portents of a fearful gale to the north-west, a rising sea now began to work the imprisoned ship up and down against the floes, threatening to drive in her bows. By midnight Hudson was getting anxious.

> . . . the quantity of floe ice appears to be rapidly increasing outside of us, or rather between us and the clear sea, and the ship continually forced with the mass of Ice towards the most permanent looking winter quarters to leeward that can well be imagined, and such as I feel no disposition to describe.[8]

Although they seemed to be making slow progress northwards through the surrounding floes, in fact they were losing ground because the whole mass of ice was being driven southward faster than the ship's rate of advance. By 3 am on the 25th the ice had abraded the outer timbers of the bow and was working away at the stem, onto which the bow planking was butted. If the stem failed there was no hope for the ship – the planking would spring open, leaving a gaping, straggle-toothed hole where the bow had been. Hudson had no choice but to drive on; it was that or be ground to pieces where they were. At 4 am they were through the thick ice and the carpenters could begin work on the rudder. It took 24 hours continuous labour to refit it 'in the best possible manner its broken condition would admit'. The ship was still within an ice bay approximately thirty miles wide, and the single narrow exit from it appeared to be closing up. For four hours the *Peacock* made short tacks in that direction and at midnight escaped. By then the opening was no more than a quarter of a mile wide.

Hudson no longer had any faith in his compasses – 'for the past week [they] might as well have been in Kamshatka as in the Binnacles' – but he recorded that during the previous 24 hours the variation had changed from easterly to westerly. The ship had crossed the magnetic meridian.

The captain reviewed his situation: '. . . rudder hanging by the eyelids, the poor *Peacock*'s feathers rumpled and the ship otherwise mangled'. Consultation with his wardroom officers confirmed that the ship was in no condition to re-engage with the ice. Lieutenant Emmons was of the view that they had only escaped because, alone of the squadron's ships, *Peacock* had been built tough for exploring service. Most of the officers felt that it would be better to use the time remaining for the present cruise to make repairs in preparation for the next, a survey of Fiji. On 26 January the *Peacock*'s head was turned towards Sydney.

In the meantime *Vincennes* and *Porpoise* had made their way west, some-times in sight of each other, ahead of the *Peacock*. On the same day *Peacock* entered her bay, Wilkes took the *Vincennes* south into another, recording appearances of land to east and west. Brought up by the ice after fifteen miles in 67°04'30"S and 147°30'E, Wilkes named the place Disappointment Bay. On the following day, 24 January, as the ship continued west, Wilkes found that Lieutenant Underwood had entered on the log slate that there had been clear water three compass points across the bottom of Disappointment Bay. Wilkes was furious and demanded to know why it had not been reported to him. Poor Underwood said that he had, but Wilkes did not recall it and put the ship about to check the report. They found no opening and Underwood was tren-chantly criticised by his captain although both knew that the ice could change quickly enough to turn yesterday's opening into today's barrier. On the day in question Wilkes had been confident that there was no opening, so why waste time checking Underwood's report? The answer can only be paranoia: from that time onwards, officers at the end of their watches officers were now required to go to the masthead and report to Wilkes what they could see, 'which will prevent any false bearing being put upon my actions by the evil minded and ill disposed'.[9]

On the 26th and 27th the *Porpoise* was in sight but declined to follow when Wilkes turned *Vincennes* south towards a line of tabular bergs, which he took to be evidence that the coast was nearby. On the morning of the 28th, as *Vincennes* dodged through the bergs, land was sighted. Lieutenant Alden, whose journal had been silent on the matter on the 19th and since, now wrote, and underlined for emphasis, 'At 9.45 am Discovered Land'. Wilkes's journal entry was more subdued: '. . . land had been reported ahead and all who had seen it felt convinced it was so'. By now he trusted nothing but the evidence of his own eyes. This he was denied by a gathering gale which forced them back the way they had come. They ran blind through the bergs in bitter cold that froze a trapped seaman to the yardarm.

After the weather moderated and the southward course could be retraced, the land again came into sight on the morning of the 30th. Between the ship and the mountains, estimated by Wilkes to be 4000–5000 feet high, lay a small bay with dark volcanic rocks showing against the white of the ice. The weather precluded any approach nearer than a few miles but the bottom was sounded in 35 fathoms. 'Antarctic Land discovered beyond cavil', wrote Wilkes in his journal. He named the bay, which he placed in 66°45'S and 140°02'30"E, for Signal Quartermaster Thomas Piner. It was the bay where the French had landed eleven days earlier.

On the same day, three degrees to the west, the *Porpoise* sighted two vessels heading northwards. Taking them for *Vincennes* and *Peacock*, Lieutenant Ringgold hauled his wind to intercept. On a closer view they appeared to be too small for the American ships and Ringgold hoisted his colours, believing that he must have come across the Ross expedition and intending 'to cheer the discoverer of the North Magnetic Pole'. When French colours and a commodore's broad pennant were hoisted in reply, Ringgold correctly concluded that it was d'Urville he had encountered.

> . . . desirous of speaking and exchanging the usual customary compliments incidental to naval life, I closed with the strangers, desiring to pass within hail under the flag ship's stern. While gaining fast, and being within musket shot,

my intentions too evident to excite a doubt, so far from any reciprocity being evinced, I saw with surprise sail making by boarding the main tack on board the flag ship. Without a moment's delay, I hauled down my colours and bore up on my course before the wind.[10]

Assistant Surgeon Silas Holmes was outraged.

A more selfish and ungentlemanly act was never committed; suppose for instance, that we had been in danger of perishing from want of provisions, what possible apology could be rendered for the refusal to assist us? We might have perished within hail of the French flag.[11]

Taking advantage of a fair wind, Ringgold hastened west towards the appointed limit of exploration, longitude 105°E, hoping that what he took to be the prevailing westerly in high southern latitudes would allow him to probe for gaps in the ice as he returned. He did not put about until the *Porpoise* was in 100°E, but to no advantage because the prevailing wind was found to be contrary, from the east. By 14 February all they had to show for their long excursion west was rock and stone recovered from icebergs. Even this was puzzling, as discoloured ice was sometimes mixed with the earth as if the berg had capsized and collected material from the sea floor, but there was no bottom at 200 fathoms. The speculation was that the bergs must have come from Kerguelen Island far to the north. Ringgold considered that the brig had gone far enough and turned east. A few days of tacking into the wind convinced him that there was nothing more they could usefully do and on 24 February he put the brig's head towards the Auckland Islands. Holmes summed up the cruise.

Nothing has been seen by us to warrant the belief that land exists anywhere in our vicinity. We have coasted along the field ice from 165°E to 100°E and have found one solid, unbroken, impenetrable barrier of ice. We have never been out of sight of it, on an average, more than two hours since we first made it, and for nearly the whole distance have had it constantly in view. We have followed with all care, every winding of this icy coast and have penetrated to the most southern point of every bight or bay, when the wind would permit . . .[12]

Porpoise was in fact the last ship of the squadron to leave the ice. From Piner's Bay Wilkes had doggedly worked *Vincennes* west, most of the time in no closer contact with the ice than Ringgold had been. He had become concerned for the health of his crew, but for a fortnight was led on by reports of land almost every other day, some of which he accepted, others not. Alden, whose previously laconic entries clearly indicated that he regarded journal-keeping as a bore, became almost effusive. He recorded land, or appearances of land, on 1, 2, 5, 6, 7, 11, 12, 13, 14 and 17 February, but still the ice made 'all further approach to the land impracticable'. Wilkes became convinced that the high perpendicular barrier sometimes visible beyond the field ice was attached to land. His confidence grew as he proceeded west, his naming of individual features giving way to, successively, 'High Land covered with snow', North's High Land, Totten's High Land, Budd's High Land and Knox's High Land. Their inaccessability frustrated him, not only because he was denied physical evidence of discovery, but because he badly needed magnetic observations free of the influence of the ship. On 7 February he had noted with astonishment a rapid increase in westerly variation, $7^{1}/_{2}°$ in half a day, and in a rare moment of self-doubt could only think that 'some error seems to have occurred in the observations'. On reflection he attributed the phenomenon to proximity to the pole but it had to be confirmed. If the land were denied him, an iceberg would have to do. In the meantime, the view over the ice on 12 February resolved any doubt Wilkes might still have had about the nature of the land they were coasting.

> The above land I think clearly determines or settles the question of our having discovered the Antarctic Continent, for we have traced it now through about 30 degrees of long[itude] – equal to 900 miles. I am in hopes we shall in our progress west be yet able to discover more of it; there seems to be little probability of reaching it from the immense quantities of ice forming so impenetrable a barrier . . .[13]

And so it proved. While heading towards the land on 14 February they passed a large, discoloured and accessible iceberg to which, when again obstructed by the ice, they returned. Wilkes landed the magnetic instruments and got a good series of observations which confirmed the rapid increase in westerly variation. To his relief, they were also able to collect a large number of samples of stone and sand, solid evidence of their discovery. The ship took on water from a frozen pond found on the berg and the sailors amused themselves by tobogganing down its slopes. Wilkes marked with a signal flag the bottle in which he placed an account of their discovery. The bottle also contained orders for Hudson and Ringgold to continue west from this longitude, the last appointed rendezvous, until 1 March. Wilkes hoped that, in the time left to him, he could join his discovery to Enderby Land, but calm seas over the ensuing days caused him to suspect that there might be a large body of ice to his north, perhaps the one encountered in 1773 by Cook.

Wilkes found water, rocks and recreation for his crew on an iceberg, but could not reach the land beyond.

On 17 February, still running west, they again came to the ice, but here it extended north and south across their bows as far as the eye could see. The variation was now decreasing. There were appearances of land to the southwest, extending northward, but with no closer approach possible, Wilkes turned away. These last appearances he named Termination Land. For three days the ship had to beat east along the northern shore of what turned out to be an ice bay 50–60 miles deep. Officers and crew became increasingly concerned that the opening through which they had entered would be found blocked. Finally, on the 21st they escaped the ice bay and all hands were mustered aft to hear Wilkes announce that their southern cruise was over. The *Vincennes* was heading for more temperate climes.

CHAPTER 6

Marking the Territory

The French expedition had returned to Hobart with d'Urville anxious both to report his second Antarctic cruise to the Minister of Marine and to make public his discovery as quickly as possible. But first he had to justify his proceedings.

> These results are, I trust, of a nature to excite general interest; and will, in particular, I venture to hope, be favourably received by the King, who, himself, directed my researches towards the Antarctic latitudes. His Majesty will see that, in fulfillment of his wishes . . . I have taken upon myself to risk another [attempt], in a direction the very opposite of that which had been indicated to me. First, the field was one wholly unexplored: no navigator having ever penetrated further than the 59th degree; secondly, from the few declinations of the magnetic needle hitherto noticed in much lower latitudes, natural philosophers had been led to place the southern pole in that direction . . . Finally, the expedition of the English Captain Ross, and the American Wilkes, contributed to my determination.[1]

He gave the Minister to understand that Adelie Land was not, in his opinion, an isolated stretch of coast, but that land 'surrounds the greater portion of the polar circle, and will present itself at nearly all points to the mariner who is bold enough and fortunate enough to clear the masses of accumulated ice which ordinarily girdle it'. He did not give a position for the magnetic pole and also failed to mention his encounter with the American brig *Porpoise*, which he had met well south of 59°; apparently only Cook's achievements were thought worthy of record. The Hobart populace showed great interest in the results of the cruise, but Jacquinot, captain of the *Zélée*, thought that their congratulations had an edge.

> . . . it was easy to detect the presence of considerable national jealousy and that our successes were causing some heartburning; especially as . . . England had entered the field by giving Captain Ross the mission to explore the south polar region and take magnetic observations. Nobody could be in any doubt that the French corvettes had already got there before the English captain, and it was enough to prick English vanity most disagreeably.[2]

After briefing Governor Franklin, d'Urville arranged for an account to be prepared for the Hobart press 'in the interests of science as well as to obviate all erroneous supposition and ridiculous exaggeration'. The *Hobart Town Courier* could see little to exaggerate about: 'although not much will have been gained by this enterprise in point of utility, it will add greatly to our geographic and scientific knowledge'. The *Hobart Town Advertiser* received the account too late for translation before its weekly deadline, but suspected that the 'large continent' said to have been discovered would prove to be Biscoe's Enderby Land. Jacquinot read this incredulity as evidence of English envy, but was confident that the evidence of their charts and the rock samples the expedition gave away would convince. Unfortunately, when the account appeared in parallel French and English texts in the *Hobart Town Courier* it only served to muddy the waters. 'Un petit nombre de phoques à fourrure'[3] was tersely translated as 'fur seals': within days sealers were planning to set out for Adelie Land. Jacquinot feared that they would be disappointed, and not by numbers alone because he was by no means sure that the four or five seals they had seen were of the desired species. Again, the French version placed the eastern limit of the discovery at 142°East; a typesetter converted this in the English version to 147°*West*, which extended the Adelie Land coast by about 150 miles or by more than 2000, depending on whether it was the error in number or the error in direction that one was being misled by.[4]

Desgraz, d'Urville's secretary, wrote to the newspapers protesting that Biscoe's discovery was 68° or 1700 miles further west, but he also gave the relative positions of Enderby Land (52°E) and Adelie Land (140°E). By the time his letter was published the expedition had left Hobart. It was just as well, because anyone subtracting his longitudes, which were correct, would have made the difference 88°. Furthermore, a degree of longitude at that latitude equates to 29 miles, not 25 as Desgraz allowed. His miscalculations would have done nothing to obviate 'ridiculous exaggeration'.

But at least Desgraz was authorised to advertise the French discovery; it was otherwise for the Americans. The *Peacock* limped into Sydney on 22 February, soon after the French had arrived in Hobart, but Hudson's instructions forbade any announcement to satisfy local curiosity. Emmons recorded that he was asked questions which he 'could not with propriety answer'. In the report he prepared for the Secretary of the Navy, Hudson wrote that he 'believed' they had sighted land on 19 January and again on the 23rd 'at least as far as *terra firma* can be distinguished where everything is covered with snow'. The *Peacock* was too large for Sydney's railway slip and so arrangements were made to heave her down in Mosman Bay which, among other advantages, put three miles between the crew and Sydney's crimps and grog shops. Examination of the bows revealed that the stem had been chafed to within an inch and a half of disaster. Another hour of grinding by the ice and the *Peacock* would have been finished.

Repairs were well advanced by 11 March when Hudson was surprised to hear that the *Vincennes* had arrived in Sydney. Wilkes had been trying to make Hobart until contrary winds forced a change of plan. Like d'Urville, he thought that the report of his discovery would reach home quicker from Australia than from the squadron's next appointed rendezvous, the Bay of Islands. He was not impressed to be greeted in Sydney by the Hobart press accounts of d'Urville's discovery of land on the afternoon of 19 January. A comparison of the *Peacock*'s log with that of his own ship was no comfort; there were no logged sightings of land on 19 January or earlier. But there was Hudson's official report, which had not yet been sent to Washington. Wilkes hurried ashore to consult the American consul, Williams, and on return was met at the gangway by Alden who remarked, with some malice one suspects, that the French had been ahead of them. Not so, said Wilkes – had Alden forgotten his reports of land on the *morning* of 19 January, several hours before the French were dating their claim? Alden had indeed forgotten them, but a look at the ship's log refreshed his memory about the incidents even though he had not entered them there. That was good enough for Wilkes; no matter that Alden's journal showed that he had not been definite about land until 28 January. Wilkes continued to build his claim for an earlier sighting – even if only by a few hours. Somehow, one copy of Hudson's report was found to refer to 'the morning of the 19th', hours before the French, although another copy only gave the date. Things were going well, but then Biscoe came to pay his respects. Had Wilkes heard the news of Balleny's discoveries? Biscoe's information was not precise – sailors' scuttlebutt – but Balleny's islands seemed to be in the vicinity of the land sketched by Wilkes on 16 January. About to beat off the French, was he now to be pre-empted by a British sealer?

Wilkes's report to the Secretary of the Navy, dated 11 March and written without benefit of the logs of the *Porpoise* and *Flying Fish*, asserted that land was seen on the morning of 19 January, a statement both more precise in time and more certain than Hudson's 'belief'. Wilkes did not mention a personal sighting on the 16th, nor that he had made a sketch of it. He told the Secretary that the results of the cruise led him to four conclusions. First, that the discovery of land through 40° of longitude[5], and the similarity of formation and position of the line of ice along and beyond it, was evidence that the Antarctic Continent existed, extending 70° from east to west.[6] Second, that at times different points of the land are free from ice. Third, that these points are frequented by seals in commercial numbers. Fourth, that the coast is a place of resort for large numbers of whales, particularly finbacks.[7]

Wilkes was bound by the expedition's secrecy instructions about discovery, but a discovery pre-empted is not a discovery at all. For the time being he could do nothing about Balleny but he could settle the French. The very next issue of the *Sydney Herald* carried the story. The paper was assured, 'on the highest authority', that 'the researches ... after a southern continent have been completely successful'. It was first seen 'on the morning' of 19 January in 64°20'S and 154°18'E.[8] To protect the interests of his own countrymen, the highest authority chose not to disclose the seals and the whales, and so left little for the *Herald* to get excited about. It could see no benefit to commerce although no doubt the discovery would be highly gratifying to Captain Wilkes and his officers.[9] This echoed the reaction of the Hobart press to the French discovery. The *Australian* was puzzled by the American change of attitude to disclosure.

> A good deal of mystery has been observed by the officers of the *Peacock* relative to the nature and extent of any discoveries they might have made of land in the Antarctic ocean. It is, from what we can learn, probably the fact, that they saw the coast of a southern continent ... The *Vincennes*, however ... appears to have been more fortunate than her consort, inasmuch as she has escaped any

danger and has been more successful in her exploration . . . but, in consequence of the icebergs, found it impossible to take possession of the territory, or to effect a landing at any point . . . These events reflect credit on the officers and men who belong to the expedition, but, while we are fully aware of the reason which has induced the explorers to maintain a reserve in speaking of the details of their voyage (namely a desire to submit the new intelligence to the American government in the first instance), we cannot feel sorry that so much has transpired, inasmuch as the cause of science is promoted thereby, rational curiosity is gratified, and we are able to afford information which may be useful to the British vessels of discovery, the *Erebus* and the *Terror*, whose arrival in our port may be almost immediately expected.[10]

Comparing the French and American accounts, the *Sydney Gazette* thought it not improbable that the newly discovered land might be a continuation of Enderby Land, in which case neither expedition could claim priority. Should science be able to profit, however, the hardships of the most recent explorers would not have been in vain. Still smarting from the Desgraz rebuke, the *Hobart Town Advertiser* read the Sydney reports as vindication.

> It appears . . . that the newly-discovered Southern continent was seen in the morning by the American sloop of war *Vincennes*, on the same day it was viewed by *L'Astrolabe* and *Zélée*, and after all it is merely a continuation of the same continent first discovered by Capt. Biscoe in the *Tula*.[11]

Leaving *Peacock* behind to complete her repairs, with instructions to rejoin at Tonga, Wilkes sailed for the Bay of Islands on 19 March. He confessed that he had worried more about *Peacock* than the other vessels because of her condition on leaving Sydney in December. On seeing the damage she had sustained in the ice he had expressed astonishment at her survival and had been full of praise for Hudson and his men. In the quiet of his own cabin he must surely have thanked Providence that she had survived, for to lose the *Peacock* and her crew after directing them to separate from *Vincennes* would have been inexcusable.

Two days after Wilkes sailed for New Zealand the barque *Acasta* arrived from London with the details of Balleny's Antarctic discoveries of the previous year, as presented to the Royal Geographical Society. Unlike Biscoe's discoveries, they were in the very quarter where the French and Americans had been exploring. The naturalist Alexander McLeay, or his son, drew the news to the attention of the Americans. It must have been Hudson they told, and he is said to have responded 'then all our labour has been in vain'.[12]

In the meantime, the French ships on the way to New Zealand had visited the Auckland Islands, long the haunt of French and other whalers. As they tacked towards the harbour of Sarah's Bosom, a departing brig had tried to catch their attention with rockets, blue lights and guns. The French probably did not see the smaller vessel, but in the ensuing days they came across evidence of its visit. In a whalers' hut they found a board on which was inscribed, in white letters on black:

> U.S. brig *Porpoise*, 73 days out from Sydney, New Holland, on her return
> from an exploring cruise along the antarctic circle, all well; arrived the 7th,
> and sailed again on the 10th March for the Bay of Islands, New Zealand.

The identity of the ship d'Urville had ignored on 30 January was now known, but he made no comment, even when a bottle was found that contained a note recording the limits of the *Porpoise*'s cruise as 64°30'S and 126°26'E. Next to the American board he placed one of his own, black letters on white:

> The French corvettes *Astrolabe* and *Zélée* left Hobart Town on 25 February
> 1840, anchored here on the 11th March, and left on the 20th of the same for
> New Zealand. From 19 January to 1 February, 1840, discovery of Adelie Land
> and determination of the South magnetic pole![13]

Shoulder to shoulder on their respective posts, Tweedledum and Tweedledee silently competed for the attention of nobody. This near encounter was not quite the last opportunity for the expeditions to make contact. Both were making for New Zealand but a visit to the South Island kept the French away from the Bay of Islands, the American rendezvous, until 26 April, by which time the Americans were well on their way to Tonga. The French then made for home through Torres Strait. Both ships grounded and were very nearly wrecked. As disasters go, it would not have been d'Urville's choice of tragic end.

> A thousand times better for us to have remained entombed in the eternal ice of
> the South Pole, where, at least, we might have hoped to deserve the interest
> that always attaches to great and noble enterprises, rather than see all our work
> wiped out by a commonplace catastrophe, by an ordinary shipwreck on coral
> reefs . . .[14]

Although it was November 1840 before the expedition reached Toulon, so keen were the French to have d'Urville's Antarctic discoveries recognised that, within a month of receiving his report and chart from Hobart, in June 1840, the latter had been engraved, officially published and distributed by the Depôt de la Marine. In London, the *Athenaeum* was generous in its praise for the 'zeal and exertion shown in making these discoveries public'. It was less impressed with d'Urville's assertion that he was the first to sail south of 59°. 'Without wishing, in any way, to detract from the merit of Capt. D'Urville', it cited the Russian, Bellingshausen, in 1820, and Weddell and Balleny. Such lesser lights were of no interest to d'Urville; his benchmark was Cook's furthest south in that sector of the Antarctic. London's *United Service Gazette* could not see that there was much to detract from: it was 'an interesting rather than important geographical discovery' of 'an island or continent with a coast of 1,700 miles . . . unavailable for tillage or settlement'. More remarkably, it had been discovered by the French and the Americans on the same day, but 720 miles apart.[15]

If Wilkes, when he entered the Bay of Islands, was relieved to find the *Porpoise*, he must have been overjoyed to see the *Flying Fish*, which had been missing since before the squadron entered the ice. After failing to rendezvous at Macquarie Island, Lieutenant Pinkney had taken the schooner south. The line of ice was reached on 21 January. Following it to the west, on the 23rd they observed dark spots to the south. Examination by telescope satisfied Pinkney that these were rocks (they were not) but the ice would not permit a closer approach. From here the line of ice had led them northward and westward, and over the next thirteen days a battering by continual bad weather opened wide the schooner's already weeping seams. The pumps had to be in almost constant use to keep the water below the level of the cabin floor. On 5 February Pinkney was handed a letter:

> We, the undersigned, the crew of the Schooner *Flying Fish*, wish to let you know that we are in a most deplorable condition: the bedclothes are all wet; we have no place to lie down in; we have not had a dry stitch of clothes for seven days; four of our number [of 11] are very sick; and we, the few remaining number, can hold out no longer; we hope you will take it into consideration, and relieve us from what must terminate in our death.[16]

Pinkney sought his officers' views. They were unanimous in the conviction that the condition of crew and vessel were such as to 'loudly demand an immediate return to milder latitudes'. Pinkney, himself ill since Macquarie Island, needed no further urging and, from a furthest west of 139°45'E, turned north. It took the bedraggled schooner more than a month to reach the Bay of Islands.

During his stay at the Bay of Islands, with the benefit of access for the first time to the logs of the *Porpoise* and the *Flying Fish*, Wilkes wrote a letter to James Clark Ross and sent it to Australia to await the arrival of the British expedition. Could he have taken to heart the *Australian*'s advice about assisting his rivals? His motivation, wrote Wilkes, was a 'desire to be useful'. He felt that his government, in spite of the secrecy enjoined on him, would expect him to make return for the assistance received from the learned societies and distinguished men of Britain. It would also give him pleasure to discharge, in a small degree, the obligation he personally owed to Ross and other promoters of the British expedition for the interest they had displayed in its American counterpart. To this end Wilkes proposed to 'enlighten' Ross on his course and offer a few hints on Antarctic navigation, even at the risk of appearing 'almost presumptuous'. There was advice about winds and currents, and about the South Magnetic Pole, which the Exploring Expedition had approached 'very

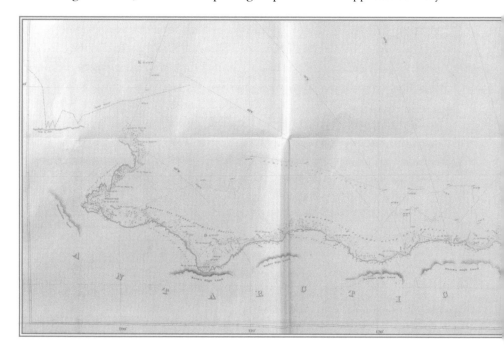

near', Wilkes's observations placing it in about 70°S and 140°E.[17] Ross would find a 'snug little harbour' at Piner's Bay and perhaps water in ponds on icebergs. Wilkes also gave Ross the benefit of his Antarctic experience south of Cape Horn in 1839. He had no doubt that, in a favourable season, Weddell's track could be followed, 'notwithstanding what the Frenchman may say', but:

> I could not afford the time to be frozen up, as my other duties were and are paramount to passing the winter in such a situation. But you are differently situated, and I should advise you, by all means, to try to penetrate between longitude 35° and 45°W.[18]

Wilkes appended his chart of 'the Antarctic Continent', which showed the track of the *Vincennes* and traced 'the land and the icy barrier'.[19] The ice and the track had been laid down by Alden, but the topography was Wilkes's own work. He was marking his territory, figuratively as well as literally. A collaborator might have taken the letter and the chart at face value, but to a competitor it was as much as to say that 'in two seasons I have, in between more important tasks, already done most of the things for which you are being sent

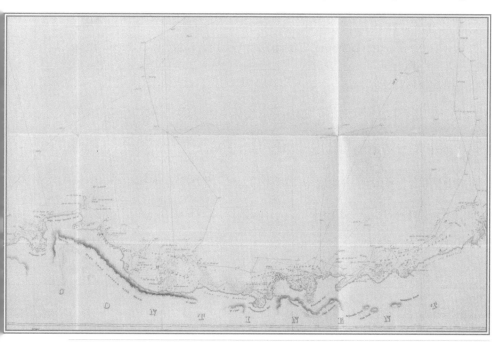

Wilkes's final version of his Antarctic discoveries.

south; you are at liberty, having far more time at your disposal, to follow up, confirm and expand my discoveries'. It is difficult to believe that even a person as insensitive as Wilkes could imagine that Ross would not take offence. It is easier to suspect that the American hoped his rival would look elsewhere for, as he later wrote, 'every one knew that Captain Ross was about to explore our very track, and thus would test our operations'.[20]

Wilkes's chart showed an almost continuous line of ice from 97°30'E to 167°30'E, with mountainous land hatched in at intervals behind it. At the eastern extremity, in 66°S, a line of hatching extended north-east to south-west between 163–166°E, well to the east of the features seen on 16 January by Ringgold, Eld and Reynolds. In the absence of a label or explanation, which was not provided, a casual reader would conclude that this represented land seen south of the *Vincennes*, whose track was the only one shown, on 12 or 13 January, or perhaps seen east of the ship on 15 or 16 January. It could also have been, although this was not evident from the chart in the absence of *Porpoise*'s track, Ringgold's sighting to the south-east on 13 January. This was where Biscoe might have approximately placed the Balleny Islands for Wilkes when the two men met in Sydney after the Antarctic cruise, but it was drawn as a continuous stretch of land many miles in extent, roughly parallel to the line of ice and with no southern shore.

With this mine left bobbing in his wake, Wilkes put the Antarctic behind him. Ahead, more than two years of Pacific surveying still lay between the Ex Ex and home.

CHAPTER 7

Victoria's Land

The magnetic agenda had made the voyage south through the Atlantic a slow affair for Ross. At the Cape Verde Islands he privately expressed his impatience to be at 'the South polar ice and the Antarctic Continent'.[1] Observations became more frequent as the ships approached the Magnetic Equator, heading as directly south by compass as the wind would allow. The intention was to cross the Equator at right angles and, in 13°45'S and 30°41'W, Ross was extremely gratified to see the agreed signal hoisted simultaneously from both ships as their dip needles reached the horizontal position. The next objective was the line of minimum total intensity, similar to the Magnetic Equator or circle of no dip, but not identical to it.[2]

The line was found in 19°S and 29°15'W, two hundred miles further north than expected. They wove a course along it, crossing it twice more. The general direction of the line was consistent with earlier observations, but in the intervening fifteen years it appeared to have been moving north at an average rate in excess of thirteen miles per year. The ships visited St Helena to set up a magnetic observatory and then proceeded to Capetown to set up another. They sailed for Kerguelen Island in the Indian Ocean on 6 April 1840, hoping to arrive in time for the May term day.

Erebus reached Christmas Harbour on 12 May and *Terror* arrived the following day, but it took two days to warp the ships up to the head of the harbour against the wind. The observatories were set up in defiance of gales which on one occasion moved the magnetic hut a foot. Ross frequently had to throw himself flat on the beach to avoid being carried into the water, and one of the seamen was driven in by a squall and nearly drowned. The observations on term day, 29 May, were worth the difficulties.

> It happened most fortunately to be a time of unusual magnetic disturbance, so that our first day's simultaneous observations (later) proved the vast and instantaneous effect of the disturbing power, whatever it might be, affecting the magnetometers at Toronto in Canada and at Kerguelen Island, nearly antipodal to each other, simultaneously and similarly in all their strange oscillations and irregular movements, and thus immediately afforded one of the most important facts that the still-hidden cause of magnetic phenomena has yet presented.[3]

The earth had demonstrated that its magnetic field was simultaneously responsive at diametrically opposite places, although the force that produced the response was still obscure. They remained at Kerguelen for the next term day and quitted the dreary place on 20 July. Gales had battered the island on most of the days spent there, and rain or snow had fallen on all but three. By sailing towards Tasmania along the 47th parallel of latitude, Ross expected to find one of the foci of maximum intensity in 140°E longitude. Fox's dip circle fully lived up to expectations. In moderate weather it gave more precise observations than was possible on land when there was local attraction such as iron, and it could be used in the heaviest gale. They did not find the focus along the parallel they were sailing and judged that it was much further south, beyond reach at that time of year. The line of no variation was crossed in 46°S and 134°45'E on 8 August. It was further east than was expected from earlier observations and contrary to the assumed westward movement of isogonic lines in the Southern Hemisphere, lending support to a remark made by Peter Barlow three years earlier that the line had changed little in sixty years. Ross concluded that it was probably as static as its equivalent off the coast of America. The regularity and magnitude of the daily change in variation along the 47th parallel also led Ross to revisit a dream as old as Columbus: where the change was as rapid and regular as this, perhaps it could be used to determine longitude more simply than by using a chronometer.[4]

In spite of all precautions the ships were separated by bad weather on 28 July and each made its way independently to the next appointed rendezvous,

Hobart. Ross's old friend Sir John Franklin greeted him with the Wilkes letter. Here, for the first time since leaving England, was recent news of d'Urville and Wilkes. Franklin also had everything ready for construction of the permanent magnetic observatory. Convicts erected it in nine days, so zealously that they had to be restrained from working past Saturday midnight into an English Sunday to complete it. How Humboldt would have smiled! Franklin himself assisted with the observations on term days, recording every two-and-a-half minutes throughout a twelve-hour shift. For non-term days Ross instituted an additional night hour of continued observation to watch for the effect of the aurora, 'which has been known to exercise so powerful an influence on the magnetometers'. The idyllic spot, in the government demesne and close by a cove for the ships, was named Rossbank as a compliment to the commander.

It was six months since the French and the Americans had left Antarctic waters. On the day he arrived in Hobart, 17 August, Ross digested Wilkes's letter and drafted one to Anne to reassure her about their prospects. He told her of the time he had spent with Wilkes in London, training him in the use of magnetic instruments. At the time Ross had been lobbying hard for the British Antarctic expedition, but in frequent conversations with Wilkes he had not withheld his views about the itinerary such a voyage would follow. He now felt that Wilkes had anticipated him to snatch 'the palm of glory'. He was not about to concede.

> ... altho' I am sorry that he did not chose some other spot than that related by myself, for there was plenty of room for all of us, yet I am not without the hope of being able to sail over this Antarctic Continent of his, which I am convinced will turn out to be nothing more than islands or ice shelf extending some distance from this Continent.

And the main objective, the South Magnetic Pole, was still unvisited.

> This [Wilkes] does not pretend to have reached ... the Frenchman Mons. Dumont D'Urville says he went down sufficiently near the pole to satisfy himself of its true position, but he will find it very difficult to satisfy others. He does not claim to have reached it, but only to infer from his observations where it is – this Gauss in Germany had already done for him and nothing short of reaching the Pole itself will satisfy the demand of science ... I feel the more confident of being able to do this – and it will be a painful stimulus to me and a

rich reward to have it in my power to surpass the Expeditions of these rivals for glory and national distinction. But a few short months work will determine this point – just about the time this letter will reach you, your birthday will have arrived and the 17th of January is the day on which I have looked forward with hope to discover something worthy of being distinguished by the name of her I love . . .5

There might even be advantage in being late to the search. Ross gave thought to Balleny's experience: south of 69° the sealer had seen open water beyond the ice, on a track to the east of that taken by Wilkes and d'Urville. The South Magnetic Pole might be more accessible from the east than from the north. And although Ross denied it, he must have had doubts about the ability of even strengthened ships to penetrate the 'awful ice' against which the French and American vessels had demonstrably failed. The meridian he would select for his southward push (170°E) was much further east than those followed by his rivals.6

Lady Jane Franklin took every opportunity to have officers of the expedition make up numbers in Hobart's tiny social circle. Crozier, Ross's second in command, was smitten with her niece, Sophia Cracroft, who rejected him and his proposal of marriage (which unfortunately for him appears to have been in writing) on the grounds that he was 'a horrid Radical and an indifferent speller'. She preferred to flirt, unsuccessfully, with Ross. Lady Jane took a rather more matronly interest in Ross, and gave him some considered career advice.

I asked Captain Ross what it (the expedition) would secure to him – it could not make him an Admiral though it could give him a title, tho' if he cared for that he could no doubt have had it long ago – he acknowledged this and said he had been offered a knighthood on his return in the *Cove*, but declined it. Afterwards . . . he began to feel a little sorry – his friends said it ought to have been forced upon him and he would not have resisted this . . . Lord Minto said he had refused it once and must take the consequences, but it would not be refused him if he applied for it; this however Captain Ross did not choose to do and he thinks it just as well as it is, for if he was called Sir James Ross, he might be mistaken for his uncle. I told him I believed the advantage of accepting the small honour as soon as it was offered was this, that the next time, when fresh honours were deserved, it must be a still higher degree which was awarded; thus, if he had been knighted after the return of the *Cove* the only next thing they could do after his return from the Magnetic Expedition was to make him a Baronet.[7]

The expedition sailed from Hobart in November, early enough to make magnetic term day observations at the Auckland Islands before tackling the ice. There they found the French and American sign boards. Ross noted that the one left by the *Porpoise* made no mention of an Antarctic Continent, but he attributed this silence to secrecy or to a more northerly course than that followed by the other American ships. The dip, which had increased gradually and predictably since Hobart, was found to be two degrees short, confirming for Ross that local attraction made observations on land uncertain and inaccurate. At Campbell Island, a day's sail to the south-east, Ross told Crozier of his intention to go south on that meridian rather than that of Hobart. Crozier 'entirely concurred' and, armed with a list of rendezvous points against the event of separation, followed his commander south.

They met their first icebergs on 27 December, table-topped monoliths 120–180 feet high, quite unlike anything Ross had seen in the Arctic. On New Year's Day they crossed the Antarctic Circle and shortly thereafter came to the line of pack ice in 169°45'E. It was further north than when encountered by Balleny, but with 'none of those evidences of impenetrability we had been led to expect'. For four days Ross reconnoitred the pack edge, looking for a soft spot and awaiting a favourable wind. On 5 January the ice beyond the wind-consolidated edge of the pack appeared to be navigable as far south as could be seen from the masthead. The weather was unsettled and the wind was blowing directly towards the ice, which would have prevented any escape to open water, but Ross made signal to *Terror* and directed *Erebus* towards the weakest point of the edge. It was time for the bombs to demonstrate their capability as ice ships.

Ice Ships

Until John Ross experimented with the paddle steamer *Victory*, all ice navigation had been in sail-powered ships. Ninety years later, Roald Amundsen, himself not averse to a calculated risk, was unstinting in his admiration for predecessors who were almost totally at the whim of the wind. When auxiliary steam first became available, it was not much more reliable and so feeble that serious icebreaking was out of the question.

Cook had set an international standard for exploring vessels, valuing carrying capacity and sturdy construction over speed and appearance. His use of Whitby colliers was noted in Europe and, by d'Urville's time, the French navy had found an equivalent – their horse transports. *Astrolabe* had most of the virtues of the *Endeavour* but unfortunately the French opted to dress her up like a proper warship. Her sides were pierced for guns and she was rated a corvette, at once better armed for self-protection and more suitable for showing the flag. The gun ports were inconvenient in big seas even when closed, and they also structurally weakened the hull. This was of no great importance in the Pacific, but d'Urville was always conscious that his ships were unsuitable for sustained contact with the Antarctic ice. Their bow plating was little more than a gesture.

But at least there had been a gesture. Most of the vessels of the Ex Ex were unsuitable for exploring service generally, much less for Antarctic exploration. Even the *Peacock*, strongly built for exploration duty, was in all other respects a typical sloop-of-war. Neither her accommodation nor her fitout made much concession to extra personnel or to scientific work. *Vincennes* had some modification made to her accommodation, but none at all to strengthen her for the ice.

Erebus and *Terror*, on the other hand, were state of the art. As former bomb vessels, they were already amongst the strongest ships afloat, but they were given an exhaustive refit. Mr Rice, of Chatham Dockyard, told James Clark Ross that his yard had stripped off all projections, including the quarter galleries. The gunwale had been doubled with eight-inch oak plank, three feet broad. Brazier's copper, twice the usual thickness, covered the bottom and the entire bow. The thwartship bulk-heads between the three holds had been made watertight, as had the holds, thus isolating each in the event of holing. Internally, the bow had been 'fortified with a solid mass of timber eight inches moulded'. The deck planking was six inches thick. Iron fittings reinforced the hull throughout. The stern was filled with timber, making it as strong as the bow 'to meet the shocks which the extremities are most likely to encounter in the ice'.[8]

If the wind were favourable and the ice not too thick, Ross had ships with hulls strong enough to break through the pack. He was the first navigator equipped to confront moderate ice he could not avoid. Sixty years later, after steam had proved its worth, wooden hulls were still favoured for their 'give' and 'ride' in the ice. Not until well into the twentieth century did the diesel-powered, steel-hulled, ice-hardened ship come fully into its own.

As usual, the edge of the pack was thicker ice than the area behind. It took an hour's thumping to get through it to small ponds of clear water and narrow leads that opened to the south. After four hours the edge was no longer visible behind them and the ships were still sailing freely, although they were occasionally sustaining shocks that would have demolished less sturdy vessels. That evening, there was an early lesson in the deceit of Antarctic horizons.

> A remarkable appearance of land was reported . . . and, continuing for many hours without any alteration of figure, several of the officers imagined it was really land they saw, assuming the appearance of many pointed hills perfectly covered with snow, and so calculated to deceive the inexperienced eye, that had we been prevented proceeding further, they would doubtless have asserted on our return to England that we had discovered land in this position. This appearance of land was, however, nothing more than the upper part of a cloud, marking, by a well-defined but irregular line, the limit to which vapour can ascend in these latitudes; below is vapour in every degree of condensation, above, the clear cold space which vapour can never attain. It is always near the margin of the ice that these appearances of land are most remarkable and most deceptive. It proved a useful lesson to some of our new hands, who could not be persuaded it was not land until we had actually passed over the place of their baseless mountains.[9]

Here was a pointed reminder of Sir John Ross's Croker Mountains, phantom barrier to the north-west passage, and a suggestion of what Wilkes might sometimes have found had he been able to take a closer look. The next day showed a water-sky to the south-east, dark with the promise of open sea, but it took another four days of buffeting before they reached clear water in 70°23'S and 174°50'E. Now free, after 200 miles, to choose a course independent of the pack, Ross followed his compass south directly towards the Magnetic Pole. As compass south was now south-west true and they had no need to proceed further in the direction of the ice, they expected to reach the pole in a matter of days. The appearance of a strong land-blink ahead of the ships in the afternoon of 10 January caused some disquiet, but the optimists took comfort from its being much paler than that seen in the Arctic. At 2 am on 11 January Lieutenant Woods, who had the watch, confirmed the pessimists' fears. He reported his sighting to Ross, who wrote:

> It rose in lofty peaks, entirely covered with perennial snow; it could be distinctly traced from SSW to SEbyS (by compass), and must have been more than one hundred miles distant when first seen. The highest mountain of this range I named for Lieutenant-Colonel Sabine, . . . one of the best and earliest friends of my youth, and to whom this compliment was more especially due, as having been the first proposer and one of the most active and zealous promoters of the expedition.[10]

As they approached the coast, disappointment about being unable to sail to the pole gave way to awe. Mount Sabine, thirty miles inland, was nearly ten thousand feet high. Its flanking ranges extended 70–80 miles to the north-west with peaks 8000–9000 feet high. Surgeon McCormick believed it to be 'a Southern Continent'. Cornelius Sullivan, armourer on the *Erebus*, found that his duties interfered with the wonder of the experience.

> My friend if i could only view and Study the Sublimity of nature – but Lo i had to pull the brails . . . The bold masses of Ice that walld. in the Land, the romantic gulf of the mountains as they glitter in the Sun Rendered this Scene Quite Enchanting. this mountain is most perpendicular mountain in the world.[11]

A bay protected by a promontory which Ross named Cape Adare appeared to offer a place to land but, when Ross and Crozier were rowed across the following morning, the coast was found to be ice-bound and had a vicious surf pounding it. They had to settle for an island in the bay and, with the weather threatening and the recall flag flying from *Erebus*, possession was taken with a minimum of ceremony. A way was forced through throngs of penguins which expressed their resentment at the annexation of Victoria Land, the 'earliest and most remote southern discovery' of the Queen's long reign. Then it was plant the flag, three cheers, drink a toast, kidnap a local inhabitant or two, gather some rocks and quickly take to the boats before the fog came down.

From the dip (86°) and the variation (44°) Ross placed the pole in 76°S and 145°20'E, about 500 miles south-west true of the ships. Should he follow the coast to the north-west, hoping that at its western extremity it turned south? Or should he follow it south, looking for a turning or an opening to the west?

Ross raised the flag on Possession Island, ignoring the protests of the inhabitants.

The latter was preferred, as being more likely to extend our researches into higher latitudes, and as affording a better chance of afterwards attaining one of the principal objects of our voyage: and although we could not but feel disappointed in our expectation of shortly reaching the magnetic pole, yet these mountains being in our way restored to England the honour of the discovery of the southernmost known land, which had been nobly won by the intrepid Bellingshausen, and for more than twenty years retained by Russia.[12]

As the ships worked south, Herschel, Lloyd and Whewell, among other magnetic crusaders, had peaks named for them. Surveying as they went required a close watch to be kept on the sea as well as on the mountains, and Ross, busy with angles, was taken aback to see an island that he would have sworn had not been there two or three hours previously. It was over 100 feet high with the summit and eastern side free of snow. A check with other officers on deck disclosed that they were missing one iceberg. Ross was sceptical that anything so covered with earth and stones could be other than land, but its slight rolling motion convinced him that he was indeed looking at a recently overturned iceberg. A cargo of Darwin's erratic boulders was on its way north. Contrary winds and thick weather took them away from the coast, inhibiting progress until 17 January when the wind veered favourably to the west and, as if to celebrate, the sun shone. Refraction brought land to the south-west into view, and then removed it. It was two days and a hundred miles on before they came to it, but the day of the mirage was more important to Ross who, true to his word, named Coulman Island 'after her father' and its southern point, Cape Anne. To his chagrin, he was unable to find a harbour from which magnetic observations could be made on the next term day, 20 January. By 7 pm on the 22nd, however, Ross was satisfied that they had exceeded Weddell's furthest south and there was an extra ration of grog to make the traditional Saturday night toast – 'Sweethearts and wives' (generally followed, *sotto voce*, by 'may they never meet').

Between Cape Anne and the mainland there was fixed land ice of the kind Wilkes had described, and Ross had to concede that it could not be penetrated, being without 'a crack or hole of water to be seen in any part of it'. Further south the ice was more amenable and a closer approach to the shore was possible. At noon on 25 January a dip of 87°54' and variation of 67°13' indicated that the pole was no more than 249 miles distant, and Ross began to contemplate the possibility, if they could not outflank the land by going south, of forcing through the ice to the shore later in the season, there to find a winter harbour.

At noon the following day the dip was 88°33' and the pole 174 miles west by south true. To the south-west by south, however, there was a landblink which soon became more definite. All hoped that it 'would prove a Cape Flyaway, as many others have done before', but the 27th revealed it to be an island. Franklin Island was no more hospitable than Possession Island had been, but Ross thought that its beaches might harbour rookeries in the seal-breeding season. The log of the *Erebus* recorded that, on the horizon beyond Franklin Island, eight other islands could be seen. The tallest was dubbed High Island and, like Topsy, as they approached it just grew. It grew into Mount Erebus, estimated by Ross to be 12,400 feet high. From the summit trailed a plume of what appeared to be snow drift. Even when it was recognised as smoke, Ross maintained his scientific composure:

The discovery of an active volcano in so high a southern latitude cannot but be esteemed a circumstance of high geological importance and interest, and contribute to throw some further light on the physical construction of our globe.[13]

Others, having passed for days through the white desolation of the ice-studded sea, were overwhelmed by the apparition that reared before them, particularly when a major eruption began at 4 pm. Hooker was rather more of a scientist than Ross, but for him it was a quasi-religious experience, causing 'a feeling of awe to steal over us, at the consideration of our comparative insignificance and helplessness, and at the same time an indescribable feeling of the greatness of the Creator in the works of his hand'.[14] As they approached it became clear that High Island was connected at its western end, by ice at least, to the mainland. From its eastern end 'a low white line' stretched eastwards as far as the eye could see. It was the second remarkable discovery of a memorable day, proving to be a perpendicular cliff of ice, perhaps 150–200 feet high, perfectly level on top and perfectly even and blank on its seaward face. It was much higher than the masthead and all that could be seen beyond it were the other 'islands', now the summits of a chain of mountains which appeared to extend as far as 79°S.[15]

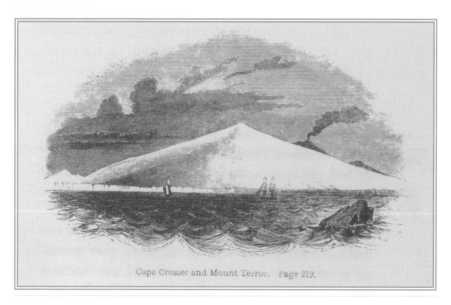

Cape Crozier and Mount Terror. Page 219.

Behind Mount Terror (centre) and Mount Erebus (right), Ross saw a mountain range (left) that he named for Sir Edward Parry.

The mountains, the southernmost parts of the globe yet seen, Ross named for Parry, so returning the compliment of his old commander, who had named the northernmost point reached in the Arctic for Ross. The ice barrier, today called the Ross Ice Shelf, ruled out any remaining hope that they could continue due south, 'for we might with equal chance of success try to sail through the Cliffs of Dover, as penetrate such a mass'. Yet it seemed to trend slightly south of east, so it was likely that a higher latitude might be reached by following it. For two weeks Armourer Sullivan watched the line of ice slip in and out of view:

> But as far and as fast as we run the Barrier apperd. the same shape and form as it did when we left the mountain . . . On the first day of Febry. we stood away from the Barrier For five or six days and came up to it again farther east, on the morning of the eight D[itt]o. we found ourselves Enclosed in a beautiful bay of the barrier. All hands when they came on Deck to view this the most rare and Magnificent sight that Ever the human eye witnessed Since the world was created actually Stood Motionless for Several Seconds before he Could Speak to the man next to him . . . Then i wishd. i was an artist or a

Ross concluded that he 'might with equal chance of success try to sail through the Cliffs of Dover' as penetrate what is now known as the Ross Ice Shelf.

draughtsman instead of a blacksmith and Armourer. We Set a Side all thoughts of mount Erebus and Victoria's Land to bear in mind the more Immaginative thoughts of this rare phenomena that was lost to view In Gone by Ages. When Captn Ross Came on deck he was Equally Surprised. to See the Beautiful Sight Though being in the north Arctic Regions one half of his life he never see any ice in Arctic Seas to be Compard. to the Barrier.[16]

Among the mysteries of the ice barrier was the fluctuation in the magnetic variation recorded on 31 January. It decreased from 96°E to 77°E and then increased 16°. Ross had seen it happen before, with Parry in the Arctic, but he could not account for the fluctuations and chose to dismiss them for the purposes of determining the position of the Magnetic Pole, 'as they would tend to throw it very considerably to the southward of the truth'. By 13 February the season was drawing in and a way east was being denied them, not by the barrier but by pack ice that threatened to trap them between its white rocks and the ice cliff. Ross turned west to make a last try for the Magnetic Pole and, failing that, to find a winter harbour nearby.

The ships returned past Franklin Island and the signs were not good.

Instead of last year's land ice breaking away, tough new ice was already forming. Ross was surprised at how early the winter was setting in by comparison with the Arctic. On 17 February they were within ten or twelve miles of the mainland coast and could see a low point with an islet close by, which might have made do as a harbour. The solid land ice which separated them from the islet made the question academic. Ross named the point Cape Gauss and gave up the attempt to reach it. He also gave up his hopes of wintering within sight of Erebus and travelling overland to the mountain and to the South Magnetic Pole the following spring.[17]

Nonetheless, being in 76°12'S and 164°E, with dip 88°40' and variation 109°24'E, Ross calculated that they were only 160 miles from the pole, some hundreds of miles closer than any predecessor. Furthermore, the mass of observations they had compiled from so many different directions would allow its position to be 'determined with nearly as much accuracy as if we had actually reached the spot itself'. A methodology he had dismissed out of hand when used by d'Urville and Wilkes had become more acceptable to Ross in the light of recent frustrations:

> It was . . . painfully vexatious to behold at an easily accessible distance . . . the range of mountains in which the pole is placed, and to feel how nearly that chief object of our undertaking had been accomplished . . . I felt myself compelled to abandon the perhaps too ambitious hope I had so long cherished of being permitted to plant the flag of my country on both the magnetic poles of our globe.[18]

There was still the north-west option, but it was very late to be taking it up. Indeed, the young ice was thickening so quickly that, although not yet strong enough to support the weight of men cutting through it with ice saws, it was sufficient to impede their progress. It became necessary to place boats ahead of the ships and then rock them until they broke through. At Cape Adare Ross attempted to land again, looking for a place to make the next term day observations and still hoping to find a winter harbour. The pack extended 8–9 miles from the shore and that was the least of it; as they continued north, every indentation in the coast was filled with solid ice hundreds of feet high. At Cape North, so named because beyond it the land appeared to extend south of west, offering perhaps a back door to the pole, the ice precluded any further progress along the coast. Again the variation changed dramatically, reducing by 74° in the space of 360 miles.

The approach of winter, heralded by the reappearance of stars at mid-night, convinced Ross that further attempts to penetrate to the west would be futile. On 25 February he turned north with the object of finding what, if any-thing, lay between Cape North and the Balleny Islands. In the back of his mind was the thought that to the north the ships might have to renegotiate 200 miles of pack, perhaps in the dark, although he hoped that, as late as this in the season, the ice would have been driven sufficiently far to the north 'to leave us a clear passage between it and the American discoveries'. Thick weather, snow showers and a heavy swell tested their seamanship:

> ... it is difficult to say whether the gales or the calms are the more embarrassing and dangerous. In the calms it is true you are less likely to meet with dangers, on account of passing over less space during their continuance, but in the event of drifting down upon the pack or a chain of bergs, you are left totally at the mercy of the waves, the high sea generally preventing the use of boats to tow you clear of them, and defeating every effort to take advantage of any feeble air of wind that in smooth water might prove effectual; and it is this constant heavy swell that renders the navigation of the antarctic seas so much more hazardous than that of the arctic ocean.[19]

The evening of 28 February afforded them their last view of Victoria Land – Mount Elliot mist-cloaked at a distance of 70 miles. As they sailed north away from the land and along the line of ice, Ross gazed west, speculating that in summer the Magnetic Pole might be attainable by persevering to the south-west between Victoria Land and the Balleny Islands.[20] On 2 March two islands were seen which Ross believed were part of the group. Two days later a good sun-sight at noon convinced Ross that these were the Balleny Islands, so Wilkes's claimed discovery had to be nearby, but when a gale blew up from the east-south-east all sail had to be set for a beat to the north-east, away from danger. The danger was on Wilkes's chart, which showed the northern shore of a mountainous land extending across their bows. How close its southern coastline might be was anyone's guess, but near or far, the gale made it a lee shore towards which *Erebus* and *Terror* were being driven.

The necessity of dodging to leeward of the icebergs they encountered cost them much ground, and the hours of darkness and fog were particularly trying, but good weather on the following morning allowed Ross to go looking for the coast which he had so strenuously sought to avoid only a few hours earlier. At sunset the ships were only 12 or 13 miles from the charted position of Wilkes's eastern point, in the midst of an empty sea. By midnight they had reached the position, found nothing, and 'shaped our course to the SW ... along the mountain range'. At 10 am on 6 March the officer of the watch on *Erebus* reported an appearance of land south-south-west to south-west by south, but from the masthead Ross could see only 'a dark misty appearance'. He was, however, prepared to concede that it might be the Balleny Islands, although they would be 70–80 miles distant. Nothing was reported in the *Terror*'s log. Just in case, soundings were taken near the centre of Wilkes's supposed land in 64°51'S and 164°45'E. There was no bottom at 600 fathoms. Another of the undertakings made to Anne had been fulfilled: Wilkes's land had been dissolved.

The observations made further south had shown that the position predicted by Gauss for the Magnetic Pole was ten degrees too far north, an error which Ross attributed to the inaccuracy of the observations on which it had been based. Although Wilkes and d'Urville had made observations closer to the point indicated by Gauss than Ross was likely to be able to reach so late in the season, it was nonetheless on the way to the line of no variation and Sabine's point of maximum intensity, both still to be visited. It took two weeks of difficult navigation west along the edge of the pack to reach the Gauss meridian and, in 64°24'S, they were still 45 miles north of his pole, but a dip of only 85°05' was near enough to that stated in Wilkes's letter to confirm that the pole was some 600 miles further south.[21]

By crossing the line of no variation twice more in different latitudes before returning to Hobart, Ross could supplement the single observation made in transit from Kerguelen the previous year. The three observations, if equidistant, could be used to compute the curve followed by the line towards the Magnetic Pole. The variation declined with pleasing regularity and rapidity until it reached zero on the night of 23 March. Thereafter it increased just as satisfactorily until Ross decided, in 127°35'E, that they had gone far enough west for the purpose and gave the order to put about. On April Fool's Day, the day after they recrossed the line of no variation, the variation diminished when it should have increased. 'Anomalous', noted Ross, but he wrote no more of using change of variation as a means of finding longitude. Under all sail the ships now made to the north-east, but a freshening gale which saw them reduced to close-reefed topsails also precluded good magnetic observations. They overran the point of maximum intensity indicated by Sabine at about 8 am on 4 April but it was an error of no importance, for later that day 'Mr Fox's invention', sorely tested in a sea high enough to carry away a quarter boat, showed less magnetic force than expected. It proved to Ross that his friend's focus of intensity, like Gauss's pole, lay well to the south, probably not far from d'Urville's Adelie Land. Two days later the ships were back in Hobart, 'unattended by casualty, calamity or sickness of any kind'.

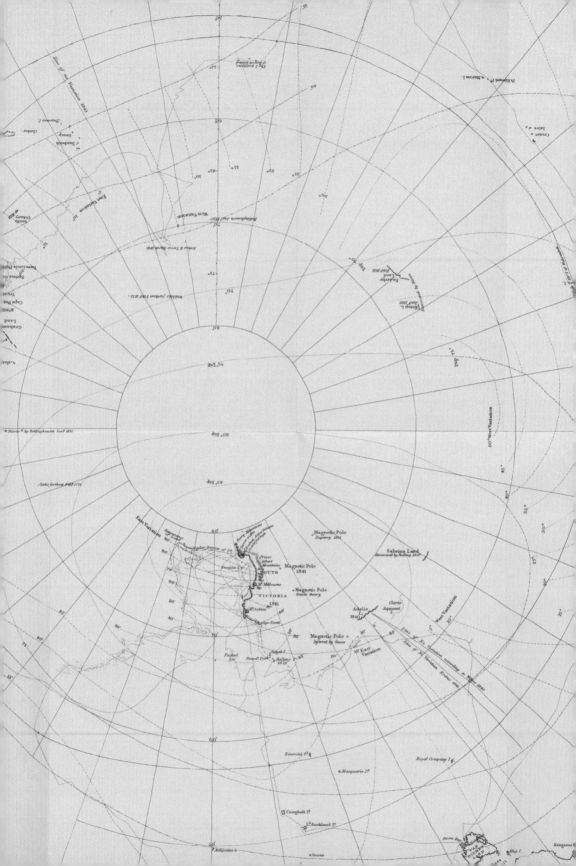

CHAPTER 8

The Economy of Life

Ross had followed Victoria Land through seven degrees of latitude, along more than 500 miles of apparently continuous, mainly mountainous coastline, but he did not declare his discovery to be a continent. To do so would be to concede that it was not possible to sail to the South Magnetic Pole – he was still optimistic that a passage might be found west of Cape North – and to admit that Charles Wilkes was right. He had grounds for caution, for had he not found that Balleny's Islands were just that? They were in the same latitude as Adelie Land, a coast of limited extent, and further south than Wilkes's eastern discoveries, which in any case were charted as discontinuous. Perhaps this sector of the Antarctic was like that off South America – numerous islands more or less concreted in ice.

In his report of proceedings, mailed to the Admiralty from Hobart, Ross relented as far as to describe his discovery as 'the great southern land'. Pack ice had been found to fill the whole space between that land and the islands 'first discovered by Balleny in 1839, and more extensively explored by the American and French expeditions in the following year'.[1] The unofficial report sent to Lloyds by its Hobart agent was more explicit about the implications: 'some

Left: Approaching from the east, Ross was able to get closer to the South Magnetic Pole than either of his rivals, and obtain a better fix on its location.

extraordinary mistake appears to have affected the calculation of the Americans who approached these regions', for not only was there sea where the American chart showed land, but one would have to sail 300 miles further south before encountering the northernmost point of the British discovery.[2]

In London, Herschel could not accept Ross's reticence about the nature of the land which had been discovered. The extremely low summertime temperatures were themselves evidence of the presence of a continental land mass covered with perennial ice. Furthermore, the fact that Arctic temperatures in the same season were higher meant that Ross had made a second discovery: 'to wit that the North Polar basin is really, as it has been of late much suspected to be, occupied not by land but by Sea'.[3] The news reached Sabine while he was with Humphrey Lloyd, visiting Fox at Falmouth. Over breakfast he read the newspaper account to the two other magnetic crusaders and any disappointment they might have felt about the pole was lost in the pleasure they felt for their friend's safety and success. Sabine did the rounds of Westminster and Whitehall so that Ross could be informed of his current standing with the great and powerful.

> You are, as you may suppose, in high favour with all classes in England. Lord
> Minto's extraordinary crotchet that because there had been no bloodshed your
> despatch ought not to be in the Gazette lost you the distinction of C.B.
> [Commander of the Order of the Bath] for the time. Beaufort wanted you
> made K.C.B. [Knight Commander] by Order in Council, but this staggered
> the routiners a little; Barrow wanted you knighted by patent, & Lord
> Haddington expressed the pleasure he should feel in asking for that distinction
> for you, provided your friends thought you will have it *by patent* and pay *£400*
> fees, or on your return by personal confer, in which case you pay only £100 fee.
> Barrow & Beaufort decided on waiting. My action was different from all; an
> address from the H. of Commons to the Queen to hasten some distinction on
> you. I have reply appointing you her extra A.D.C. [Aide De Camp] till your
> return. However I daresay you will have your fill of honour before you have
> done as perhaps you may like as well to continue to be distinguished as *Le
> Jeune* Ross instead of a title which might mix you up with achievements of a
> different character from your own.[4]

In Paris, François Arago laid Ross's track chart before the Institute of France but was not particularly laudatory. Other scientists were more appreciative. Humboldt, who was in town, was delighted and asked for a copy to be made that he could send to Berlin. Those of d'Urville's officers who enquired seemed put out that their leader, who not in Paris, had been 'outstripped so far and with so little fuss'.[5]

In a letter to Francis Beaufort, the hydrographer, Ross privately expressed his disappointment at not being able to reach the Magnetic Pole. He confessed that the 'complete repulse' they had suffered made him doubt that they would be able to do it next year 'in so high a latitude as I consider to be worthy of the time it will occupy'. Any Cape North route to the pole would be too far out of the way and in too low a latitude to be worth spending a season on – the opportunity cost would be too high. Instead, Ross foreshadowed an early start eastward from the point reached on the ice barrier in 78°S, intending to cross to Weddell's furthest south 'for I am perfectly certain that if there be no land at the [geographic] pole we shall find no ice to prevent us – and I think it probable that after rounding the Eastern end of the barrier we may find the Land trend to the Westward again'.[6] Ross was hoping that the ice barrier was not attached to land along its southern margin and might therefore be outflanked to the east, again opening the possibility of sailing to the Magnetic Pole. If that was not to be, perhaps they could follow the barrier east around the globe as far as the Weddell Sea.

The expedition returned the hospitality of Hobart by giving the most splendid ball the place had ever seen. The ships were moored together, one outside the other, and were reached from the shore through an illuminated grotto laid over a bridge of boats. The illumination was truly the highlight of the ships' decoration, owing its brilliance to artful placement of the expedition's supply of trinket mirrors intended for the natives of Antarctica. The covered deck of the *Erebus* was the ballroom and supper for 300 was served on the *Terror*. It took two full days to clear heads and wreckage. On 7 July the expedition sailed for Sydney.

Ross had hoped that it would be possible to use Fort Macquarie for his magnetic observations, which would then be exactly comparable with those of Wilkes, but he found the site so cluttered with cannon and shot that he was obliged to set up his observatory on nearby Garden Island. The locals' anxiety to make good Sydney's defences in the wake of Wilkes's surprise arrival had put yet another American-laid obstacle in Ross's way. Ross did not encounter Biscoe but he met the men who had conversed with the Americans about their discoveries: the McLeays, father and son, told him that they had shown the Americans, on their return from the Antarctic, the issue of the London *Athenaeum* in which the latitude and longitude of the Balleny Islands had been first published. Ross took this to be a conversation with Wilkes, but as the *Athenaeum* did not reach Sydney until after Wilkes had left for New Zealand, the McLeays can only have been speaking to William Hudson, who did not see Wilkes again until after the infamous chart had been sent to Ross.[7] Ross was mistaken to think that Wilkes knew the exact location of the islands when he prepared his chart. It would prove to be a mistake of some consequence.

Ross's schedule called for an extended visit to New Zealand before sailing to the Antarctic again. As the ships crossed the Tasman Sea, night watch was

William Hudson, who feared America's labour lost.

kept for the meteorite showers expected in those latitudes in mid-August. More observers were needed than could be found among the officers, and some of the keener seamen were trained in the duty. It says much for the enthusiasm inspired by Ross as a leader that there was no difficulty in finding volunteers, one going as far as to refuse relief when his half hour was up. Although he had seen no falling stars in that time, 'he was sure two or three would fall in a few minutes; he had been watching them, and could see they were shaking'.[8] They reached the Bay of Islands on 17 August and there found the USS *Yorktown*, under the command of Captain John Aulick. Aulick had been one of the officers senior to Wilkes who had offered to command the Ex Ex rather than see such violence done to naval precedence. Ross could not have known this, but it was unfortunate that, of all the officers in the US Navy, Aulick was the first with whom he had the opportunity to discuss Wilkes's chart.

Aulick was expecting to find Wilkes's squadron at Honolulu, and Ross decided to take advantage of what he thought was friendship between the two Americans to apprise Wilkes in 'the most delicate mode' that he, Ross, had sailed over some of his supposed land. Aulick agreed that Wilkes's chart as overlaid with Ross's track clearly showed that this was the case and undertook to pass the information on to Wilkes. Ross chose not to confirm this message in writing, although he had yet to acknowledge Wilkes's letter of the previous year. In a formal age, such a lack of courtesy was incompatible with the consideration Ross claimed to be showing.

Another visitor to the Bay of Islands was the French corvette *Héroine*, whose commander was able to give Ross a chart of d'Urville's discoveries. After three months of observations, with the Antarctic sailing season approaching, the British expedition sailed for the Chatham Islands. They repeated Thursday 25 November by crossing the meridian of 180°, the international date line, from west to east and two days later reached the islands. Unable to land and unwilling to wait for better weather, Ross bore south-east towards the second focus of greater magnetic intensity. Its supposed location, about 60°S and 125°W, was too far east to fit into the Antarctic itinerary, so Ross contented himself with aiming to cross the lines of equal intensity 'in such places as should be best calculated to secure its accurate determination'. On 13 December even this limited aim was abandoned; observations were showing that the second focus lay far to the south. They had reached the meridian chosen by Ross for the season's attempt to penetrate the Antarctic, 150°W, and the ships altered course to the south.

Ross was expecting to find land. He subscribed to the theory that large masses of ice could not form in the open ocean and he knew that both Cook and Bellingshausen had encountered them in low latitudes on this meridian. If he did not find land he could expect to arrive at the most easterly point of the previous year's cruise from a direction as different as was practicable. There were many reported sightings of land, each subsequently identified as cloud. On 18 December the pack blinked its presence, stretching from east to west across their course in 62°30'S. The ice was light and open and Ross had no hesitation in running in, but within 30 miles it had compacted so much that they were forced to head more to the west. Until 30 December every opportunity was taken to push from pond to pond, by which date all outlets had iced up. The ships were moored on either side of 'the largest piece of ice we could get hold of' and the water tanks filled with ice because, contrary to Wilkes's advice, the pools of water they found on the berg were too brackish to drink.

On New Year's Day they found that the pond in which they were trapped had carried them across the Antarctic Circle, 1400 miles east of where they had crossed it on the same day of the previous year. They were already 250 miles into the pack, which had been only 200 miles deep altogether in 1841, with no clear water visible to the south. What could they do? They could hold another ball. John Davis, second master of the *Terror*, took charge of the decorations.

> . . . Hooker and myself went on the ice and cut out in hard snow the figure of a woman, which we called our 'Venus de Medici'. She was made sitting down and about eight feet long, and the snow froze very hard . . . after dinner we all went to a ball on the ice, a ballroom having been previously cut, with sofas all around, of course all made of snow . . . Captain Crozier and Miss Ross opened the ball with a quadrille; after that we had reels and country dances . . . Ladies fainting with cigars in their mouths, to cure which the gentlemen would politely thrust a piece of ice down her back . . . At about one o'clock as the captains left we first pelted them with snowballs and then cheered them, both of which honours they took with equally good humour.[9]

For nearly three weeks the ships were largely at the mercy of the ice, sometimes making a few miles to the south and then losing those, and more, over the next few days. The season was slipping away. At last, on 18 January they broke out and were able to make some progress again, although the fog was so thick that, to avoid separation, the ships were made fast to a piece of ice which acted as a fender. It was found that under reduced sail the ships could persuade their fender to accompany them southwards but, even as the ice seemed to be opening ahead, a rising swell began snapping the hawsers like twine. They cast off and waited in the lee of a berg for the fog to clear. Instead, a northerly gale blew up, breaking waves over the highest bergs and driving the ships into the pack ice to leeward.

> Soon after midnight our ships were involved in an ocean of rolling fragments of ice, hard as floating rocks of granite, which were dashed against them by the waves with so much violence that their masts quivered as if they would fall at every successive blow; and the destruction of the ships seemed inevitable from the tremendous shocks they received. By backing and filling the sails, we endeavoured to avoid collision with the larger masses; but this was not always possible . . .[10]

'Like standing in an earthquake', according to Hooker.

Hooker likened it to standing in an earthquake. *Terror*'s rudder was destroyed and that of *Erebus* so badly damaged as to be useless. By the time the sea subsided and they were able to make repairs, they found that they had been carried back to the Antarctic Circle, near enough to the spot they had left three weeks earlier. Not until 2 February did they clear the southern edge of the pack, 56 days and more than 800 miles after entering it. They reached the ice barrier on 23 February and followed it eastwards through another ten degrees of longitude. There in 162°20'W it was intersected by the pack and all hope of further progress to the east ceased. They were just six miles further south than their furthest in 1841. The barrier was lower here and as viewed from the masthead it appeared to rise to an undulating horizon. No doubt with Wilkes in mind, Ross was unwilling to risk 'the chance of some future navigator under more favourable circumstances proving that ours were only visionary mountains'. He charted them as an appearance of land only, extending through thirty degrees to the south-east, but they led him to revise the opinion that he had formed the previous summer. He had come to the view that an 'extensive continent' lay to the south of the great barrier.[11]

Ross now knew that he would be denied a triumph like that of the previous year. He opened the sea chest in which lay the silk Union Jack that he had hoped to fly at both magnetic poles. Beside it was a small book of moral philosophy given him by his sister many years before. The inside cover of *The Economy of Human Life* was inscribed 'written on board the *Endeavour* in Latitude 82¾°N 27th July 1827 Jas. C. Ross'. To this he now added, 'HM Ship *Erebus* 23rd Feb 1842 in Lat. 78°10'S', and signed his name. It seemed that the economist of human life, to save him from hubris, intended to ration him to one magnetic pole, but he had been furthest north and furthest south, and surely not even the Almighty would deny him the satisfaction of it. It was a record that would stand for most of the century.

The ships ran to the west of north along the pack edge looking for any opening to the east that might offer a shorter route to the Falkland Islands than by way of Cook's *Ne Plus Ultra*. On 27 February they weathered the westernmost point of the pack and were able to continue northward along its margin, with decreasing likelihood that it might yet again intercept their track. In 60°S Ross felt that they were far enough north of the ice to run the easting down to Cape Horn with little risk, and still in a high enough latitude to get good observations of the second focus of magnetic intensity. For several days his theory held good but, on the afternoon of 12 March, bergs were encountered and the combination of thick snow and a brisk north-west breeze persuaded Ross that to continue running through the night would be hazardous. Before midnight the topsails had been reefed and all preparations made for rounding to until daylight. The large berg that suddenly loomed ahead was dealt with as a matter of course; *Erebus* was hauled to the wind, port tack, to weather it. What was not seen from *Erebus* was the even larger berg on the port beam, where *Terror* was stationed, and Crozier's ship had to haul to starboard to avoid it, which put the ships on opposite tacks and converging courses:

... just at this moment the *Terror* was observed running down upon us, under her topsails and foresail; and as it was impossible for her to clear both the berg and the *Erebus*, collision was inevitable. We instantly hove all aback to diminish the violence of the shock; but the concussion when she struck us was such as to throw almost every one off his feet; our bowsprit, foretopmast, and other smaller spars, were carried away; and the ships hanging together, entangled by their rigging, and dashing against each other with fearful violence, were falling down upon the weather face of the lofty berg under our lee, against which the waves were breaking and foaming to near the summit of its perpendicular cliffs.[12]

The collision saved *Erebus*, because she could not have weathered the berg to port. The surge of the waves violently separated the ships and Ross saw with relief that the *Terror*, whose rigging was not much damaged, was able make sail for the western end of the berg. He would have followed suit but *Erebus* was in such chaos, and stern on, that he was forced to resort to the most desperate of measures; she would have to weather the berg stern first. Surgeon McCormick, who had had his differences with Ross from time to time, nonetheless regarded this as one of his captain's finest hours:

Captain Ross was quite equal to the emergency, and, folding his arms across his breast, as he stood like a statue on the afterpart of the quarterdeck, calmly gave the order to loose the main sail. His whole bearing, whilst lacking nothing in firmness, yet betrayed both in the expression of his countenance and attitude, the all-but despair with which he anxiously watched the result of this last and only expedient left to us in the awful position we were placed in.[13]

So great was the danger that, when the order was given to back the mainsail, McCormick was one of several who, disregarding rank, lent a hand to the maintack. As the *Erebus* gathered sternway, the gig and quarter boats were swept overboard and the lower yardarms scraped along the berg, only the backwash preventing the ship from being overwhelmed. As they reached the corner of the berg, Thomas Abernathy reported that there was another beyond it, but that a dark patch might be an opening between the two. Ross had no option but to find out. The opening, if opening it was, was too narrow to attempt stern first, but there was just enough time to go about before they were driven, pell-mell, into a passage no more than three times the width of the ship. The lantern that greeted them at its end was a double blessing: *Terror* had made it through and so, it seemed, had they. Crozier confessed later that he had not the slightest idea of what he had done at the time or how *Terror* had come through. Davis recorded that 'the men on the whole behaved very well throughout; only one was running about out of his senses, but two or three were crying'.[14]

Erebus and *Terror* in collision while trying to avoid icebergs.

Remarkably, both ships had escaped serious structural damage, although for some days *Erebus* carried a reminder of the forces to which she had been subjected. One of her largest anchors was fixed upside down at the starboard bow, its palms embedded 7–8 inches in the solid timber. After repairs had been made, Ross resumed course for the predicted position of the second focus of magnetic intensity. It was reached on 18 March and, although the swell caused the observations to be less 'accordant' than they might have been, Ross was satisfied that they provided no support for the two-foci theory. He was now inclined to believe that there was only one southern focus – in the vicinity of the South Magnetic Pole. The season's tasks completed, the ships made for their winter base, Port Louis in the Falkland Islands, which was reached on 6 April 1842.

During the winter, observations were made at Port Louis and Hermite Island, near Cape Horn. Neither had the attractions of Hobart, or Sydney, or even the Bay of Islands, and Ross was hard-pressed to maintain morale. There was the work of repairing and refitting, and hunting the wild Falklands cattle for fresh meat was a useful diversion, but by the end of July there was little to keep the men occupied and Ross had to fall back on make-work. This he could disguise as an act of Antarctic remembrance. Some years earlier, Matthew Brisbane, the commander of Weddell's tender *Beaufoy* on his celebrated Antarctic voyage, had been murdered at Port Louis and his body left under a pile of stones. Ross had the bones removed to the local burial ground and set his men to enclose the ground with a stone wall. Reflections on the mortality of Antarctic explorers would have been reinforced by mail from Europe. Ross learnt that d'Urville was dead.

On 8 May 1842 d'Urville, his wife and their only surviving child, Jules, had been seen boarding the 5.30 pm train from Versailles to Paris. The train was three minutes late and the engineer had been trying to make up time. On the downhill past Bellevue he had worked his two locomotives up to 80 kph. At a level crossing the lead locomotive jumped the rails and ploughed into the embankment, with the carriages behind piling up to a height of ten metres. The fire boxes of the locomotives ignited the locked wooden carriages stacked above them and, in the space of a few minutes, 59 people were incinerated, many beyond recognition. When it was rumoured that d'Urville had been seen boarding the train and was now missing, Arago proposed to a meeting of the Academy of Science that they should assist by searching for the family among the injured. The Prefect of Police regretted to have to inform them that it would not be necessary: the bodies had been identified among those recovered from the front carriages. No member of d'Urville's family, nor of his wife's, attended their burial at Montparnasse.

On 17 December 1842, *Erebus* and *Terror* left Port Louis for a third season in the Antarctic, into the regions visited by d'Urville in 1837 and Wilkes in 1838. Ross's plan of campaign was to re-locate d'Urville's discovery and follow it to the south-east, keeping between the land and the pack ice. Should that fail, he would cross to Weddell's track and follow it south to the limit of that navigator's 'clear sea'. The ships made landfall on 28 December but found that d'Urville's Joinville Land did not extend far to the south-east. Rather, its coast turned south-west and, as the ships followed it into what Ross named Erebus and Terror Gulf, he could see an inlet to the north-west that suggested a passage between Joinville Land and Louis Philippe Land. Viewed from the south, the flat western half of Joinville Land was dominated by a 'very remarkable tower-shaped rock' of considerable height near its centre. This feature had been mapped from the north by d'Urville as an *isle supposée*, as he had been too distant to see the low land on which it stood. Ross was impressed by its solitary grandeur and named it d'Urville's Monument, 'in memory of that enterprising navigator, whose loss not only France, but every civilized nation must deplore'.[15]

The gulf contained a great quantity of loose ice, with the main pack about twenty miles offshore. Even when the hoped-for westerlies blew, they did little to clear the ice from the shore. Here was no open water like that off the east coast of Victoria Land. On 6 January 1843 Ross and Crozier were able to land on Cockburn Island at the south-western extremity of the gulf to take possession, but the mainland remained beyond reach. The following day found them in 64°34'S and 57°10'W. The land could be seen to continue to the west but across their bows, from west to south-east, was fixed land ice. Not only was it impenetrable, but to stay in its close vicinity was to risk entrapment, which became a common and exhausting, if temporary, experience over the ensuing weeks. On 12 January Ross resolved to waste no more time in 'this perplexing navigation' and attempted to follow the edge of the land ice south-ward. The ships were soon sandwiched between the land ice and the pack and Ross began to fear that they might be frozen in. His only option was to run northwards into the pack until stopped, and then to warp, heave and bore until the ships could be manoeuvered again. It took five days to get clear. They per-severed with the pack until the end of the month, but were carried northwards by it as fast as they could cut a way south. They had, however, demonstrated that the land south of d'Urville's discoveries ran south-west rather than south-east. This Antarctic land was at best a peninsula, and perhaps no more than a chain of islands separated by ice-choked straits.

There was not much of the season left. It was time to try Weddell's route. The ships followed the margin of the pack eastwards in about 64°S, searching for an opening to the south. They crossed Weddell's track but what for him had been a clear sea confronted them with impenetrable pack. They were only a degree or so further south than d'Urville had penetrated but, unlike the Frenchman, Ross was prepared to conclude that 'Weddell was favoured by an unusually fine season, and we may rejoice that there was a brave and daring seaman on the spot to profit by the opportunity'.[16] The line of no variation was crossed on 22 February in 61°30'S and about 22°30'W. The dip was 57°40', which gave a position for the South Magnetic Pole in remarkable accord with that determined by Ross in 1841 and 1842. The position he had then assigned to the pole was found to be exactly halfway between where they now were and where they had been in New Zealand when the identical dip had been observed. Ross could now refine his assigned position for the pole, which he

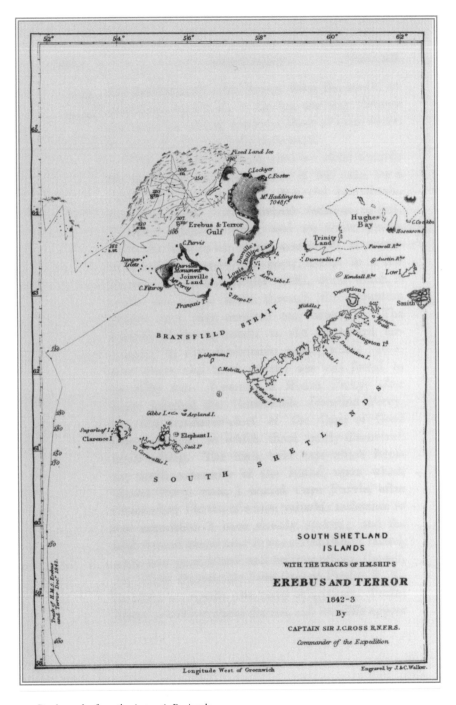

Ross's repulse from the Antarctic Peninsula.

fixed as 75°5'S and 154°8'E. This was only 2°30' south of its position as theoretically computed by Gauss, but much further from the position he had then
been misled into predicting by double-counting the erroneous Hobart observations. Ross was struck by the fact that the theory placed both magnetic
poles 2–3° south of their positions as observed by him. His quality observations
would, he hoped, enable Gauss to perfect his theory.[17]

The pack now trended southward of east and hopes rose when, on the
27th, it disappeared to the south and the ships were able to steer south-east
across a clear sea. They were fast approaching the Antarctic Circle when the
wind swung dead ahead. Ross could have beat into it but, reflecting that
Bellingshausen in January 1820 had almost reached 70°S on a course barely a
hundred miles further east without seeing land, he turned away. He was
again being spared the embarrassment of too much success: 400 miles further
south-east lay what is now called Princess Astrid Coast, possibly free of sea
ice at that time. It was with Ross as it had been with Weddell; open sea ahead,
but other priorities calling.

They entered the Antarctic on 1 March, steering south-west, only three
days earlier than they had left it in previous seasons. On 5 March they again
encountered the pack and were soon obliged to enter it to continue south.
After 27 difficult miles Ross called a halt; the ice was too close and heavy. It
was time to leave. They were in 71°31'S and 14°51'W, nearly two degrees
further south than Bellingshausen but well short of Weddell, and between the
tracks of the two. A paper recording the event was signed by all officers
and thrown overboard in a cask. The ice had denied them another discovery:
45 miles to the east was the Princess Martha Coast. The exit from the pack was
uneventful but a rising gale drove them back towards an ice bay on its
northern margin. Fortunately, the ice was also being blown southwards and
by setting every stitch of canvas that the quivering masts would bear it was just
possible to keep off the edge of the pack. Huge seas broke over the ships,
leaving spray frozen on the rigging. In the intense darkness the ropes were
difficult to handle but at least the effort focused attention inboard. Had they
been able to see the bergs lumbering past on both sides they might well have
concluded that there was no avoiding them.[18]

They left the Antarctic for the last time on 11 March and, after an unsuccessful search for Bouvet Island, made for Capetown, where they arrived on
4 April. Five months later the ships anchored off Folkestone. Ross got his
knighthood, the Founder's Medal of the Royal Geographical Society and, 'that
which afforded me, if possible, still greater pleasure', the Gold Medal of its

sister society in Paris. On 18 October he married Anne and at the age of 43, as promised, put polar exploration behind him. He began work on his book of the voyage and on the large collection of marine organisms that he and Hooker had painstakingly gathered. Hooker was sure that retirement was not a reluctant decision:

> Capt. Ross says he would not conduct another Expedition to the South Pole for any money & a pension to boot. Nor would any individual of us join it if he did; I am sure I would not for a Baronetcy.[19]

CHAPTER 9

Paper Warfare

The French could not claim to have discovered more Antarctic land than Wilkes or Ross, but they had the advantage of getting home first. The Americans might dispute priority, but second-hand and confusing accounts in Australian newspapers were not authoritative. Washington released Wilkes's despatches as they were received, but he was not there to elaborate. All of this d'Urville understood, and he wasted no time in seeking approval to publish an official account of the voyage he intended would surpass that of his earlier expedition in the number and splendour of its volumes. In his despatches from the Pacific he had taken pains to demonstrate the value of these earlier works as official propaganda: at Macassar, he assured his superiors, the authorities had been lost in admiration of the *Astrolabe* atlas, whose availability to the world he contrasted with the exclusivity about discoveries characteristic of 'the enlightened English'. When this backhanded comment was reported in London, the *Athenaeum* was exasperated.

> What the 'enlightened English' do, or have done, cannot affect the merit of the French government. As, however, Capt. Dumont d'Urville has been pleased to institute a comparison, we may be allowed to observe that the English have, during the period referred to, surveyed the Eastern and Western shores of Africa, . . . of America, and the whole of Australia; while 'the magnificent atlas of the *Astrolabe*' does not contain 300 miles of newly-explored coast.[1]

This could only have encouraged the French Government to believe that there was as much credit to be earned with a small discovery attractively packaged as with a large one left to find its own place in public conversation. Promoted to rear admiral, made an Officer of the Legion of Honour and awarded the Gold Medal of the Geographical Society of Paris, d'Urville was posted to that city to prepare the results of the voyage for publication. The work was to be entitled *Voyage au Pole Sud* [*to* the pole, not *towards* it] *et dans l'Oceanie*. Ten volumes of narrative and thirteen of scientific results were intended, but only three volumes of the narrative had been published and a fourth written before d'Urville's death. His readers were left stranded at Fiji in October 1838. The task of fleshing out his outlines of the remaining volumes of narrative and supervising the technical volumes fell to Jacquinot and Vincendon-Dumoulin, neither of whom was confident of his ability to do the voyage justice. The self-doubt was justified: their narrative volumes are repetitious and contain much peripheral matter. The last of these appeared in 1846 but it was not until 1854, fourteen years after the expedition's return, that the 23-volume set was completed.

The new editors found that they did not have the field to themselves for long. A month after d'Urville's railway accident Wilkes arrived in New York. The Exploring Expedition which returned to the United States in June 1842 was not the squadron that had sailed four years earlier. For one thing, only two of the original ships, *Vincennes* and *Porpoise*, remained. *Peacock*, the tough old bird which had weathered all that the Antarctic could subject her to, had been wrecked on the bar of the Columbia River in 1841; the *Flying Fish*, worn out on duties far beyond her design strength, had been sold at Singapore. Then again, whatever goodwill had existed between Wilkes and the other officers in 1838 had long gone. They might have preferred never to see each other's faces again, but feelings ran too high even for that. Charge and counter-charge filled the in-tray of the Secretary of the Navy. What should have been a triumphal return dissolved into a messy series of courts-martial.

Within a fortnight of arrival Wilkes was addressing the National Institute in Washington. His presentation was billed as a synopsis of the voyage, but it was mainly a defence of the second Antarctic cruise, characteristically vigorous and unsparing of d'Urville, Ross, Aulick and even Balleny. Wilkes noted that the French account – by which he meant d'Urville's report from Hobart – did not mention the encounter with the *Porpoise*. He felt that any comment he could make on this refusal to speak would be superfluous. Without mentioning d'Urville by name he described 'the discoveries of others' as less important than his own, and claimed priority by 'a few days'. Ross was accused of an unfounded statement about sailing over Wilkes's land, and Aulick was condemned for giving it currency (which he had done by spreading the story in Hawaii, where he had missed Wilkes). Furthermore, as Ross's despatch from Hobart had not reported a sighting of 'Bellamy's Islands', although they appeared on his chart 'where he ought to have seen them if they existed', it remained to be seen whether the American discoveries might yet prove to be the first sightings of land of any description, island or mainland, in that part of the globe. What really irked Wilkes about Ross's chart, as presented to the House of Commons in August 1841, was that it acknowledged the French discoveries but entirely ignored the American.

The darts that he hurled at his competitors reveal that Wilkes was fully informed of their claims and the challenge they posed to his own. It is the more remarkable then, that Wilkes's own claims, as set before the National Institute, raised as many questions as they answered. The Antarctic Continent, from 160°E to 97°E, had been discovered, he said. At Sydney, he had only claimed from 154°18'E when, 'on the morning of the 19th of January, on board the *Vincennes* and *Peacock* land was ascertained positively to exist, though they were separated some miles'.[2] What had occurred in the interim? As the journals of Eld and Reynolds had been available to him in Sydney, recording sightings further east on 16 January, he must at that stage have discounted them in the light of Hudson's doubts. The 160°E claim had been first made from New Zealand, after Wilkes had learnt of the 'large, dark and rounding' feature seen by Ringgold from the *Porpoise* on 16 January. This was independent corroboration of the midshipmen's sightings from *Peacock*, three days before the French discovery. Even more tantalising was Ringgold's account of distant mountains seen south-east on the 13th. Could this be confirmation of Wilkes's suspicions that land lay to the southward and eastward of the *Vincennes* on 15 January? How could he separate fact from fancy amid these clouds of conjecture? He did not try.

> . . . as we sailed along the icy barrier, I prepared a chart, laying down the land, not only where we had actually determined it to exist, but those places in which every appearance denoted its existence, forming almost a continuous line . . .[3]

It was a strange methodology for a man whose primary mission was to remove the uncertainty of phantom islands and doubtful shoals from existing charts. Worse, in his own charts, both as sent to Ross and appended to the printed

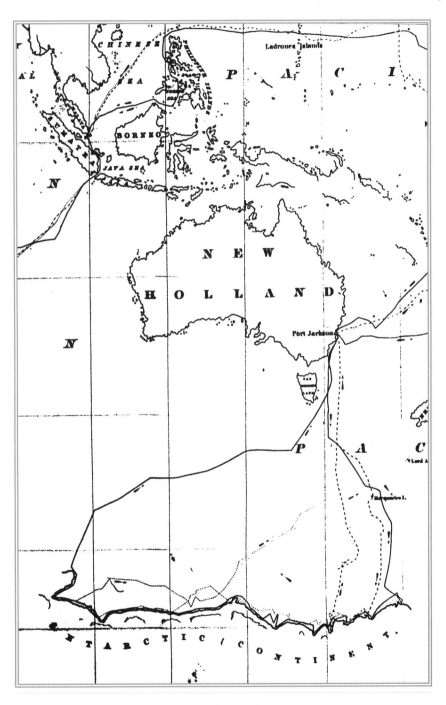

The chart that accompanied Wilkes's National Institute lecture.

version of his Synopsis, Wilkes did not distinguish between existence and appearance. The Synopsis chart shows the Icy Barrier as continuous from about 166°E, but the most easterly feature behind it is in 150°E. The chart is disgracefully crude and too much cannot be read into it (which was perhaps Wilkes's intention) but, with the omission of the discoveries east of 150°E that he had placed on the chart he sent to Ross, it was hardly a document to inspire confidence in the discoveries it did show.

There was a way out. If Wilkes had been prepared to concede that his eastern discoveries were no more than appearances of land, there would have been little loss of face in allowing that Ross might have sailed over one of them; but it was not in Wilkes's nature ever to take a backward step and, in truth, one such concession might have called everything into question, for he had landed nowhere. No, attack was the best form of defence: Ross and Aulick must both have been blind not to see that the easternmost land shown on Wilkes's chart was 'Bellamy's Islands', which was labelled 'English discovery' on his original. That label, for some unaccountable reason, seemed to have been omitted from Ross's copy. Wilkes offered no explanation as to why these islands were represented as mountains, or why they appeared to be part of his 'almost continuous line'. To this point his case was tenable, if tendentious, but his last stroke was just dishonest. He simply asserted that if Ross had sailed over land it was Balleny he was discrediting, not Wilkes. Ross had 'not approached near enough our positions, either to determine errors or verify results'. And yet he acknowledged that he had seen Ross's chart, which showed the Balleny Islands in the position indicated by the *Athenaeum*, nearly a degree further south and a degree west of where Wilkes placed them in 164–5°E. No one except Wilkes had ever charted land in the latter location and his cartography was entirely the product of Ringgold's account and his own wishful thinking. He seems to have retained it on his chart for as long as there was any possibility that Ringgold might have seen land on the 13th. That possibility had not been extinguished by Biscoe's information, hence its appearance on the copy of the chart sent to Ross. And if Ross had only minded his own business, and stayed away from the American sphere of operations, the possibility would have remained alive and there would have been no need to explain away the embarrassment of Ringgold's phantom. The *Athenaeum* was scathing.

> [The Americans] seem to have rested satisfied in general with faint indications of land, and not to have sought the actual proof. The long line, therefore, of the Antarctic Continent, discovered by them, will probably soon fall to pieces;

and, melting away already at its eastern extremity, it will disappear in a few years before the researches of more persevering and more accurate explorers.[4]

Wilkes's audience at the National Institute had been polite, although it contained a number of critics and sceptics. His court-martial was more of a trial, and not just because it had little in common with the normal run of disciplinary proceedings. Among other things, the court was asked to consider whether the claim of discovery on 19 January, like that of the 16th, might not also have a little retrospectivity in it. Charles Guillou, Assistant Surgeon of the *Porpoise*, alleged that Wilkes's claim of land being seen on the morning of 19 January 1840 was a deliberate and wilful falsehood. It was a tit-for-tat charge, one of a number made against Wilkes by officers themselves being court-martialled at his insistence.

In his own defence, Wilkes summed up the charge against him in a way that implicated others. He was being accused, he said, of colluding with Hudson and Ringgold to deny the French the honour of discovery. This was as much a reflection on them as on him. In rebuttal he cited Hudson, Ringgold, Eld, Reynolds, Davis, Alden and Williamson. He relied most heavily on Eld's testimony which, being definite about a sighting of land on the 16th, made the timing and credibility of sightings on the 19th irrelevant, at least as far as priority of discovery was concerned. There remained the question of veracity. Wilkes tackled it head on. What did it matter that the original of Hudson's report of 3 March 1840 to the Secretary of the Navy, seen by Wilkes before dispatch, referred to 'the morning' of the 19th (that is, some hours before the French), a reference that Hudson had disavowed? It must have been a clerical error because he, Wilkes, had been able to put before the court a copy that did not contain the offending phrase. The key document was his own report, which he said had been written before his return to Sydney (but it bore the date of his arrival, 11 March), had been read out to Hudson (but, as the latter had been out of town, not before Wilkes could have learned of the French claims) and claimed only what Alden and Williamson of the *Vincennes* had vouched for. Extraordinarily, Wilkes was here repudiating his own Synopsis, which also had referred to the morning of 19 January.

The court turned to Lieutenant Ringgold. When had he first realised that Antarctic land had definitely been seen on 19 January? Not until Wilkes had told him of it much later, in New Zealand. So, Wilkes had not mentioned it when their ships had come together in the ice on 26 January? No, said Ringgold. The prosecution put it to Wilkes that this was 'strange'. But I did mention it on the 26th, said Wilkes. Then why did Lieutenant Ringgold not recall it? Wilkes chose his words carefully: he said he had asked 'have you seen *the land*', to which Ringgold had replied in the negative, but it was blowing fresh, the sea was high and it was almost impossible for the ships to be kept within hail. He speculated that Ringgold might have misheard him to be asking some other question like 'do you want anything?' It was a plausible explanation that served two purposes, dismissing Ringgold's ignorance while testifying to Wilkes's own confidence in discovery on the 19th. And who among the witnesses on Wilkes's quarterdeck would have been willing to swear, given the conditions, that the commander had not used the definite article, which presupposes the existence of land, rather than merely ask 'have you seen *land*', which does not?

Another difficulty with which the court had to contend was the absence of sightings in the ships' logs. Ringgold's Knoll, for example, on which Wilkes hoped to rest so much, was logged as no more than a supposed island south by east. There was also no one more senior than a petty officer who could testify to Wilkes's belief that land had been seen on 19 January. Wilkes was sure that the court would understand.

> Those who are unacquainted with the isolation in which the etiquette of the navy places the commander of a strictly disciplined ship of war, may express surprise that no interchange of opinion on the subject of land took place between myself and the officers, such discipline being maintained we had little communication, and I felt satisfied that from all the appearances increasing, as we proceeded to the westward, we should soon again see most indubitable proofs of the land, and place its existence beyond cavil, which we did in a few days afterwards. It might also be inquired by the same persons, why land, seen by me, was not entered in the log book? You know that the commander of a vessel exercises no control over the log book for which the officer of the deck is responsible.[5]

Hudson, who had ordered a log slate entry erased, must have been surprised to hear of this doctrine. And then, how could it be that commissioned officers had to be kept at a distance for the sake of discipline, but petty officers could be engaged in social conversation?

> The Court will understand how highly the tact of a veteran, such as Gunner Williamson, is to be relied on in such a case. The Quarter-Masters who were

on duty at this time, I have not been able to find; I well recollect their
coinciding in opinion in what I saw, and fully corroborating it.

And while the logs might be silent, the defendant's journal could speak if
the court would allow it. The room was cleared while the bench considered
the request. It decided that the journal could not be evidence inasmuch as
it differed from the log book, which was 'the true record of all occurrences
and facts'. Further, Wilkes's argument that his 11 March report confirmed his
19 January journal entry could not be accepted. Here the court was trying to
avoid saying that between the two dates Wilkes could have revised his journal.
Although Wilkes felt that some members of the court were hostile to him, he
remained outwardly confident of the outcome and in hopes of something
better than mere acquittal.

> . . . may I not venture to say that a bare verdict of not guilty is far less than
> the nation has a right to require at your hands? Its honour, its glory, the
> untarnished lustre of its unconquered flag, have all been assailed through
> me. With you rests the power of vindicating that honour, exalting that
> glory, and wiping off any stain which these proceedings have cast upon
> that banner.[6]

Wrapping himself in the flag almost worked. Of the charges preferred against
Wilkes, only that of authorising illegal punishments was upheld and he was
sentenced to no more than a public reprimand. The specification of false statements was found to be unproven (the court giving Wilkes benefit of doubt)
and therefore the verdict on Guillou's charge of scandalous conduct had to be
'not guilty'. Another man might have been content with getting off so lightly,
but Wilkes was outraged. He foresaw that anything less than total exoneration
would leave a cloud hanging over all the works of the expedition, no less than
over him, and so it proved. In Paris, the hydrographer Pierre Daussy concluded
from the Synopsis and the court-martial evidence that there was no certainty
about discovery until 28 January. He pointed out that if, on 22 January, 'an
unforeseen circumstance had forced the American expedition to leave those
parts, it would not have had any certainty of the existence of a southern continent'. There was insufficient information to permit verification by subsequent
navigators. The map attached to the Synopsis was inadequate, as was Wilkes's
response to Ross. What was needed, Daussy said, was:

... publication of the chart itself with exact indications of the sightings from each ship. We hope that we will not have long to wait for this publication, and that it will be of such authenticity that it will be impossible to have the least doubt of its accuracy.[7]

Wilkes feared that the task of publication might be denied him. As he saw it, one cabal, his court-martial, had been succeeded by another: the Administration had someone else in mind to write the official record of the expedition. Wilkes manoeuvered to secure the job by organising a successful resistance among his friends in Congress. His *Narrative of the United States Exploring Expedition* was published in 1844 as the first five volumes of 24 planned, which were to be accompanied by 11 atlases. The set was still a few volumes short when Congress finally cut off funding thirty years later. The title chosen by Wilkes is revealing; where the expedition came from was regarded as of greater significance than where it went. His account of the expedition's origins was highly selective. Poe for one was disgusted, and in a column for the *Columbia Spy* he pointedly referred to the Antarctic Exploring Expedition 'originated by Jeremiah N. Reynolds'. If Wilkes's ambition had been to produce one volume more than the French, it was not realised, but the splendour of the American publication outshone even theirs and was said, with pride, to be almost entirely the work of American scientists, artists and craftsmen. Wilkes remained at the helm, only occasionally interrupted by distractions like the Civil War, for the whole period of publication. More than a year went by after his return in 1842 before the Navy saw fit to promote him to commander. In spite of the controversy that surrounded some of his achievements, the British were more ready to acknowledge them with the award, in 1845, of the Founder's Medal of the Royal Geographical Society.

Wilkes was not the only leader to be tormented by a gadfly, but at least he was alive to the sting. Dumont d'Urville had been in his grave only a few days when one of the *Zélée*'s surgeons published, in the *Annales Maritimes*, what Vincendon-Dumoulin described as a 'libellous and insulting notice to his memory'. Curiously enough, this libeller of the dead not only shared a profession but bore a surname almost identical to that of his American counterpart. Elie Le Guillou was reacting to d'Urville's criticism, in volume two, of his protests against the sickness that had carried off so many on the passage from Java to Hobart. His counter-charge of callous disregard by d'Urville contained an element of truth, but his own conduct had been mischievous and self-serving, motivated by a desire to have the *Zélée* sent home. Later that year

Le Guillou published his own account of the voyage, in which he was again highly critical of his commander, because 'the death of the admiral [d'Urville] has not interrupted publication of his work, which contains allegations against me of a kind that compromise my honour, and false recriminations, and I must respond'.[8] Le Guillou's book was edited by Jacques Arago, the brother of d'Urville's old antagonist. A chapter was devoted to the *expeditions rivales*, in which Le Guillou professed himself convinced by American 'proofs' that they had sighted land earlier than the French on 19 January, but it was Ross that he lauded. Not the least of the Englishman's achievements was the complete absence of sickness in his crews. In France, people were comparing d'Urville to Cook. That was not how Le Guillou saw it: the immortals were Cook and Ross. By implication, there was no place on the pedestal for another.

Scientific notes were appended to Le Guillou's book, among them a reappraisal by Duperrey, d'Urville's associate on the *Coquille* voyage, of the position of the magnetic poles.[9] Duperrey compared what was then known of the magnetic results from the three recent voyages and found d'Urville's to be the most convincing: he had followed a magnetic meridian south and his observations fitted admirably into a consistent series, compiled over several voyages, which included some of Duperrey's own. The 1840 observations, projected by Duperry to the south of Adelie Land, placed the Magnetic Pole in 75°20'S and 130°10'East (of Paris – add 2°17' for Greenwich). The particular merit of this spot was that it coincided in latitude and differed by no more than 80 miles in longitude from the position Duperrey had deduced from the magnetic meridians in 1837. He was unable to say much about Wilkes's results because, as he complained, they were still unpublished. Those of which he was aware filled him with astonishment, the observations in Disappointment Bay being explicable only by observational error or local attraction. He believed that Ross was wrong because he had not taken into account the way in which the magnetic meridians pressed against each other in places where polar currents lower temperatures[10]; Ross could not have been closer than 400 miles to the Magnetic Pole, certainly not 160, when he observed a dip of 88°40'.

In the context of rough handling of all three expeditions, a preference for d'Urville was damnation by faint praise, but it did not matter. The surgeon's was a lone voice. In death, the discoverer of Adelie Land could be forgiven boorishness, irascibility and even crew neglect. Thereafter, as the official volumes flowed, d'Urville's version of the events of his voyage went largely unchallenged in his own country. Wilkes knew that it would be otherwise for him, but could not contain himself. The American narrative, for which he claimed copyright, borrowed shamelessly, often without acknowledgment, from the journals of his subordinates. Wads of material were lifted from earlier writers to pad out the histories of countries visited. The passage of two years since the Synopsis had made him no less prickly about the claims of his French and British rivals.

> The credit of these discoveries has been claimed on the part of one foreign nation, and their extent, nay, actual existence, called into question by another; both having rival expeditions abroad, one at the same time, the other the year succeeding. Each of these nations, with what intent I shall not stop to inquire, has seemed disposed to rob us of the honour by underrating the importance of their own researches, and would restrict the Antarctic land to the small parts they respectively saw.

Wilkes was prepared to concede that d'Urville had landed at Piner's Bay, but three days after the Americans had first seen land. The Frenchman had only *believed* it to be a vast tract of land, whereas what the Americans had seen had left them in 'no doubt'. Ross had coasted 'some distance along a lofty country connected with our Antarctic Continent', thus confirming it was such and not just a chain of islands. He, Ross, had clearly been guided by Wilkes's chart, the receipt of which he had never acknowledged. Of this, Wilkes said, he did not complain, but only sought to maintain his 'indisputable claim'. And just in case his continent should prove, after all, to be islands.

> . . . who was there prior to 1840, either in this country or in Europe, that had the least idea that any large body of land existed to the south of New Holland? and who is there that now doubts the fact, whether he admits it to be a vast continent or contends that it is only a collection of islands? Examine all the maps and charts published up to that time, and upon them will any such traces of land be found?

It was artful rhetoric. Balleny did not count: he had found only tiny islands and an appearance of coast, questionable discoveries so insignificant that Wilkes felt that he could leave them out of the atlas which accompanied his narrative. Again, Balleny's discoveries might date from 1839, but it was undeniable that no chart of them had been published before 1840. And, as everyone knew, Biscoe's discoveries were not south of New Holland.

We ourselves anticipated no such discovery; the indications of it were received with doubt and hesitation; I myself did not venture to record in my private journal the certainty of land, until three days after those best acquainted with its appearance in these high latitudes were assured of the fact; and finally, to remove all possibility of doubt, and to prove conclusively that there was no deception in the case, views of the same land were taken from the vessels in three different positions, with the bearings of its peaks and promontories, by whose intersection their position is nearly as well established as the peaks of any of the islands we surveyed from the sea.[11]

Who would imagine from this description of deliberate and careful triangulation that it refers to the uncoordinated observations of 16 January which had to be retrieved from memories after the date became significant? The sighting of 13 January is not entirely disowned, but set down as no more than the view of one best acquainted with the appearance of land in high latitudes. If this is a reference to Ringgold, it was a misleading description of one who had first sailed polar seas in 1839. And what of the chart for which Daussy had pleaded two years earlier? In Wilkes's atlas the line of coast that had represented Ringgold's first sighting or, as Wilkes now would have it, Balleny's Islands, had disappeared without explanation. It was not the only omission: Wilkes might be excused for ignoring Ross's discoveries, although he was hardly then in a position to criticise Ross for having done as much to him, but why was there no representation of d'Urville's discoveries? Even Wilkes could not try to deny that the French had landed in Piner's Bay days before his own unsuccessful visit.[12]

The easternmost Antarctic land featured in Wilkes's atlas bears the label Ringgold's Knoll. It is the large, dark and rounding object seen from the *Porpoise* on 16 January and should entitle Ringgold to be acknowledged, at least by his countrymen, as the first man to set eyes on that sector of Antarctica. Not so. In the narrative Wilkes prints what he describes as an illustration of this feature: it is his own journal sketch, explicitly timed on the original at 4.30 am on 16 January. The feature in the sketch is not dark, nor particularly rounding. This is not a confirmation of Ringgold's claim: it is the remnant of a counter-claim. If the court-martial had been prepared to accept Wilkes's journal as a true record of events, made on the dates of occurrence, there would have been on the record a sighting some hours earlier than that made by Ringgold. As it was, by identifying his sketch with the feature Wilkes was laying claim to at least a share of the personal glory.

Wilkes's publication of 'what I myself saw, and have called Ringgold's Knoll on the chart'.

Not surprisingly, the most perceptive and critical of his American reviewers was a fellow officer. Like Wilkes, Charles Davis was a naval lieutenant and a hydrographer. He wrote anonymously in the *North American Review*, but his readers could have been in little doubt that his views represented the considered judgment of Wilkes's peers. He gave credit to Wilkes for rescuing the expedition from the ridicule associated with its tardy departure, but condemned 'the Captain' for his usurpation of rank. On Wilkes's evidence, he considered that the claim to discovery of a continent was fairly stated but, whether future research confirmed or disproved the title, the importance and extent of the discovery to the westward of 150°E was indisputable. To the eastward, however, 'the existence of land and its limits are rendered uncertain by the statements of Captain Wilkes himself'. The discrepancy of thirty or forty miles between 160°E and Ringgold's Knoll in about 158½°E 'we are unable to reconcile with the idea of a determinate discovery'. Davis scoffed at the notion that the logbooks had failed to record land until 28 January because discovery was not anticipated. He pointed out that Biscoe in 1831 had revived expectations in that regard and that Antarctic discovery had been part of the Ex Ex mission. As to the relative merits of the American, French and British discoveries, and resolution of 'the disputes to which they have given rise', that would have to await the publication of Ross's account. Daussy, he thought, had tried to be 'just and temperate', unlike other foreign commentaters. However, Davis was not aware that Wilkes had excised 'Bellamy's Islands' from his chart, and so could not see how Ross could claim to have sailed over part of the American discovery:

> If it should be proved hereafter, that there is no excuse or pretext for this
> assertion . . . it will be incumbent on him [Ross] to make an apology for

suffering his name to be used for such a dishonorable purpose as the dissemination of a false report, injurious to the honor of a foreign officer, and to the character of his nation. We leave here the subject of the land ... merely adding an expression of our regret, that the inconsistencies of Captain Wilkes should have promoted and justified, both at home and abroad, such discussions and doubts respecting the date and extent of this discovery, as involve, though we trust they will not in the end impair, the national honor.[13]

Notwithstanding, what most offended Davis was the way in which Wilkes had used the narrative to continue his vendetta against subordinates. In Europe too, this pettiness was regarded as unworthy of a great enterprise. Davis concluded that the partial and self-serving nature of Wilkes's criticism of others showed him to be 'deficient in some of the requisite qualities of a good commander'. He looked forward, in due course, to reviewing the volume wherein Wilkes would be reporting on matters in which Davis could bring to bear his own expertise – Physics.

Copies of the Wilkes *Narrative* reached Paris in time for Vincendon-Dumoulin to notice it in volume eight of the interminable *Voyage*, although he had relied mainly on the Synopsis for his account of the American expedition. He devoted an entire chapter to comparing the French, American and British expeditions, with particular emphasis on rebutting Wilkes. Vincendon-Dumoulin was at pains to emphasise that the views expressed were his own, d'Urville's journals being silent on the subject of Wilkes save for his version of the encounter with the *Porpoise*. To this, Vincendon-Dumoulin added the support of his own testimony: he had heard d'Urville order that the guns be held ready to salute the American flag. If anyone had been trying to keep secrets it was the Americans, who had been forbidden by Wilkes to reveal their discoveries in Sydney.

Vincendon-Dumoulin confessed himself to be as unsure as anyone about the American claims, the Synopsis being too insecure a foundation on which to base a judgment. If Wilkes was right and it was a continent, the honour of discovery must be Balleny's. Wilkes could not have it both ways: if his Totten's High Land and Budd's High Land existed, and were part of a continuous coast, then Balleny's Sabrina Land, which lay between them in the same latitude, must be part of the same continent. If it was not a continent, as Vincendon-Dumoulin believed, then the only coastal sighting confirmed by a landing was that made by the French. As far as the controversy with Ross was concerned, he thought that in all probability the British had indeed sailed over land that Wilkes claimed had been seen on 15, 16 and 17 January. He made great play with the court-martial evidence that called into question the veracity of the American's original claims to discovery on 19 January, expressing regret that the detailed descriptions of land in Wilkes's journals had not found their way into his official report. It would have been the surest way of satisfying his antagonists who, as Vincendon-Dumoulin saw it, 'were in sufficient agreement to raise serious doubts about his sincerity'.[14]

With the reports attributed to Ross, Vincendon-Dumoulin had less difficulty. He thought he could detect certain allusions directed more or less at d'Urville, but contented himself with the observation that, if the French expedition had been less happy in its results than its successors, it conceded nothing in intrepidity and perseverance. Like Wilkes, he noted that Ross had been greatly aided by having his choice of route informed by the French and American experience in 1840. Vincendon-Dumoulin also made peace with the British about the credibility of Weddell's furthest south: d'Urville had been wrong to query it on the basis of his own unhappy experience in 1838. In return, he hoped:

> . . . the happy Captain Ross, when he writes the story of his fine voyage, will display towards the work of the French expedition a little more deference and that he will render to our intrepid chief the share of glory due to him for his discoveries in the icy regions, and for the persistence and courage which he brought to his research.[15]

On the issue that touched his own professional reputation most closely, the position of the South Magnetic Pole, Vincendon-Dumoulin chose not to dispute Duperrey's favourable judgement, although his own calculation of its position placed the pole fully three degrees further north. However, he cautiously noted that Ross might not have been able to sail along a magnetic meridian in circumstances favourable to determination of the pole. He seems to have appreciated, as Duperrey did not, that there was more to come from Ross, and:

> . . . until we know the results of his observations and the use that he makes of them to solve this important question, we believe we must abstain from all discussion on the subject.[16]

CHAPTER 10

Contradictions

Two years of silence followed the flurry created by the Wilkes narrative. In England, Edward Sabine worked at Ross's magnetic data, reporting from time to time in the *Philosophical Transactions of the Royal Society*. Maps of variation, dip and intensity based on his first season's observations were published in 1843 and those from the second season in 1844. The latter compared theoretical intensities of Gauss with the observations of Ross. The discrepancies between the two allowed Sabine to make the point that more observations would be needed if the theory were to be perfected. Humboldt felt vindicated. Joseph Hooker began issuing his *Flora Antarctica* in parts in 1844, with the government making a £2 grant towards the cost of each plate. The *Zoology of the Antarctic Voyage* also began appearing, similarly subsidised. The question being asked by many, and most pointedly by John Murray, the publisher, was when would Ross's narrative be available?

Unlike the French and American publications, the narrative was to be a private venture. In 1843 Murray had agreed to pay Ross £500 on publication. Three years had gone by, public interest in the voyage was waning, and Murray feared that he might be left with something unsaleable. As only two volumes were planned, to be written mainly from the ships' logs and Ross's journals, the delay seemed inexplicable. It was the sort of book that could have been written on the voyage home, and it threatened to be dull as well as late.

'I am well aware you cannot invent adventures', Murray wrote, but 'a leaven' of incident and anecdote would be welcome, and at the very least would Ross please refrain from striking them out.[1] It seemed that Ross had retired mentally as well nautically. Although he was only in his early forties the strain of the voyage had exhausted him and his promise to Anne and her family was an honourable release from sea duty. The dashing young figure had thickened. The handsome head was still crowned with a thatch which always looked as if blown by a polar gale, but jet black had given way to snowy white with remarkable swiftness. Without the spur of Wilkes's criticisms, John Murray might have waited even longer for his book.

The two volumes appeared in 1847. Both d'Urville and Wilkes were accused of forestalling the British attempt on the South Magnetic Pole, 'for the exploration of which they were well aware, at the time, that the expedition under my command was expressly preparing'. It was not a promising start to what Vincendon-Dumoulin had hoped would be generous assessment of the French effort. Ross identified the western point of d'Urville's *Côte Clarie* as Balleny's Sabrina Land but insisted that in so doing he had not 'the least intention of disputing the unquestionable right of the French to the honour of this very important discovery'. As disclaimers go, it was rather lame.[2]

Defence of Balleny also provided a vehicle for criticism of Wilkes. Ross pointed out that the Americans had been very close to Sabrina Land on 10–11 February. They must have failed to see it, as there was no mention in Wilkes's narrative. 'I suppose, therefore, he has placed it on his chart on the authority of Balleny, but under a different name' – Totten's High Land. Balleny, Ross said, should not be deprived of his due share in the honour of a discovery.

> . . . for the priority of which the Americans and French are contending with each other, and to which, should this land eventually prove to be a continent extending to Kemp and Enderby Land, as they suppose, it follows that neither of them have the smallest claim whatever; although equal praise is due to them for their exertions and perseverance as if they had really been the discoverers, for at that time they could not have known that Balleny had been there the year before them.[3]

A chapter which Ross did not publish – perhaps some of the excision that Murray had pleaded against – included a stinging critique of the Ex Ex, in which the Americans were scorned for their first 'unfortunate' attempt at discovery and patronised for their 'zeal without knowledge'.[4] Spleen thus purged, Ross confined himself in the printed work to a rebuttal of Wilkes. He published the letter Wilkes had sent him from the Bay of Islands and, although the American was finally thanked, the manner of it was at best snide and at worst little short of hypocritical. The relevant passage began by noting that the 1840 Sydney newspaper accounts to which Wilkes had later referred Ross and the American captain Aulick, to enable them to correct their misunderstanding of the American discoveries, were nothing but uncertain conjectures and contradictory statements. Ross was inviting his readers to ask themselves why Wilkes had drawn attention to unauthorised reports. Surely Wilkes had not been suggesting that the newspaper accounts had official status, given his government's instructions about secrecy? And if they were official, what need was there for his letter?

> I felt therefore the more indebted to the kind and generous consideration of Lieutenant Wilkes, the distinguished commander of the expedition, for a long letter on various subjects, which his experience had suggested as likely to prove serviceable to me, under the impression that I should still attempt to penetrate to the southward on some of the meridians he had visited; a tracing of his original chart accompanied his letter ... These documents would, indeed, have proved of infinite value to me, had I felt myself compelled to follow the strict letter of my instructions; and I do not the less appreciate the motives which prompted the communication of those papers, because they did not eventually prove so useful to me as the American commander had hoped and expected: and I avail myself of this opportunity of publicly expressing the deep sense of thankfulness I feel to him for his friendly and highly honourable conduct.[5]

What followed had a more genuine ring, although a reference to the duration of the American campaign in the ice invited unfavourable comparison with the author's own more extensive efforts:

> The arduous and persevering exertions of this expedition, continued throughout a period of more than six weeks, under circumstances of great peril and hardship, cannot fail to reflect the highest credit on those engaged in the enterprise, and excite the admiration of all who are in the smallest degree acquainted with the laborious and difficult nature of an icy navigation: but I am grieved to be obliged to add, that at the present time they do not seem to have received either the approbation or reward their spirited exertions merit.[6]

Ross published the notorious 1840 chart with his own track overlaid. Comparison with Wilkes's original in the Admiralty archives has confirmed that the published version is a fair representation of it. The only oddity is the Balleny Islands, which Ross added in order to show their position relative to Ringgold's coast; they are centred in the part of the ocean where Balleny had placed them, and more or less correctly oriented, but they are fly specks, smaller even than they appear in the larger-scale polar chart which accompanied Ross's despatch from Hobart. It seems that Ross too was not beyond misrepresentation to support his case, for the implication was inescapable: how could anyone chart those dots as fifty miles of coast?

In the book Ross thanked Aulick for his recent public confirmation of their discussion at the Bay of Islands, a confirmation which had subjected Aulick to yet another published denunciation by Wilkes for supporting an attack on fellow Americans. Like Davis before him, Ross had difficulty with the inconsistencies in Wilkes's story. If the Americans had charted appearances of land as well as confirmed land, why was Ringgold's sighting of 13 January not in their atlas? He turned the American's own rhetoric back on him: why, if that bit of coast was meant to be the Balleny Islands, was it charted in the wrong place, although so near the tracks of the American ships as to have been well within sight? Aware of what the McLeays had told the Americans about the Balleny Islands, Ross all but called his rival a liar for denying precise knowledge of their location.[7] And as for Wilkes's practice of charting appearances of land:

> [it] is not only entirely new amongst navigators, but seems to me likely to
> occasion much confusion, and even to raise doubts in many minds whether the
> existence of some portions of land that undoubtedly were seen might not also
> be of an equally questionable character with those laid down from appearances
> only, unless some distinctive mark were given by which they could be known
> from each other.[8]

This was Ross's justification for leaving the American discoveries off his chart, and he concluded by warranting his own:

> . . . I may here further remark, once for all, that the whole line of coast laid
> down as our discovery, was really and truly seen, and its continuity determined
> in such a manner as to leave not the smallest doubt on the mind of any officer
> or man of either of the ships, and that no part has been laid down upon mere

appearances or denotations except in those places where it is distinctly marked 'appearances of land'.[9]

With this as a standard, the inclusion of d'Urville's discoveries on Ross's chart implicitly became the acknowledgment of them that Vincendon-Dumoulin had hoped for, and the Briton's final word on the 'Antarctic continent' offered more comfort to the French than to the Americans, even as it put both of them in their place.

> There do not appear to me sufficient grounds to justify the assertion that the various patches of land recently discovered by the American, French and English navigators on the verge of the Antarctic circle unite to form a great southern continent. The continuity of the largest of these *Terre Adélie* of M. D'Urville has not been traced more than three hundred miles [that Hobart newspaper again!], Enderby's land not exceeding two hundred miles: the others being mostly of inconsiderable extent, of somewhat uncertain determination, and with wide channels between them, would lead rather to the conclusion that they form a chain of islands. Let each nation therefore be contented with its due share, and lay claim only to the discovery of those portions which they were the first to behold.[10]

By English navigators, Ross meant Balleny and Biscoe and, like Wilkes, he tried to have it both ways. He did not believe that it was a continent, but should future navigators prove the conjecture to be correct, their discoveries 'will set at rest all dispute as to which nation the honour justly belongs of the priority of discovery ... for I confidently believe with M. D'Urville that the enormous mass of ice which bounded his view when at his extreme south latitude was a range of mountainous land covered with snow'.[11] But not a continent.

Ross wrote as though he were the adjudicator of a debate in which he was not a participant. Wilkes, for his part, saw the intervention for what it was, the summing-up of the case for the negative, and immediately went to the American press, rejoicing 'that the time has at last arrived when I can meet my accuser, as it were, face to face'. Ross, he wrote, was guilty of bad taste and egotism and was wrong about being forestalled: the instructions that directed the Americans to explore south of Tasmania pre-dated those issued to Ross. He, Wilkes, had not spoken to the McLeays after the Antarctic cruise, had only seen the relevant issue of the *Athenaeum* since reading Ross's book, and had never uttered the words that Ross said the McLeays had attributed to him – 'then all our labour has been in vain'. The declaration that accompanied his repudiation – 'I pronounce the whole … without foundation and utterly untrue' – would have had more force had it not been qualified by the words 'so far as regards myself'. As Wilkes had been the only person ever mentioned by name in this context, he might here have been allowing for his own suspicion of what had passed between Hudson and the McLeays in Sydney after his departure – maybe even a remark about labouring in vain. Perhaps, like the true position of the Balleny Islands, this was something best not to know: he might then say, with a clear conscience, 'nor do I believe the information was in possession of any officer in the squadron. I certainly never heard of it'.

By Wilkes's reckoning, the easternmost mountainous land on his original chart, which he had explained as the 'English discovery' – the Balleny Islands – was only 27 miles in length, not 80 as engraved in Ross's book (it was in fact something between the two) 'and as much unlike in every other respect'.

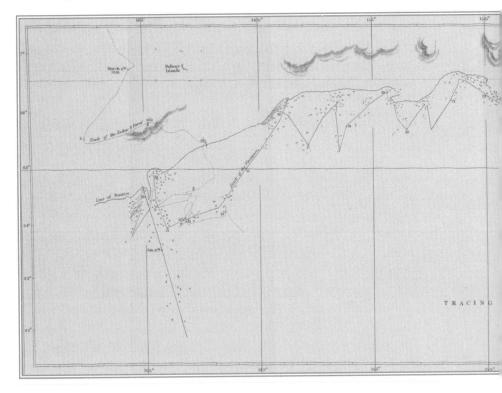

Ross published the chart Wilkes sent him from New Zealand, with his own track across its eastern 'discovery'.

The explanation he offered for representing islands as mountainous land was that Biscoe had marked the position on his chart but had provided no other information, not even the discoverer's name. He did not offer any explanation as to why a single point in 65°50'S and 164°27'E should be represented by even as little as 27 miles of mountain. Instead, he made an elegant segue, first referring to 'Bellany's Islands', then to 'Bellany's Island' and finally to 'Bellany's Land', by which time its name was compatible with the topography Wilkes had given it. It did not appear in his atlas, he said, because he had not seen it (but Ringgold thought that he had seen it, and did not Wilkes claim to have charted all *appearances* of land?). But, and for the first time, Wilkes was prepared to concede that there might have been errors in the letter and chart he sent to Ross.

> The whole was hastily prepared, and my letter shows the feelings under which I acted. If I had supposed any errors it might have contained were to have been

A Copy of the

OF THE ICY BARRIER ATTACHED TO THE ANTARCTIC CONTINENT DISCOVERED

Communicated by Lieut. Wilkes to Captⁿ James

taken advantage of in any way to the prejudice of the Expedition or myself, it certainly would not have been sent. But I relied on the character and standing of a British officer. If I have been mistaken, and have suffered by the persecutions it has caused me, I can take pleasure in the consciousness that I was led to the act by a feeling which I hope may ever be alive in my own breast, as well as in those of my countrymen.[12]

Aulick did not escape another mauling, but to accuse a fellow United States officer of lying would risk being challenged to a duel. Ross was a safer target. He was said to be guilty of misstatements, because Aulick could not have represented himself as a friend of Wilkes, which he was not, nor could he have undertaken to deliver a message to Wilkes as all relations between them had ceased. 'I cannot believe that he would have deceived Capt. Ross in this way'. Very economical: two rivals downed with the one shot, but the debate was a sterile one in the absence of any means of confirming the discoveries. Wilkes hoped that he would be vindicated by contemporaries rather than by posterity.

It is in the power of neither Capt. Ross nor myself to affect the final estimation in which the labours of the two expeditions will be held. When the results are fully before the world, I make no doubt a proper judgment will be passed upon them, and I have the fullest confidence to believe that we shall then receive the reward which our exertions and labours merit. Captain Ross and myself serve different governments; the one has it in its power to confer titles and decorations, while the other must leave its servant dependent upon the final decision of public opinion. I have great confidence in the latter, although it may act slowly; yet upon its final judgment I am willing to rely, assured that it will be not only just but generous.[13]

When he read this in London Ross was nonplussed. How could one deal with an opponent who, however badly handicapped by his own inconsistencies, refused to concede? He began drafting a response, starting with an apology for stating that Wilkes had endeavoured to anticipate his purpose, an error which Ross said he had been led into by the acknowledgment of d'Urville to that effect. There he lost heart, and turned to his friend Beaufort, the Admiralty's hydrographer.

I have given up all thoughts of answering Lieut. Wilkes' letter; for a man that will so unblushingly deny the work of his own hands will say anything however false that he may think will suit his purpose – but I will be glad to be guided by your advice – all I could do would be to flatly contradict what he said about the map not being a correct copy of his and state that I preferred believing Mr McLeay's account rather than his denial of the truth of it. The other points are minor and of no public consequence.[14]

Beaufort counselled against a 'war of pamphlets', but believed that some of the American's assertions should be contradicted somewhere on the public record:

A few short paragraphs – written with great temper but with equal firmness – and put together in a plain manly English style without any of his sophistry and subterfuges, would cost you but little trouble, would be very satisfactory I think to your friends here as well as to the Americans, and would hereafter be a useful appendage to the history of your voyage, because it is one of the few modern voyages that will go down to posterity.[15]

Ross let the opportunity pass and thereby conceded the last word to Wilkes, but the matter was unresolved. There was rough justice in this. Wilkes's motives in writing to Ross from the Bay of Islands may have been less than pure, but so was Ross's resolve to discredit his rival's discoveries. And if sophistry and subterfuge were the crimes of one party, hypocrisy and discourtesy characterised the other. Wilkes's case was too weak to have persuaded any but the most partisan, but he succeeded in bluffing his opponent out of the debate. It could have been otherwise. In 1850 an Enderby captain, Tapsell, sailed the whaler *Brisk* west from the Balleny Islands to 143°E on a course to the south of that taken by Wilkes. Unlike Ross, he sailed over what Wilkes was still claiming were his eastern discoveries. The record of Tapsell's voyage, so damningly innocent of any suggestion of land, was misplaced by the Royal Geographical Society. Charles Enderby's recollection of it was not published until 1858. By then, Ross was past caring.[16]

Not until the Civil War, when the Union needed every naval officer it could find who was not wearing grey, was Wilkes allowed to go to sea again. It was a mistake. The Secretary for the Navy subsequently came to the view that, desperate as things were, they were not that desperate. Wilkes had learnt nothing. He obeyed orders only when it suited him, but required prompt and unquestioning obedience to his own. Single-handedly he almost drew Britain into the war on the side of the Confederacy by intercepting the British steamer *Trent* and removing Confederate commissioners on their way to Europe.

Britain took exception to any other power behaving as she did on the high seas, but Wilkes was arguably within his rights and was briefly the popular hero he had always believed was his due for the Ex Ex. In 1864 he disobeyed orders once too often and was suspended from service for a year. The suspension effectively finished his naval career, although the seniority he had once over-turned eventually brought him a rear admiral's flag. The cessation in 1874 of Congressional funding for the expedition's publications caught the last volume, Physics – which included the magnetic results – in the press. It was never issued, a strange fate after 32 years for the work which Wilkes told his son was amongst the most important of the expedition. Perhaps he was no longer sure about the effect of ocean currents on magnetic variation. He died in 1877, still waiting to have his achievements recognised by his countrymen. Most of the obituaries focused on the *Trent* affair. Some failed to mention his command of the Ex Ex at all.

Ross's determination to remain at home was soon tested. With *Erebus* and *Terror* again available, John Barrow persuaded the Admiralty to make one last attempt at the north-west passage. It went without saying that Ross would have first refusal of the command, but refuse it he did, despite the baronetcy and pension that gossip said had been offered with it. The candidate who most strongly pressed for the command was Franklin, recently recalled from Tasmania following a concerted campaign by some of his subordinates there to have him removed. He wanted to restore his reputation. At 59 he was far too old for polar duty, but his keenness was one reason Ross gave for 'declining an honour which a few years ago was the highest object of my ambition'. Another reason was the proposal to equip the ships as steamers. Ross remembered the *Victory*.[17]

When Franklin sailed in May 1845 he had Crozier as his second-in-command and one of Ross's companions at the North Magnetic Pole, Thomas Blanky, as icemaster. Before the expedition parted from its escorting transport in July, Crozier wrote to Ross. He wished the *Terror*'s unreliable engine back on the Dover railway line, whence it had come, and the engineer with it. He was concerned about how late in the season it was, and feared they would 'blunder into the ice and make a second 1824 of it'. Did Ross shiver when he read this reference to the loss of the *Fury*? He would probably have been more concerned about the low spirits of his old shipmate, which Crozier openly confessed were caused by Ross's absence and, although expressed more guardedly, by a slight lack of confidence in Franklin. Later that month the expedition was seen by two whaleships and then disappeared into the ice.

Late in 1847, when nothing had been heard from Franklin for three summers, some concern was expressed, but it took no more urgent form than preparations for a search in 1848. This was a duty that Ross could not refuse and Anne, who was fond of Crozier, did not try to dissuade him, declaring that 'both our hearts are ardent in the cause'. He sailed in the *Enterprise* in June 1848 with Thomas Abernathy as icemaster, accompanied by the *Investigator* under the command of Edward Bird, who had been his first lieutenant in the Antarctic. The second lieutenant of the *Enterprise*, Francis Leopold McClintock, immediately warmed to his captain. 'He seems a very quick, penetrating old bird, very mild in appearance and rather flowery in his style. He is handsome still . . . and has the most piercing black eyes.'[18] The regard was reciprocated.

Ross believed that Franklin might have tried to penetrate south along the west coast of the Boothia Peninsula, a good guess. He wintered his own ships at the entrance of Prince Regent Inlet and, in the spring of 1849, pushed out sledging parties across Barrow Strait and down both sides of the Boothia Peninsula. He took the west coast route himself, but the coastal ice was so severe that on 5 June he named a nearby point Cape Coulman and resolved to return to the ships. Ross and two of the men pushed on for one more day, and from their furthest point could see, fifty miles further on, 'the extreme high cape of the coast' which he named Cape Bird. He was then about 170 nautical miles from his magnetic pole of 1831, from where he might almost have been able to see Franklin's abandoned ships, locked in the ice north of King William Island. Franklin himself had already been dead for two years.

Ross had hoped to reach his pole again, but was forced to acknowledge that the state of his men would not allow it. They regained the ship on 23 June after a round trip of nearly 500 miles. It was effectively the end of the expedition, for the ships were beset by the ice of Barrow Strait at the beginning of September and then carried eastward by it to be unceremoniously ejected into Baffin Bay. Two months later the ships were paid off at Woolwich. Ross was criticised by some, including his uncle, for abandoning the search – John Ross accused his nephew of being more interested in exploration – but the Admiralty signalled its satisfaction by awarding James a good service pension of £150 a year.

As a member of the Arctic Council James Clark Ross continued to be consulted while the search for Franklin continued, but he did not go to sea again. When promotion to rear admiral came in 1856, it reflected no more than his seniority on the Navy List. The boundaries of his world contracted from the poles of the earth to a country house near Aylesbury in Buckinghamshire, where he found all the society he wanted with his wife and children. Even his interest in biology waned, and work on the Antarctic collection of marine organisms was neglected. Happiness built on such a narrow foundation is easily overthrown and Ross was dealt a blow in 1857 from which he never recovered. His beloved Anne died of pleural pneumonia at the age of forty. Neither responsibility for their four children nor a belated attempt to re-engage with the scientific life of the nation through the British Association and the Ordnance Survey rallied him. He was chairing the geographical section of the association meeting in Aberdeen in 1859 when news came through that his protege McClintock had finally found conclusive evidence of the end of Franklin and Crozier. Unable to free the ships, Crozier had abandoned them after the death of Franklin. The whole expedition had perished dragging boats across ice and land in an attempt to find clear water. Although hope of finding Franklin and Crozier alive had long been abandoned, even by the indomitable Jane Franklin, confirmation of their loss must have reinforced Ross's sense that life no longer held much for him. He began drinking heavily and died on 3 April 1862, having confided to a friend only weeks earlier that:

> Since I returned from my magnetic tour in October, I have lived the life of a recluse, which is now more congenial to my feelings than the laborious trifling and heartless intercourse with the world . . .[19]

Hooker was curious to know what had become of the marine invertebrates that he and Ross had so assiduously collected in the Antarctic twenty years earlier. When he was sent to Aylesbury by the Admiralty after Ross's death to recover some instruments, he looked around until 'I found in the backyard of the house a huge pile of rubbish amongst which were the broken and unbroken empty bottles that contained his collections, the contents of course destroyed'.[20] Hooker did not speculate about Ross's motive for this sad vandalism, and might not have called to mind a peculiar circumstance of their original work together. The expedition had carried no preserving alcohol, and in its place the specimens had been bottled in ship's rum.

Hooker had not been able to save the marine collection, but Sabine had taken charge of the magnetic observations from the moment of the expedition's return. His work on the first season's observations of variation had shown that they did not agree with the estimate made by Gauss of where the magnetic meridians would converge. Herschel, in spite of his reservations about Sabine's insatiable appetite for more and better data, supported his request to the Admiralty for high-latitude observations from the meridians between 0° and 125°E, which Ross had lacked the time to make. These were obtained in 1845 by Thomas Moore, formerly master's mate in the *Terror*, who was sent back to the Antarctic in the *Pagoda* for just that purpose.

Sabine did not complete his reduction of all the data until 1868. By then he had long since parted company with Herschel, who had been looking for an elaboration of theory rather than the collection of ever more data, but Sabine was by then so entrenched in the government's councils of scientific advice that his views on geomagnetic research almost invariably prevailed. And at least one of his discoveries, although serendipitous, was a triumph for the inductive method. In 1852 his wife Elizabeth had been translating Humboldt's *Cosmos* into English. Sabine noticed that it included the first results of Heinrich Schwabe's studies of the timing of sunspots. He noted the correlation between Schwabe's observations and those of magnetic storms recorded at the colonial observatories. Further work on the statistical relationship between the phenomena led to recognition that the earth's magnetic field has both a terrestrial and a (smaller) cosmic component. Observation, undertaken globally at vast expense, had revealed that Gauss's purely terrestrial theory of magnetism was not a complete explanation. Sabine concluded his 1868 paper, the final magnetic fruit of Ross's Antarctic expedition, with a tribute to his fellow crusader.

> . . . I should be unjust to the memory of Sir James Ross and to my own high regard to his memory, if I failed to record my conviction that . . . he has established a claim to be regarded as the first scientific navigator of his country and of his age.[21]

And although d'Urville and Wilkes were nowhere mentioned, Sabine's maps of dip and intensity showed their discoveries as lines of coast, with occasional dotted stretches between.

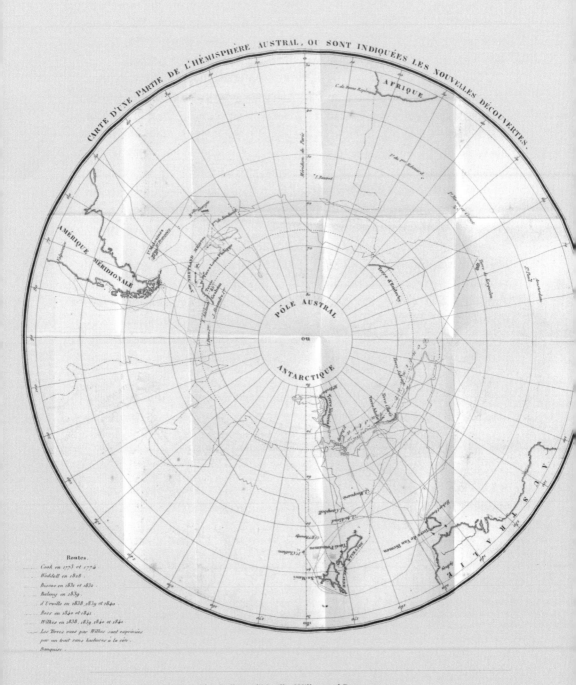

The Antarctic regions after Balleny, d'Urville, Wilkes and Ross.

INTERLUDE

The Sphinx in the Ice

Although the British colonial observatories continued to function throughout the 1840s, the Magnetic Crusade was practically at an end, and so was official European and American interest in the Antarctic. An enterprise that had started as cooperation between like-minded scientists throughout Europe had become dependent on state support. From there it had been but a short step to becoming an arena for international rivalry and a hostage to national budgets. Even if British scientific interest had been maintained, the Antarctic would have been unable to compete for funding priority while the obsessive search for Franklin continued. The first historian of Antarctica, Hugh Mill, described the half-century that followed as the generation of averted interest but, in truth, it was a hibernation in which the sleeper was occasionally prodded but not awakened. The more honour then, to the solitary figure

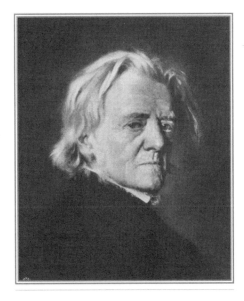

Georg von Neumayer, who kept the magnetic faith.

who continued the crusade for forty years, struggling against indifference which would have turned aside a lesser man.

Georg Neumayer was born too late and in the wrong place. By the time he took his doctorate in science, at Munich in 1849, victory had been declared in the Magnetic Crusade and the captains and kings had departed. Neumayer's interests lay in oceanography, magnetism and meteorology and, judging that it might be a long time before a Bavarian navy took an interest in exploration, he sailed to South America as a common seaman to gain experience in astronomy and navigation. On return he sat for and won his mate's ticket. In 1852, after holding a chair in physics at Hamburg and participating in the magnetic survey of Bavaria, he sailed to Australia, and for two years worked as a gold miner and seaman and did research at the Hobart magnetic laboratory established by Ross. Neumayer returned to Bavaria convinced that Australia was the place for magnetic and meteorological research. He enlisted the support of Humboldt – indefatigable Humboldt – and campaigned to persuade King Maximilian II to fund a physical laboratory. He also laid his plans before the British Association, where they were welcomed by the old magnetic crusaders, Whewell, Airy and Faraday. In 1857 he established the Flagstaff Observatory in Melbourne, and between 1858 and 1864 travelled many thousands of miles making observations for his magnetic survey of Victoria. Before he returned to Europe he revealed his ambitions to an audience of fellow expatriate Germans.

> It would be a glorious moment in the next period of my career if I could seek the Antarctic regions in a German ship, and perhaps sometime you will see me return to these shores accompanied by the pick of the youth of all Germany, bound on a voyage to the South Pole.[1]

This looks much like the glory-hunting that had so powerfully motivated the Ex Ex, but Neumayer's purpose was serious. With every year that passed, Ross's observations were less useful for contemporary purposes. Without a magnetic survey of the Antarctic it would not be possible to advance terrestrial magnetic theory. Neumayer persuaded the German naval power of the day, Austria-Hungary, of the value of an Antarctic expedition. Unfortunately, the 1870 Franco-Prussian war intervened. After the creation of the German Empire Neumayer was appointed hydrographer to the Reichsmarine and then, in 1876, director of the Hamburg Oceanic Observatory. He could only look on in envy as the British mounted the *Challenger* expedition of 1872–76, which became famous for the extent and quality of its oceanographic work in southern waters. It achieved its furthest south in the area recommended by Neumayer as most likely to allow ice-free access to the Antarctic, but spent only nine days south of the Antarctic Circle and saw no land. This was itself of some significance, because Captain Nares had taken the *Challenger* looking for the westernmost of Wilkes's discoveries, Termination Land. On 23 February 1874 the *Challenger* was only twenty miles east of its charted position, in good viewing weather. A sounding found bottom at 1300 fathoms. At the cost of collision with an iceberg on the following day the ship was worked to within fifteen miles of the reported location but there was still no land to be seen. Wilkes's discoveries had now been undermined at both their western and eastern ends while, paradoxically, his assertions about the nature of the land mass were being proved, because the rocks dredged up by the *Challenger* along the Antarctic Circle were of the kind associated with continents rather than with oceanic islands.

Neumayer's failure to excite interest in a German national expedition had its advantages for science. He re-directed his enthusiasm into the concept of an International Polar Year. In 1882–83 Western scientists made simultaneous meteorological and magnetic observations at the highest attainable latitudes around the North Pole. Southern observation was limited to stations in the three southern temperate continents and at South Georgia in the far South Atlantic, but the limitation itself was enough to re-ignite the spark of interest in Antarctic exploration. Veterans of the Ross and *Challenger* expeditions began urging the British Association to advocate another. Their efforts were seconded by members of the learned societies of Victoria, but British governments, imperial and colonial alike, could not be prevailed upon to vote funds for the purpose and the initiative lapsed. In 1893 Sir John Murray, of the *Challenger* expedition, took another tack.

> Is the last great piece of maritime exploration on the surface of our earth to be undertaken by Britons, or is it to be left to those who may be destined to succeed or supplant us on the ocean?[2]

The spectre thus conjured up was Germany and, although Neumayer's was a solitary voice, the rise of German naval power made the Reich a convenient bogey for anyone interested in exciting public interest and political response in Britain. Stirring the pot in this fashion suited the purposes of scientists in both countries. In 1898 the Berlin Geographical Society, concerned about flagging interest in its own proposals, went as far as to write to its English and Scottish counterparts suggesting that the prospect of a British expedition should be publicised because this would stimulate a German reaction.

As in the 1830s, the reluctance of politicians to fund Antarctic exploration was both challenge and opportunity for the imaginative. Like Poe before him, Jules Verne regarded the South Pole as a setting in which the further shores of the possible could be explored without interference from inconvenient facts. Verne had long been dissatisfied with Poe's inconclusive ending to *The Narrative of Arthur Gordon Pym*, and in 1897 undertook to 'find' the lost chapters. Poe had left his hero and a companion in the Weddell Sea south of 84°, their boat being drawn inexorably southward by the current towards an immense falling curtain of vapour – Poe's explanation of the aurora. Through momentary rents in the curtain they could see 'a chaos of flitting and indistinct images'. As a chasm opened to receive them, a shrouded human figure rose in their path, 'very far larger in its proportions than any dweller among men. And the hue of the skin of the figure was of the perfect whiteness of the snow'.[3]

Verne picked up this 'fantastic and baseless climax' where Poe had left it, but ignored the white giant.[4] Instead, he took on board the discoveries of 1840–41 and confined himself to exploiting the still unknown. According to Verne, Pym's companion escapes the impending chasm and the Antarctic. He offers to lead a rescue party, believing that the indistinct images seen through the curtain of vapour could have been appearances of land, islands or continent, where Pym, 'poor Pym, is waiting . . . until aid comes to him'. The party sails south to be marooned on an iceberg. They drift across or past the South Pole and in 86°S and 114°E land on a barren volcanic coast.[5] After following it north for several days to 75°S and 118°E (via what Verne mistakenly took to be Ross's return route from the area of the South Magnetic Pole[6]), they behold a huge mound resembling an enormous sphinx.[7] Their boat inexplicably gathers speed as they approach. Suddenly, their iron equipment flies off towards the sphinx. Fortunately the boat itself is of native construction, entirely free of iron, and can be safely beached. They find their utensils firmly attached to the mound and, hanging six feet above ground level, pinned by the iron barrel of the musket slung across his chest, the frozen corpse of Pym.

Where Poe had chosen to leave the South Pole to his readers' imaginations, Verne, having completed the story, was now obliged to provide an explanation for these 'astonishing phenomena'. Could it have been proximity to the South Magnetic Pole that produced such effects? Surely not, when all that had been observable at the North Magnetic Pole was a dip needle standing vertically.[8]

Was the sphinx, then, a prodigious magnet? Verne's generation had lived to see the electromagnet emerge from Faraday's laboratory to power many of the wonders of late Victorian civilisation. They could still be teased about what might be possible, but would not be taken for fools. Verne hypothesised that not all of the electricity in clouds was dissipated by storms, leaving a large surplus of 'electric fluid' that accumulated at the poles, causing the aurora. The continuous electric currents could be seen to confuse compasses. Could they not also act on a block of iron and transform it into an immense magnet?[9]

The electric coil could be supplied by the windings of a metallic lode in the soil which connected with the sphinx at its base. If it were at the Magnetic Pole it would act 'as a sort of gigantic calamite, from whence the imponderable fluid whose currents made an inexhaustible accumulator set up at the confines of the world should issue'. So was this electromagnet located at the Magnetic Pole? Verne knew that this would be going too far, and took refuge in feigned ignorance: the disorder of the compasses made it impossible to say, but the location of the 'artificial lodestone' mattered little by comparison with the way the clouds and the metallic lode gave it power. Verne's narrator was highly pleased with himself: 'in this very plausible fashion I was led to explain the phenomenon by instinct', and his companions, he said, had no difficulty in accepting his explanation as conclusive.[10] His readers were expected to do the same.

Verne had deliberately placed his sphinx many degrees to the west of any of the calculated positions for the magnetic dip pole. It was in fact another beast entirely, the geomagnetic South Pole, an arithmetic abstraction without any physical manifestation except floodlighting by the aurora. Gauss had calculated the positions of the geomagnetic poles as the points on the Earth's surface that gave the best fit for a magnetic dipole that passed through the centre of the planet. Unlike the dip poles, the geomagnetic poles are antipodal and the geomagnetic axis is at an angle of approximately 10.5° to the axis of rotation. It was these that Sir David Brewster had mistaken for the dip poles (see the Prologue).

The Geomagnetic Poles

In 1881 Hermann Fritz had concluded from his study of the frequency and distribution of the aurora borealis that its displays centred neither on the geographical North Pole nor on the magnetic (the north end of the earth's dipole axis), but rather on the axis of the earth's total magnetic field, dipolar and other. A decade later Kristian Birkeland in Norway was able to reproduce the aurora experimentally. Like William Gilbert, he made a small magnetised sphere, and like Gilbert's it was bipolar. He exposed it to electron discharge in a near vacuum and observed the formation of luminous rings. This, together with the coincidence of the aurora with sunspot activity, suggested to him that the aurora is the product of charged particles emitted by the sun interacting with the earth's magnetic field.

Birkeland's laboratory aurora oriented themselves about his geographical and magnetic poles, which were identical. The discovery by Fritz that the real aurora centred somewhere else was taken as evidence that Gauss had been correct: the presence of centres of intensity away from the dip poles indicated that some part of the earth's magnetic field was not bipolar. The places where the axis of the earth's total magnetic field passes through the planet's surface into space became known as the geomagnetic poles. Jules Verne, the alchemist, had again been entertaining his readers by transmuting emerging science into plausible fiction.

Verne had diverted Poe's narrative to the South Magnetic Pole to exploit popular interest in electromagnetism. He would have been truer to Poe's object, the geographic pole, had he drawn on another scientific discovery of his day, one that offered the prospect of a non-magnetic compass. In 1852 Verne's fellow countryman, Leon Foucault, had invented the gyroscope. Foucault had the idea that, if his spinning device were free to move horizontally, it would align its axis with that of the rotating earth and adjust itself parallel to the geographical meridian, thus becoming a true north-south pointing compass. In 1884 a patent was sought to improve the mariner's compass by replacing its magnetic needle and card with an electrically spun wheel. So Pym need not have been trapped at the South Magnetic Pole. The searchers could have found him at the geographic pole after all. What if the Earth long ago had been a huge gyroscope? The sphinx could have been its pivot and a solid spherical core rotating in fluid in the centre of the planet its flywheel. Because the sphinx would have been spinning much faster than the surrounding crust, it would have kept the planet in stable orbit during its formative ages. It would be reasonable to assume that friction had since gradually slowed rotation of the sphinx until it was barely faster than that of the planet, and imperceptible to Pym until he attempted to jump across to the monolith. When he missed his footing, the only thing that could have saved him from falling into the narrow gap between ice and sphinx was his musket sling, which must have caught on the rock. What at first must have seemed a providential escape became a slow death, because he was too weak to free himself. With one bound he was trapped.

Be that as it might have been, at the turn of the century it seemed that for the first time there could be an alternative to the hitherto indispensable magnetic compass. If so, magnetic science would lose its strongest practical underpinning, its importance to navigation.

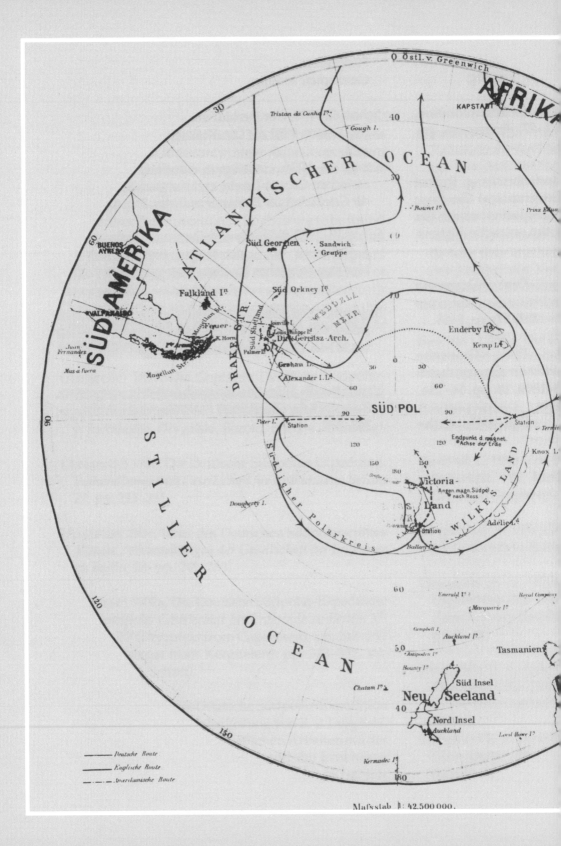

O Östl. v. Greenwich

AFRIKA

KAPSTADT

30 10

Tristan da Cunha Iⁿ. Gough I.

ATLANTISCHER OCEAN

Bouvet Iⁿ. Prinz Edua

SÜDAMERIKA

BUENOS AYRES 60

Süd Georgien Sandwich Gruppe

VALPARAISO

Falkland Iⁿ. Süd Orkney Iⁿ.

WEDDELL MEER

Enderby L

Juan Fernandez

Magellan Str.

K. Horn Süd Shetland

Joinville I.

Louis Philippe Iⁿ. Die Geritsz. Arch.

Kemp L.

DRAKE STR.

Fener Palmer Iⁿ.

Graham L.

Mas á Fuera

Magellan Str.

Alexander I. L^d.

30 0 30

60 60

90 SÜD POL 90 Station Termi

Peter I. Station

120 120

Endpunkt d. magnet. Achse der Erde

Knox L.

STILLER

150 180 150

Großte Isl. Victoria- WILKES LAND

Angen. magn. Südpol nach Ross.

S. Land Adélie L^d.

Dougherty I.

Südlicher Polarkreis

Station

Balleny

60

Emerald Iⁿ? Royal Company

Macquarie Iⁿ.

OCEAN

Campbell I. Auckland Iⁿ.

Tasmanien

50 Antipoden Iⁿ.

Bounty Iⁿ.

Süd Insel

Chatam Iⁿ. Neu Seeland

40 Nord Insel

120

Auckland Lord Howe Iⁿ.

150

Kermadec Iⁿ. 180

——— Deutsche Route
——— Englische Route
—·—·— Amerikanische Route

Maſsstab 1 : 42.500 000.

THE SECOND CRUSADE 1898–1914

Beobachtetes Packeis
Äusserste Packeisgrenze
Äusserste Eisberggrenze

Neumayer's Germany planned to resume the Magnetic Crusade, while Markham's Britain opted for 'naval adventure'.

PART TWO THE SECOND CRUSADE 1898–1914

	Borchgrevink & Bernacchi (Australia)	Robert Scott (Britain)	Erich von Drygalski (Germany)	Ernest Shackleton (Britain)	Douglas Mawson (Australasia)
1899	To Cape Adare				
1900	'Locate' SMP				
1901	Bernacchi with Scott	To McMurdo	To Antarctic	With Scott	
1902	Bernacchi at McMurdo	Furthest south	At Gaussberg	With Scott	
1903	Bernacchi on Ice Shelf		Ordered home	Sent home	
1904	Bernacchi to Britain	Returns to Britain			
1905					
1906					
1907				To McMurdo	With Shackleton
1908				At McMurdo	Climbs Erebus
1909				Furthest south	Near SMP
1910		To McMurdo			
1911		At South Pole			To Adelie Land
1912					Bage near SMP
1913					
1914					To Australia

CHAPTER 11

Poles Apart

Verne had written only just in time to be more or less believable. His work was itself a sign of widening public interest in the Antarctic. The impetus had been twofold. Whalemen equipped with steam catchers and explosive harpoons had come looking for the whales reported by Ross half a century earlier, both in the Ross Sea and around the Antarctic Peninsula. Scientists again began hitching rides, as they had during the search for the north-west passage, to pursue their interests in virgin fields. In 1894 a Norwegian migrant to Victoria, H. J. Bull, persuaded the originator of steam whaling, Sven Foyn, to fit out a whaleship, the *Antarctic*, for a southern cruise. A young colonial of Norwegian descent, Carsten Borchgrevink, wanted to join as scientific observer but was shipped as a 'generally useful hand'. No concession was originally made for scientific pursuits, but he was able to get ashore at Possession Island on 18 January 1895, and five days later was in a party which landed at Cape Adare, so becoming one of the first humans to touch the primeval rock of the Greater Antarctic mainland. Although the cruise was commercially unsuccessful, as the whales were few and far between, both Bull and Borchgrevink were subsequently much in demand as speakers in Australia. T. W. Edgeworth David, professor of geology at the University of Sydney, told the Linnean Society of New South Wales that the rocks collected by Borchgrevink at Cape Adare strongly implied the continuity of Victoria Land with Adelie Land. Bull wished to return, believing that it was possible to winter at Cape Adare, 'with a fair chance of penetrating to or nearly to the magnetic pole by aid of sledges and Norwegian ski-es'[1] but support was not forthcoming and he faded from the scene. Borchgrevink, on the other hand, took his presentation to the Sixth International Geographical Congress in Britain.

The 1895 Congress served to focus interest on Antarctica in the same way as the meetings of the British Association had sixty years earlier. Everyone was there. Neumayer advocated three simultaneous expeditions, south from Kerguelen, New Zealand and Cape Horn. Hooker, now Sir Joseph and the doyen of botanical science, postulated that there were three unknowns – the location of the South Magnetic Pole, Antarctic meteorology and Antarctic geology. Borchgrevink's forceful presentation, and his offer to lead a small expedition to locate the South Magnetic Pole, stirred the meeting in a way that the academic papers could not. The congress recommended that the scientific societies of the world should pursue 'the greatest piece of geographical exploration still to be undertaken'. Cost and official indifference in Britain and Germany seemed to present insuperable obstacles, but Borchgrevink was not to be deflected: he persuaded a British publisher, Sir George Newnes, to fund a private expedition.

The *Southern Cross* was a former whaling barque. She was fitted with a new auxiliary engine and the expedition departed from London on 23 August 1898. Its physicist was Louis Bernacchi, a young Tasmanian of Italo-Flemish origin. Bernacchi had studied astronomy, magnetism, meteorology and physics at the Melbourne Observatory and had attempted to join the Belgian Gerlache expedition to the Antarctic Peninsula a year earlier. The recruitment of ninety Greenland and Siberian dogs with two Lapp handlers foreshadowed some determined sledging. Borchgrevink was careful to speak only of 'locating' the Magnetic Pole, which could be done without visiting it, but it can hardly be doubted that to stand on the spot was his ambition. South from Hobart, Borchgrevink directed the *Southern Cross* towards the Balleny Islands, 'anxious to be enabled to judge for myself the cause of Captain Wilkes' mistake'. They crossed Wilkes's track a little further east than Ross had, and Borchgrevink concluded that Wilkes must have seen the most northerly of the Balleny Islands and that, mistaking the distance, he had taken it for a new discovery. The ship was unable to break through to Cape Adare until 17 February 1899, but ten men and three prefabricated huts were then quickly unloaded in Robertson Bay and left to face the Antarctic winter. Hopes of penetrating inland were soon dashed by the realisation that the Admiralty Mountains would be impassable to a sledge party.[2]

The dog sled journeys undertaken during the winter involved little scientific field work, and the systematic magnetic and meteorological observations were made from base camp. The rigours of observing from an open tent in temperatures of as low as -25°C convinced Bernacchi of the need for simple, robust instruments. He was intrigued by refraction, noting that on 15 August a number of icebergs 30 miles to the north, usually invisible, appeared level with the top of Cape Adare, nearly 900 feet high. On clear days the coast around Cape North, 100 miles distant, was frequently seen. The aurora was more of a puzzle.

> . . . a phenomenon at the same time cosmic and terrestrial, which on the one hand is confined within the atmosphere of our globe, and stands in close connection with terrestrial magnetism, and on the other hand is dependent on certain changes in the envelope of the sun . . . It is impossible for one who has not seen it to even feebly understand its great beauty. How little we understand the nature of its origin. It appears as if Nature has reserved for these cold climates of the pole its most astonishing, soul-inspiring, and baffling phenomenon.[3]

The *Southern Cross* returned to Robertson Bay on 28 January 1900, embarked the sojourners and sailed south towards the Ross Ice Shelf. Bernacchi made observations as they went. A landing was effected at Wood Bay, near Mount Melbourne. To the south of the mountain the gradient inland appeared gradual, but Bernacchi did not assume that it offered an easy approach to the Magnetic Pole; he cautioned that it was still to be determined whether the coast of Victoria Land was an archipelago or the edge of a continent. The dip was 88°2'31", the highest observed by the expedition. Borchgrevink confidently proclaimed that, taken together, the magnetic observations indicated that the pole was approximately 220 miles distant from Wood Bay in 70°20'S and 146°E. Bernacchi, who did not think much of Borchgrevink as a leader and still less of him as a scientist, was sceptical of such precision.[4] He had little doubt that the Magnetic Pole lay much further to the north and west than it had in 1841, 'but, of course, it is impossible to accurately locate its position from such scanty data'.[5]

At Mount Erebus the ship turned east along the ice shelf, which was found to have receded thirty miles since Ross's day, and in longitude 195°50'E, it was low enough to permit a landing. A ten-mile dog sled excursion over the surface of the shelf gave Borchgrevink a furthest south record of latitude 78°50'S. Bernacchi recorded that Ross's 'huge' Parry Mountains ran parallel to the coast

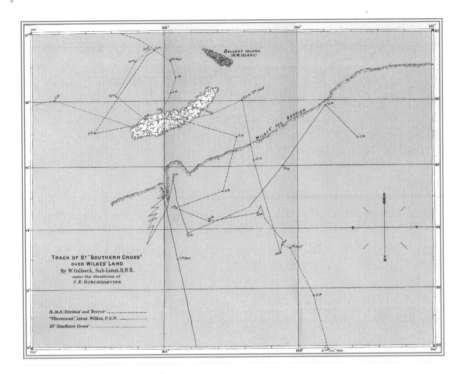

Borchgrevink steamed over Wilkes's eastern discovery, confirming Ross's obliteration of it.

and appeared to be a continuation of the great spinal ranges of Victoria Land. As seen from the *Southern Cross*, they seemed to extend much further south than Ross had shown them on his chart. The expedition did not see Ross's 'appearance of land' to the south-east, but Bernacchi guessed that it might be the eastern shore of a bight containing the shelf. He also feared that the good surface the shelf offered for travel towards the south would make it a magnet of an undesirable sort, attracting those who were more interested in being first to the geographic pole than in undertaking serious scientific exploration.

> A dash to the South Pole is not, perhaps, of very great scientific importance, but it is a goal for which most expeditions will strive . . . What is rather desired is a steady, continuous, laborious and systematic exploration of the whole Southern Region with all the appliances of the modern investigator, and discovery will lead to discovery.[6]

Reiterating his caution about the nature of the region's land masses, he warned that there could be open sea between the southern edge of the shelf and the

South Pole. He also pressed the claims of further magnetic research, arguing that, while the mathematical theory had been developed, of the physical theory of 'that mysterious force of nature, we are yet in perfect ignorance'.[7] What was needed was a systematic survey of land and ocean which would be 'of infinitely greater value than the determination of the spot where the needle stands vertical'. He might have added that it was also a much harder task, for it would require observations to be made at places all around the pole, some of which would be much further from the coast of Victoria Land than the Magnetic Pole itself. But, echoing Neumayer, he had no doubts about the utility of the task, if only to correct navigational charts for the inconstancy of the magnetic forces.[8]

The opportunity to take more observations came more quickly than he might have foreseen. While the *Southern Cross* expedition was wintering in the Antarctic, preparations had set in train for an official German expedition and a semi-official British one. Although he was now too old to go himself, Neumayer's time had finally come. As they had in the Britain of Ross's day, proponents played on nationalist sentiment and found the politicians responsive. In the Reichstag, Deputy Grober claimed to be speaking for the whole house when he said:

> I stress that the question of dispatching a South Polar Expedition has now become a matter of national honour . . . Once upon a time Germany could not seriously have considered sending such an expedition . . . Then, our German scholars were obliged to turn to others to test their theories and to conduct practical experiments. Today we can expect the aspirations of German scholars to be realized by German expeditions. Germany has today very nearly, if not quite the second most powerful navy in the world . . .[9]

The Reich authorities agreed to construct an auxiliary barquentine, the *Gauss*, for an expedition to be led by Erich von Drygalski, professor of geography at Berlin University and noted Greenland explorer. This was exactly what the proposers of the Britain expedition, notably the President of the Royal Geographical Society, Sir Clements Markham, needed to prod the government into providing financial support and naval volunteers to man the society's own new auxiliary barque, the *Discovery*. She was built of solid oak with a large part of the hull entirely free from magnetic influence. In the context of growing Anglo-German naval rivalry, this second crusade showed every sign of becoming a contest like that of the 1840s, but Neumayer remained firm in his conviction that cooperation was the key to maximising scientific results.

Paradoxically, he was originally lukewarm about the expedition, prompting Drygalski later to accuse him of having 'an essential separation in his mind between the actual realization of an expedition and campaigning for the idea of such a thing'. Someone more sensitive might have recognised an old man's disappointment at seeing his ambition of forty years realised by another.

A program of complementary explorations and simultaneous observations was arranged. The Belgians had gone south of Cape Horn, as might Swedish and American expeditions if they eventuated, and the British would follow Ross's track. In Neumayer's scheme for widespread coverage, this left empty the Antarctic sector south of the Atlantic and Indian oceans, specifically the blank between Termination Land and Kemp Land. If they were found to be connected, it would strengthen the case for the existence of an Antarctic continent. If not, how far south could one sail in that sector? The area was also relatively close to the Magnetic Pole and known to have a strong magnetic force field east of 80°E. It was there that the *Gauss* was directed. She sailed from Kiel on 11 August 1901, five days after the *Discovery* left Cowes. The commander of the British vessel, Robert Falcon Scott RN, had been hand-picked by Markham. The physicist they wanted, however, failed the medical and they were hard-pressed to find another. In the end, Louis Bernacchi found himself again bound for Victoria Land.

The respective motives and objectives of the two expeditions are neatly summarised in a map prepared for the Berlin Geographical Society in 1899. It shows a proposed German station at 72°S and 90°E, from which radiate the tracks of a sea voyage to the south-west and a land journey south-east towards Ross's Magnetic Pole, past a point described as the 'endpoint of the magnetic axis of the Earth', the geomagnetic pole. The track of a third journey, the most distant of the three, points towards the geographic South Pole. By contrast, the only track from the proposed British station at Cape Adare passes within a hundred miles or so of the South Magnetic Pole without so much as a nod in its direction. It points directly to the geographic pole. The same single-mindedness is evident in another proposed British track southwards from a station in the vicinity of Peter I Island in 90°W. Bernacchi had been right. The geographic pole was exercising its inexorable attraction. It was to the credit of Neumayer, Drygalski and the German scientists that they had resisted, but they could not escape its influence. Fund-raising propaganda had fixed in the mind of the European public a yardstick against which it would measure all Antarctic exploration for the next decade: had the expedition in question got further south than its predecessors?

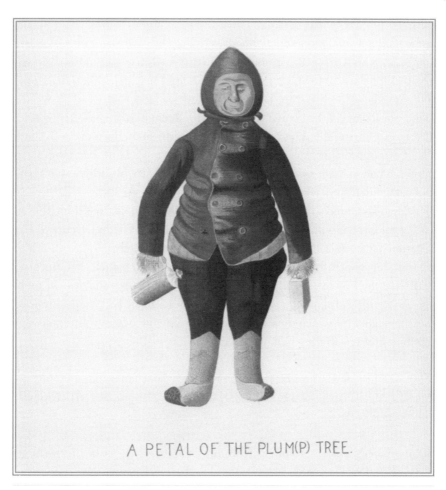

A PETAL OF THE PLUM(P) TREE.

Louis Bernacchi, 'Loadstone'.

The experiences of the German and British expeditions were as different as their expectations. The *Gauss* attempted to penetrate the Antarctic in about 90°E to test Neumayer's theory that a warm current from the Indian Ocean would keep the area relatively ice-free and perhaps open as far as the Weddell Sea. By 21 February 1902 they were within sixty miles of Wilkes's Termination Land and land was seen in that direction, but Drygalski doubted that it could have been seen from the *Vincennes* in 1840. The onset of a severe storm denied him the opportunity to investigate further and left the *Gauss* trapped. As if contemptuous of Neumayer's prediction, the ice would not even allow the ship to cross the Antarctic Circle. After battening her down for the winter, members of the expedition sledged fifty miles south until they reached a black and naked volcanic nunatak, 300 metres high. The Gaussberg, as Drygalski named it, reared from the monotony of its flat white surrounds as though expelled for non-conformity. It was the only land reached, although, from a balloon tethered to the ship, Drygalski could see land to the east as well as to the south beyond the Gaussberg. With the advent of spring all efforts were directed to freeing the ship, but even blasting proved ineffectual. In the end, a lead through the ice was manufactured by creating a fault line: ashes from the ship's boilers were spread with other dark rubbish to absorb the sun's heat and partly melt the ice beneath.

The expedition's magnetician, Friedrich Bidlingmaier, spent his year in the ice making observations with great attention to detail and accuracy. His instruments were a Bamberg Deviation Magnetometer, which could also measure horizontal force and dip, and a Lloyd-Creak dip circle, an improved version of the Fox instrument of sixty years earlier. In an ironic case of more not necessarily being better, the scale of this instrument had been so refined that the quality for which the Fox circle was originally so highly esteemed – its suitability for use at sea – had been degraded.

> It had to be read with a magnifying glass, thus compounding our problems, in that the oscillations of the needle were usually so great that they went beyond the field of the glass.[10]

Bidlingmaier's technique for overcoming the deficiencies of his instruments was simple but exhausting. He repeated his observations and took their mean value. He was not satisfied that he had taken a sufficient number until the mean value was within the margin of error of each observation. In the end he had eight series of observations taken across the Atlantic, Indian and Southern oceans, sufficient, it was hoped, to establish whether the magnetic force had the same potential across the globe, as land observation seemed to suggest, or whether the potential of the oceans was different.[11] The voyage of the *Gauss* generated twenty volumes of scientific results between 1905 and 1931 but was widely regarded as a failure. As a supporter bitterly remarked, even if Drygalski had sledged as many miles as Scott, he would still have been north of Scott's starting point, and that was the beginning and the end of interest for the German public.

Notwithstanding, the German public had reason to be aggrieved because Scott had landed, not at Cape Adare as 'agreed' in 1899, but much further south, at McMurdo Sound in the shadow of Mount Erebus. This was one of the outcomes of a bitter struggle between the Royal Geographical Society, or more precisely its President, Markham, and the Royal Society. At stake had been the very nature of the expedition. The Royal Society had wanted a scientist to lead. Markham, with an obsessive nostalgia which had its origin in his own experience as a midshipman during the search for Franklin, was adamant that only a naval officer could be entrusted with a voyage of discovery, even if it involved much land work. No matter that the first of the two principal objects of the expedition was the magnetic survey; no matter that any wintering party would be engaged in land exploration, and that it would be unwise for the commander to harbour his ship in the ice unless it were unavoidable. In a masterly display of committee politics, Markham had his way and the Royal Society all but withdrew in disgust. Scott's final instructions maintained the primacy of the magnetic work, but it was plain to all that scientific work was to be subordinated to 'naval adventure'.[12]

While McMurdo Sound was undoubtedly superior as a winter harbour to either Robertson Bay or Wood Bay, the choice left Bernacchi disappointed, as much for Scott's agenda as for his own.

> And so, perhaps, was lost an opportunity for reaching the South Pole years before it was finally accomplished, for Wood Bay leads immediately and easily to the Polar Plateau, reached in later years at a much less accessible spot. The mileage would have been greater, but the travelling easier, and at least we could have reached without difficulty the South Magnetic Pole, at that time only about 150 miles from the bay. It was one of those 'might-have-beens' which change the course of polar history.[13]

To Scott, McMurdo Sound seemed ideally placed for the geographical explorations set out in his instructions: west to the mountains of Victoria Land, south towards the geographic pole, and in the volcanic region around Mount Erebus. While the magnetic survey, in accordance with the program of the British and German committees, called for observations, there was no remit for an attempt to visit the magnetic pole. That was left to the Germans.

The first of Scott's geographical discoveries was that the Parry Mountains were just a few small hills. They were as unlike as a hawk and a handsaw, and he found it difficult to understand how a reliable observer like Ross had been so deceived: 'I am inclined to think that in exaggerating the height of the barrier in this region, he was led to suppose that anything seen over it at a distance must necessarily be of very great altitude'.[14] Scott did not realise that it was refraction which had enabled Ross to see the mountains, and that they were both more distant and higher than even Ross had believed. Unlike Ross and Bernacchi, Scott was not favoured by refraction, which would have lifted his gaze from the hills to the mountains far beyond. If he had been, he would have realised that the 9000–10,000 foot peaks he later named Mounts Field, Wharton and Albert Markham were Ross's Parry Mountains. But, having queried one Ross discovery, he then confirmed another: east of the ice shelf, near where Ross had reported an appearance of land, Scott saw exposed rock standing out from snow-covered slopes. He named it King Edward's Land.

Scott himself was not particularly interested in magnetic work and, indeed, complained that it totally consumed Bernacchi's time to the exclusion of his other responsibilities as physicist. The magnetic program could not be neglected, but Scott excused himself from being enthusiastic about it:

> The general reader may well wonder why so much trouble should be taken to ascertain small differences in the earth's magnetism, and he could scarcely be answered in a few words. Broadly speaking, the earth is a magnet, and its magnetism is constantly changing; but why it is a magnet, or why it changes, or indeed what magnetism may be, is unknown, and obviously the most hopeful road to the explanation of a phenomenon is to study it.[15]

With these few words of his own he dismissed what was, in the eyes of the Royal Society, the most important of all the expedition's tasks, but the work itself was in safe hands and Bernacchi was adept at finding opportunities to advance it in the face of competing priorities. Writing as Loadstone[16], he contributed a succinct account of the state of magnetic knowledge to the *South Polar Times*, which as the expedition's house journal was the first magazine published in Antarctica. With illustrations drawn by the expedition's doctor and father figure, Edward Wilson, the article was a nicely judged piece of domestic propaganda.[17] For nearly two years Bernacchi tended the instruments at McMurdo Sound, during which time Scott, with Wilson and a merchant navy officer, Ernest Shackleton, achieved a furthest south, 82°16', along the western margin of the Ross Ice Shelf. It was a harrowing journey of three months for little gain, in the process killing all of the dogs and so reducing Shackleton through scurvy that, against his will, he was evacuated on the relief ship *Morning*.

Most of the resources of the expedition's 1903 spring campaign were earmarked for another southern journey and for Scott's own push into the western mountains. Enough men remained to make one other small party which, because it would be unsupported, could not be expected to go far. Bernacchi put it to Scott that they had no idea of the topography of the ice shelf south of its edge and east of its mountainous margin. Since his first voyage Bernacchi had suspected that there might be open water no more than fifty miles south of the edge, as Ross had hoped. If not, it was still a wonderful opportunity to make a prolonged line of magnetic observations, free of local attraction, on a solid footing. Scott agreed and Bernacchi was able to get his observations, but 180 miles of 'pulley-hauley' to the south-east revealed nothing but the shelf, and then more shelf, all the while sloping imperceptibly to the east.

When the *Discovery* was freed from the winter ice of McMurdo Sound in February 1904 Scott steered along the coast of Victoria Land searching for Ross's hoped-for passage to the west around Cape North. Not until he neared the Balleny Islands was he able to pass to the west, the first navigator to find an ice-free passage between the islands and the mainland. All aboard were conscious that the ship was heading towards Wilkes Land, and twice Scott had to dismiss reports of land that proved to be no more solid than 'the fantastical cloud forms that fringe our horizon'. By 4 March he was satisfied that this was an empty sea.

> The sky has been dull, but the horizon quite clear; we could have seen land at a great distance, yet none has been in sight, and thus once and for all we have definitely disposed of Wilkes Land ... We have been standing NW true, and on such a course we should have sighted Eld's Peak and Ringgold's Knoll on our right had these places existed. It is therefore quite evident that they do not, nor can there be any land in this direction, as the long ocean swell has never ceased to roll steadily in from the north ... Tonight Cape Hudson should be in sight on the port bow, but that is also conspicuous by its absence. After reading Wilkes' report again, I must conclude that as these places are non-existent, there is no case for any land east of Adelie Land.[18]

For all that, he acknowledged that Wilkes's soundings were a guide to the limits of the continental shelf, which ran approximately along the Antarctic Circle. Shortage of coal precluded any further exploration and the ship made for New Zealand. In the appendices to his account of the voyage Scott published lengthy notes on the geology and fauna of the Antarctic. The magnetic work was dismissed with half a page, but he was confident that 'the mass of material obtained will go far to accomplish the main object which was named by the Royal Society'.[19] The society entrusted the task of reduction to Commander Chetwynd of the Royal Navy's Hydrography Department, with Bernacchi reduced to the role of assistant. Chetwynd was careful to cross-check his inclination result for the pole by comparing it with an independently calculated declination result. Remarkably, the positions agreed to within two minutes of latitude and ten minutes of longitude. Chetwyn declared their mean, 72°51'S and 156°25'E, to be 'in all probability a close indication of the centre of the polar area'.[20]

Scott predicted that a period of 'reaction and quiescence' would set in after the British and German expeditions. There would be others, but only in the fullness of time. He had not reckoned with the dynamism and impatience of Ernest Shackleton.

CHAPTER 12

Thereabouts

Ernest Shackleton was not the kind of man to be put off by a bout of scurvy. Evacuation from McMurdo Sound in 1903 had deeply wounded his pride. He was determined to return to the Antarctic and, although a merchant marine officer by profession, he sought the position of Secretary to the Royal Scottish Geographical Society, and for four years laboured to put together a cut-rate expedition with himself as leader. His main objective was the geographic pole and he proposed to start from the Edward VII Land end of the Ross Ice Shelf rather than from McMurdo Sound, a saving of ninety miles. The magnetic pole was nominally included in the expedition's itinerary, but it was a long way from Edward VII Land and money was tight, so when the sealer *Nimrod* sailed from the Thames, on 30 July 1907, there was no magnetician aboard. It was only after the expedition had reached New Zealand, and the Australian and New Zealand governments had agreed to contribute, that Douglas Mawson, a young Yorkshire-born lecturer at the University of Adelaide, was offered the post as physicist on the recommendation of Professor Edgeworth David.

Mawson's Antarctic interest was glaciation, which he had hoped to satisfy in a summer's round trip on the *Nimrod*, but he could not resist the opportunity to go, even if as physicist he would have to stay for a year and more. Nor could his mentor. David likewise had planned only a summer's work, intending to return to New Zealand with the *Nimrod*, but Shackleton persuaded him to stay on. At the age of 50 he was by far the oldest member of the wintering party but Shackleton now wanted him available for a task that had unexpectedly come to the fore. The Edward VII coast had been found to be impenetrably ice-bound and it had become necessary to establish winter quarters at McMurdo Sound, near Scott's old base. From there the magnetic pole was realistically within reach. As a test, David was given command of the advance party which, in March 1908, made the first ascent of Mount Erebus. His companions on the mountain were Mawson and one of the expedition's doctors, Alistair Forbes Mackay. They seemed to make a good team, and Shackleton told them that in spring they would be off to the magnetic pole by way of the coastal ice, as advocated by Bernacchi. Contrary to Bernacchi's advice, however, it was planned that the party would turn inland south of Mount Melbourne rather than con-tinue around it to the gentle slopes which he had been sure would allow easy access to the polar plateau.

As with Scott's expedition, most of the late winter work was devoted to establishing depots for the southern party. Neither ponies nor dogs could be spared for David's northern party. The best that could be done to start them on their way was to have the expedition's motor car carry their stores 15 miles out onto the ice of the sound. On 5 October 1908 their two sledges were likewise towed out but visibility was poor, and after two miles it became too dangerous for the car to continue. The party slipped into harness, toggled on to the sledges, and started hauling for the western shore.

Fully loaded, the sledges were too heavy to be pulled together. They had to be relayed forward one at a time unless the wind was in the right quarter, when floorcloth sails on tentpole masts could carry all along together. On 18 October a change was made to the order of march. David, who was suf-fering from snow-blindness, relinquished the leader's position at the front of the sledge rope to Mawson. He never resumed it, Mawson having 'proved himself', as David put it, 'so remarkably efficient at picking out the best track . . . and steering a good course'.[1] For his part, Mawson believed that 'the Prof' was not pulling his weight. More allowance might have been made for his age had David adapted better to the routine of sledging. As it was, he sat up late at night and invariably woke the others when he finally clambered into the three-man sleeping bag. He wore so much clothing that he took up half the bag and always claimed the middle, warmest position. He seldom helped to pack the sledge but still managed to be the last man ready to resume the march in the morning.

They were averaging only four miles a day using the relay method and at that rate there was no prospect of reaching the magnetic pole and returning by early January. They decided to reduce their load by travelling on half rations along the coast, supplementing them with seal meat, and depoting the remainder. Mawson pointed out that even if they reached the pole there would be insufficient time to cross the polar area and make detailed observations. He would have preferred to forego the pole and concentrate on coastal survey and geology but, outvoted, insisted that they must have at least six weeks of full rations at the time they turned inland. His concern arose from observations he had made with the dip circle on 11 November. The pole appeared to be further inland than Chetwynd had placed it for epoch 1903. If anything, it should have been closer, because Chetwynd's comparison of his inclination results with those of Sabine had shown that the pole was moving east, towards them. The glacier-fed Drygalski Ice Tongue added more miles. Their first attempt to cross it failed. Earlier in the season they might have tried to go around it, but it projected 35 miles from the coast and by December its seaward edge would already be melting. There was no option but to try again, further east. A route was found, but it took eight days to cross and left them even further from the pole than Mawson had made allowance for. From their Drygalski depot, on an inlet where a ship could dock against the ice, they had to allow for a journey to the pole and back of 500 miles, which would take seven weeks at an average of 14–15 miles a day.

Here was no gentle ascent, not even the low, sloping shore promised by their Admiralty chart. The mountains in the vicinity were upwards of 4000 feet high and separated by glaciers. It was a daunting prospect for three men who would have to pull 670 pounds of sledge, stores and equipment (the dip circle and its tripod alone weighed 30 pounds). Even David's public account of the journey, which made light of his personal difficulties, acknowledged that the mountains gave them cause for concern.

> We were doubtful, in our then stale and weakened condition, whether we should be able to pull such a load over the deep loose snow ahead of us, and then drag it up the steep ice slopes of the great glaciers which guarded the route to the plateau.[2]

The party set out for the mountains on 16 December, everything carried on a single sledge. Mawson by then had come to a low opinion of Mackay. He felt that the doctor had been lazy in camp and was generally unskilful at everything other than plain, hard manual work: 'he would make a good soldier but no general'. They now had no margin of time for error. In the event that they failed to return to McMurdo on foot as planned, it had been arranged that the *Nimrod* would look for them along the coast in the first few days of February. There was no Plan C.

The party first headed for the Reeves Glacier between Mount Nansen and Mount Larsen but soon found itself in a 'perfect labyrinth of crevasses and pressure ridges'.[3] They turned south-west to see if the Larsen Glacier north of Mount Bellingshausen offered better going. The glacier was steep, broken and rugged, but a small branch flowed around the slopes of Mount Gerlache and offered difficult but practicable access to the higher reaches. Even so, they could only haul half of the stores up at a time and it was Christmas Eve before they reached 1200 feet. From there the ascent was more gradual. On 27 December they were able to depot their mountaineering gear and, on New Year's Eve, boiling the hypsometer gave an altitude reading of nearly 5000 feet. The sledge meter had been clicking off 11–12 miles a day, but it was not enough. The journey would take longer than planned. They agreed to shorten rations and create a reserve of one-eighth of their food. The tent was fraying, as were tempers, but the main concern was David, as Mawson confided to his diary:

> Something has gone very wrong with him of late as he [is] almost morose, never refers to our work, shirks all questions regarding it, never offers a suggestion. Well anyway, he is getting the value of our blood as we (Mac and I) do our level best at pulling and generally pushing on the expedition.[4]

Four days later, as they gradually climbed, a note of alarm found its way into Mawson's diary. David was affected by the altitude and unable to do anything between hauls. His memory seemed fainter. He was doing his best, but it was less than could have been asked of a younger man. Mawson also found that the time, strength and distance equation was becoming more difficult to solve. His continuing magnetic observations showed that the dip was not increasing as much as it should have. They were not closing on the pole quickly enough.

The going was easier on the plateau but sastrugi two to three feet high cut across their line of march and soft snow in the hollows between these ridges slowed their progress. It was all they could do, as shortage of food began to pinch, to pull ten miles a day, five in the morning and five in the afternoon, with a halt in between for a meal, which only reminded them how hungry they were. Navigation was simple but uncertain on the featureless expanse of the plateau: they marched along the magnetic meridian as indicated by the south end of a prismatic compass needle which was, of course, pointing north-west true. By 11 January 1909 the instrument was very sluggish, which drew a quip from David: 'This pleased us a good deal, and at first we wished more power to it: then amended the sentiment and wished less power to it'. On the evening of 12 January Mawson carefully re-read his advance copy of Chetwynd's magnetic report from the *Discovery* expedition. Although the report nowhere drew attention to the fact, comparison of the absolute declination data sets for 1902 and 1903 showed that the pole was moving *west*, away from them. The data confirmed Mawson's own observations, yet the position Chetwynd had assigned to the pole for 1903 lay nine degrees *east* of that given by Sabine on the basis of Ross's 1841 observations. Either the pole's track had made a dogleg or someone was wrong:

> It is a revelation and great sorrow – we shall have to go farther than otherwise. The others very glum. We got up this morning [13th] and discussed situation. Prof [says] go on, Mac first states he will be willing to go on (thought 4 days [to Pole] 4 days [back]) but says we cannot get back if we do. I make proposal by which only 3 days extra at most needed, and then 13 m[iles] per day return to coast required to exactly pan out provisions on already reduced scale. Mac then protests strongly against going on, says if we go on past the 15th we cannot get back as head winds and bad weather will retard us, and 13 m per day impossible. At last we agree to this plan by which 57 m shall if necessary be added to our run [from] today if required, allowing for our return on morning of 18th at latest. Mac wants us to swear we will do 13 m per day return; it is done.[5]

The dip was then 89°10'. By 15 January the needle was only fifteen minutes from the vertical but Mawson felt that the outlook for safe return had become 'really serious'. He calculated that the pole might be as little as 13 miles ahead and announced that if they were to take continuous magnetic observations where they were for 24 hours, most probably the pole would at some time pass beneath their feet.[6] That evening they resolved to try for its approximate mean position even though they could not afford the two days at the current rate of progress it would take to get there and return to their present camp. They would have to sprint.

On 16 January they hauled two miles and cached the heavy gear, including the dip circle. At further successive two-mile intervals they set up the legs of the dip circle and the theodolite as route markers, and two miles beyond that erected their tent, where they took 'a light lunch'. A post-prandial

Mackay, David and Mawson raise the flag in the area of 'approximate verticality' of the dip needle on 15 January 1909.

stretch of five miles, carrying only camera, tripod and flagpole, took them to 72°25'S, 155°16'E, 40 miles north-west of where Chetwynd had placed the pole. If both Mawson and Chetwynd were correct, the pole was moving about seven miles a year. At 3.30 pm the Union Jack was hoisted and David read 'in a loud voice' the form of words given to him by Shackleton: 'I hereby take possession of this area *now* containing the Magnetic Pole for the British Empire'. The wind muffled the click as David pulled a string that triggered the camera shutter. The identical photograph could have been taken anywhere within a radius of a hundred miles or more. As evidence of discovery it was nothing, which was somehow appropriate: it was a souvenir, nothing more. Without the dip circle it was not even possible to observe the inclination. In the awkward silence that followed Mackay suggested three cheers for the King. David's exhaustion was temporarily relieved by the glow of achievement.

> It was an intense satisfaction and relief to all of us to feel that at last after so many days of toil, hardship and danger we had been able to carry out our leader's instructions, and to fulfill the wish of Sir James Clarke Ross that the South Magnetic Pole should be actually reached, as he had already in 1831 reached the North Magnetic Pole. At the same time we were too utterly weary to be capable of any great amount of exultation.[7]

Mawson was more conscious of the limitations of what they had done, claiming only to have reached the area of 'approximate verticality'. His prismatic compass was the only magnetic instrument to hand and, by gently tapping it, the needle could still be made to point north-west true. As the horizontal force was still acting, they were not at the pole, although Mawson was inclined to think that diurnal motion had 'merely carried it to the north-west of its central position'. Confirmation would require a large number of readings taken at a number of positions surrounding the pole, an impossibility for manhaul sledging parties like theirs.[8]

By 10.30 pm they were back at the cache of heavy gear, 249 miles from the Drygalski Glacier depot and with just fifteen days to reach it if they were to rendezvous with the *Nimrod*. Providentially, the south-easterly wind that had helped them over the last few miles to the pole died away and was replaced by a north-westerly, hurrying them home. More than sixteen miles a day was now required of them, but on the 20th Mawson had good news – they could afford to revert to nearly full rations. On 21 January they lost the track of their outward march, which led to a discussion about whether they were to the right or left of it. Mawson, who was setting the course, insisted that they were more or less on line. On the 24th they picked up a short section of track that had not been obliterated, confirming Mawson's skill as a navigator. Four days later a 25 mph blizzard at their backs enabled them to make twenty miles under sail. It was David's fifty-first birthday and they had a special meal to celebrate. Wrestling with the sail had proved so exhausting that they did not set it on the following day, but wind and the downhill slope allowed them to maintain the pace. That evening they reached their depot at the head of the Larsen Glacier.

Mackay was in favour of descending by their outbound route, the Backstairs Passage. David and Mawson were fearful that the thaw would have destroyed the ice path and opted for a direct descent of the Larsen Glacier. It was a decision that three days later they would happily have revisited. The slope was far steeper than expected, with innumerable pressure ridges and crevasses. No one escaped a fall or two and, on one occasion, David and Mackay only prevented themselves going through a snow bridge by throwing out their arms to catch the edge as they fell. Mackay had no patience left for David and called him 'a bloody fool'. Mawson thought that the Prof was half-demented: 'the strain has been too great. He says himself that had he known the magnitude he would not have attempted it'. To make things worse they encountered a new phenomenon – tiled ice which curved up from the surface. Its edges caught the sledge and the men often crashed through up to their knees. David afterwards likened it to sledging over a wilderness of glass cucumber frames set at an angle of 45°. While Mawson was reconnoitering ahead, Mackay, in his capacity as party doctor, confronted David.

> . . . I have deposed the Professor. I simply told him that he was no longer fit to lead the party, that the situation was now critical, and that he must officially appoint Mawson leader, or I would declare him, the Professor, physically and mentally unfit. He acted on my proposal at once.[9]

In fact, another two days were to go by before David raised the matter with Mawson and in the meantime his physical condition had deteriorated further. On 1 February they were still 16 miles short of the Drygalski depot. There were only two days' rations left but soon there would be seal and penguin to hunt. However, the crucial question was whether they would arrive in time for the *Nimrod*. A fortuitous mirage enabled Mawson to detect the depot flag on 2 February. They had been pulling too far to the east and the Drygalski inlet lay between them and the depot. David was spent.

Prof's boots were frozen on and foot gone. Mac now reports that his feet are more or less gangrenous. During most of day the Prof has been walking on his ankles. He was no doubt doing his best in this way, and Mac appears to have kicked him several times when in the harness.[10]

That evening, when they were within seven miles of the depot, David struggled up to Mawson, after Mackay had again threatened to certify him unfit, and asked his former pupil to take command of the expedition. According to Mawson:

> [David] asked me to consider myself leader of the expedition since
> [30 October] – as indeed, he said he had always considered me. He said he
> would draw it up in writing and get me to sign it. I said I did not like it and
> would think on it. Whilst Mac was away killing seal he drew out his pocket
> book and began writing out my authority as leader of the expedition and asked
> me to sign it. I said I did not like the business and stated he had better leave
> matters as they were until the ship failed to turn up.[11]

After a day and a night's continuous trudging they turned into the sleeping bag at 7 am on 3 February, camped atop an ice cliff within three miles of the open sea but still on the wrong side of the inlet. Sleep instantly claimed them. Fifteen minutes later the *Nimrod* passed the spot, steaming north. Drifting snow hid both tent and depot flag from the ship. The three men rose at 11 am and spent the reminder of the day attempting to reach the depot. They were still a mile short when a halt was called at 10.30 pm but it was near enough for Mackay to visit while he was on night watch. In the tent on the afternoon of 4 February they considered their position. The *Nimrod* was late, or they might have missed her. Should they wait or start back for winter quarters, hoping to reach them before the equinoctial gales of March? Mackay favoured the latter, but Mawson and David were disposed to wait until the end of February. Neither option was particularly appealing and no decision was taken. They were dispiritedly packing their belongings for the short march up to the depot when the sound of a double explosion, startling in the stillness, invaded the tent.

> Mawson gave tongue first, roaring out, 'A gun from the ship!' and dived for
> the tent door. As the latter was narrow and funnel-shaped there was for a
> moment some congestion of traffic. I dashed my head forwards to where I saw

a small opening, only in time to receive a few kicks from the departing Mawson. Just as I was recovering my equilibrium, Mackay made a wild charge, rode me down and trampled my prostrate body. When at length I struggled to my feet, Mawson had got a lead of a hundred yards, and Mackay of about fifty. 'Bring something to wave', shouted Mawson, and I rushed back to the tent and seized Mackay's ruck-sack.[12]

David reappeared to see the *Nimrod* steaming into the inlet, her crew cheering, but Mawson had unaccountably disappeared. 'He's fallen into a deep crevasse', yelled Mackay, 'look out, it's just in front of you!' Mawson had fallen eighteen feet but was unhurt. His companions were unable to get him out unassisted and Mackay ran down to the ship shouting a memorable greeting: 'Mawson has fallen down a crevasse and we got to the Magnetic Pole'. Within minutes First Officer John King Davis had recovered Mawson and had all three of them safely on the ship.

The *Nimrod* had proceeded north as far as Cape Washington, at the foot of Mount Melbourne, and then, as arranged, had turned back. The snow of the 3rd had given way to clear, fine weather and now both depot and tent could clearly be seen. The explosion heard by Mawson had been a double distress detonator. It was quite apt: David's account describes their position at the time as 'somewhat critical'; Mawson's unspoken reason for choosing to wait for the ship was his conviction that David would be unable to start for some time; only Mackay was able to confront how close to the edge they had come.

> We were relieved from a very real peril of death. I had made up my mind that if the ship did not turn up on the 5th or shortly after, we might pretty well give her up. We would then have started down the coast, with all our rations exhausted, that is to say, nothing to live on but seal meat, and with our tent and clothes utterly worn out. The professor could not have lived many weeks and his weakness would have delayed us to such an extent as to finish us. The whole thing is enough to make a man turn religious.[13]

The *Nimrod* reached the winter quarters at Cape Royds on 11 February. As there had been no word of Shackleton's southern party, preparations were made to send relief in accordance with his instructions. Those same instructions called for command of the relief party to be offered to Mawson who, in spite of having the rigours of the trek only a week behind him and the distinct possibility of another winter in the Antarctic ahead, accepted. The party was ready to depart when smoke was seen rising from Scott's old base further down the sound at Hut Point. Shackleton had set fire to Bernacchi's magnetic hut to attract attention. His party was safe, but he had to lead the relief back along his track to bring in two of its members.

Had Shackleton reached the geographic South Pole? No, he had been forced by weather, starvation and exhaustion to abandon the attempt on 9 January. The party had reached 88°23'S, fewer than 100 miles short of the prize. They too had made a last lunge without the sledge, 'half running and half walking', and had taken a photographic record of the ceremony which marked the end of the event. On the positive side, there could be little doubt that the remaining 100 miles of plateau to the pole were exactly like the 150 behind.

> While the Union Jack blew out stiffly in the icy gale that cut us to the bone, we looked south with our powerful glasses, but could see nothing but the dead white snow plain. There was no break in the plateau as it extended towards the Pole, and we feel sure that the goal we have failed to reach lies on this plain.[14]

In a rational universe that would have been the end of the matter. Even the because-it's-there school of exploration should have been disarmed because, in all probability, there was no *it* to find. Moreover, because Shackleton could locate but not quite reach the geographic South Pole, he had to acknowledge that he had failed. David and Mawson, on the other hand, could not be sure where the South Magnetic Pole was, but were confident that it was nearby, and on this basis felt justified in claiming success. Both parties had made prodigious efforts. Shackleton and his men had covered 1725 miles, but had the advantage of support parties. The David party trekked 1260 miles, unsupported after the first 15, a record which stood for the entire manhaul era of Antarctic exploration. David was apologetic about the scanty nature of their magnetic, geological and meteorological observations, but was more positive about Mawson's survey of the coast between Mount Erebus and Mount Melbourne and satisfied that 'at all events we have pioneered a route to the Magnetic Pole'. In the realm of what might have been, he reflected that the seals found along the coast would have supported a dog team. A quicker rate of advance to the pole would have given Mawson the time he needed to make a series of observations. A party with dogs, landed near Backstairs Passage in early December, could make at least fifteen miles a day towards the pole. It could spend one or two weeks in the vicinity and still be back on the coast by early February.

With the entire expedition now aboard, Shackleton directed the *Nimrod* towards Cape North. He hoped to follow the mainland coast westwards, inshore of the Balleny Islands, until it joined up with Adelie Land. Scott's *Discovery* had sailed over part of Wilkes Land but its existence 'in any other position' was still an open question. They pushed along the edge of the pack ice to 69°47'S and 166°14'E, and on 8 March had a clear view of the coast for 45 miles beyond Cape North. It extended first to the south, as Ross had hoped, but then continued west. It comprised ice cliffs with a few bays and in David's opinion it was the northern edge of the polar plateau. They were in danger of becoming beset by ice and followed the edge of the pack north, still hoping to pass beyond the Balleny Islands and find Wilkes Land. A temporary entrapment on 9 March put an end to dicing with the ice and, on the following day, the *Nimrod* was turned towards New Zealand.

David, feet somehow intact, returned to his career as a distinguished academic and did not go south again. For Mawson the voyage was only the first episode in what was to become an Antarctic argosy. Mackay had similar ambitions, and more or less convinced Clements Markham that a dog-hauled, seal- and penguin-fuelled, unsupported land party could survey the entire unknown coast between the Antarctic Peninsula and Edward VII Land. No backers could be found for this experiment of living on the bounty of the ice, and Mackay instead signed on for Stefansson's Canadian Arctic Expedition. Its ship was crushed in 1913 and the crew wintered in a hut built on the ice. In February 1914 Mackay led a party towards land and met another group which was returning from an unsuccessful attempt to reach Herald Island. Although his party was in poor condition, Mackay refused their offer of help. Survivors of the expedition reached Wrangel Island in March, but Mackay and his companions were never seen again.

CHAPTER 13

Jemima's Secret

Douglas Mawson once told his fiancee that, had he lived before the twentieth century, he might have been a crusader. It would not have been the magnetic crusade he had in mind. The remark revealed something in him that from an early age had been as obvious as his intellectual ability. His headmaster is said to have prophesied, as he left school for university at the age of sixteen, 'that if there be a corner of this planet of ours still unexplored, Douglas Mawson will be the organiser and leader of an expedition to unveil its secrets'.[1] After the Shackleton expedition he had emphatically rejected any suggestion of returning to the Antarctic. Less than a year later he was in London angling for an expedition of his own.

The competition was fierce. Scott was preparing to go back, with the geographic pole the explicit object of what would this time be an official expedition. Shackleton, temporarily distracted by get-rich-quick schemes, nevertheless attempted to divert attention from Scott by hinting that he had Antarctic plans of his own. Scott, acting on David's recommendation, promised Mawson a place on his polar sledging party and was surprised to find that the Australian was only interested in hitching a ride as far as Cape Adare. Mawson wanted to explore the unknown coast to the west of the cape, unvisited since d'Urville's day, and perhaps as far as Gaussberg. He described it as his 'Land of Hope and Glory'. Scott displayed quiet interest, but it was Shackleton who, with his customary enthusiasm, encouraged Mawson to expand his ideas and, more importantly, undertook to find financial support. Enthusiasm bred enthusiasm until Shackleton said he would lead the expedition himself, with Mawson as chief scientist. Mawson was more than happy to be thus freed of fund-raising responsibility, particularly as the program he had devised was now hugely ambitious, a three-year undertaking involving three separate landing parties totalling 16–19 men. They would explore 2000 miles of coast, observe the magnetic pole from east, west and north, and sledge towards the point previously reached by David's party, but from the opposite direction.

For a year Shackleton procrastinated. He obtained promises for only a small fraction of the funds required and his involvement prevented Mawson from making approaches to other possible contributors. It was almost a relief when, in December 1910, Shackleton cabled that he could not go but would give the expedition his wholehearted support. Scott had already sailed. In January 1911 Mawson laid his proposals before a meeting of the Australasian Association for the Advancement of Science. He spoke of economic and scientific advantages, and of national interest, but his rhetoric was not just that of maritime enterprise as a demonstration of national virility, nor was Britain the nation he was referring to. He was an Australian staking a claim in Antarctica against the possibility that other nations would 'step in and secure this most valuable portion of the Antarctic continent for themselves, and forever from the control of Australia'. The association voted to donate £1000, a third of its liquid assets, to help finance the expedition. Its participation meant that the chauvinism had to be of a regional rather than a strictly national character: Australasia included New Zealand.

Mawson again took his appeal to Britain, and in April had the satisfaction of receiving a donation of £500 from the Royal Geographical Society, as much as they had given to Scott. In this there was a hint of criticism of Scott's program, one distinguished member remarking that there was 'something undeniably heroic' in Mawson's omission of the geographic pole from his objectives. Mawson also laid before a meeting of the society an alternative to current views about the geomorphology of Antarctica. He supposed that the Antarctic Peninsula and the lands south of Australia and Africa were a single continental unit and that the area between the Ross and Weddell seas was occupied by barrier ice, archipelagoes or lowland, with no passage between. The main land mass undoubtedly lay in the Australian Quadrant, as theorised by the society's own map curator, E. A. Reeves, from the differential deflection of the lines of magnetic force caused by land and sea. The accessibility of the

Ross Sea and the lure of the geographic pole had led to neglect of the coastline west of Cape Adare, said Mawson. The discoveries of Wilkes, d'Urville and Balleny had been fragmentary, leaving scope for 'great geographical successes', and the society's own secretary, Dr H. R. Mill, had only recently suggested that it was time to revisit the area.

Hugh Mill was present at the meeting, and remarked that all expeditions sailing west along the coast in question had made discoveries and initiated controversies. He wished Mawson the joy of discovery and 'new controversies that will stimulate exploration right on through the century'. Mawson's need for funds tempered his rhetoric about claiming discoveries for Australia. For his British audience, the Australian nationalist's message was that he wanted authority to raise the Union Jack and take possession for the British Empire.[2] Shackleton's financial contacts had started to come good, but not to the extent expected. There was also disappointing news from the south. The party that Scott had intended should explore Edward VII Land had arrived at the Ross Ice Shelf to find Roald Amundsen already there and preparing to race Scott to the geographic pole. As a fall-back position, this British party was landed at Cape Adare in February 1910, effectively depriving Mawson of the eastern base from which he had intended to observe the magnetic pole.[3] Scott had pre-empted him in the same way that Amundsen had pre-empted Scott, a gambit of which Scott had been highly critical. Mawson also feared that Scott might attempt to use his ship to make a quick sweep along the coast west of Cape Adare, and so it proved. Before the Australasian expedition could sail it was announced that Scott's *Terra Nova* had discovered two patches of new land in 164°30'E and 158°53'E – Oates Land – which extended the known coast to at least 280 miles west-north-west of Cape Adare.

With neither the *Discovery* nor the *Nimrod* available to him, Mawson settled on a Dundee-built sealer, the *Aurora*. She was found for him by J. K. Davis, his rescuer from the crevasse in 1909, who had agreed to captain the expedition's ship 'even had we to go in a cutter with no equipment'.[4] Contributions from the Australian Government and from some of the Australian states ensured that it did not come to that, but the expedition was still inadequately funded when it sailed from Hobart on 2 December 1911. The magnetician was Eric Norman Webb, a 22-year old New Zealander who as a boy had watched Scott sail from his home town of Lyttelton in 1902. He had prepared for his role by working on a magnetic survey of Australia being carried out by America's Carnegie Institution. The assistant magnetician, who was also astronomer and tide recorder, was Lieutenant Robert Bage of the Royal Australian Engineers. Among the other members of the expedition was Frank Hurley, an adventurous Australian photographer. The only Antarctic veteran, Mawson and Davis aside, was Frank Wild, who had been with Shackleton when he reached his furthest south.

Davis attempted to push through the pack ice along the meridian of 156°E, which would have enabled Mawson to set up his eastern base about 100 miles west of Cape Adare and as nearly north as possible of the magnetic pole area. The pack did not oblige and the ship steamed west looking for an opening to the south. On 6 January 1912 they sighted the forbidding ice cliffs of the Mertz Glacier Tongue. By now Mawson was calculating that there might only be time to find landing places for two parties, and on 8 January he seized 'the first available spot' for a base station, a section of coast where rock projected beyond the ice to form a headland with a small boat harbour. Cape Denison, on Commonwealth Bay, was at 142°40'E. The western promontory of the extensive bay was d'Urville's Cape Discovery.[5] It took eleven strenuous days to ferry the stores ashore, after which Mawson released the *Aurora* to find a base for the second, western party. On the evening of her departure, toasts to d'Urville and Wilkes were drunk in Madeira which had been carried on HMS *Challenger* forty years earlier.

As Davis pushed westwards, often further to the south than all previous

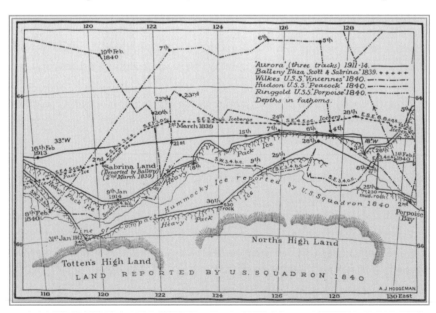

Aurora's track eliminated Balleny's Sabrina Land, as it had earlier eliminated d'Urville's Clarie Coast and Wilkes's Cape Carr

explorers, his wake obliterated one after another of their discoveries. On 23 January the *Aurora* sailed over the charted position of Clarie Coast. Later that day Wilkes' Cape Carr suffered the same fate. Four days afterwards they passed where Balleny's Sabrina Land should have been and saw nothing. Wild, who had command of the western party and was supposed to be landing at Wilkes's Knox Land, must have begun wondering whether the second glass of Madeira had been warranted, but better cheer followed. In the evening of the day when Cape Carr was found to be missing, the *Aurora* continued south to 65°45'S and 132°40'E. Land was first seen twenty miles distant but ice made it impossible to approach closer than twelve miles. As it had no feature matching the description of Cape Carr, it had to be a new find. In a gesture that was as political and politic as it was polite, Mawson later called the discovery Wilkes Land.

> . . . as it is only just to commemorate the American Exploring Expedition on the Continent which its leader believed he had discovered in these seas and which he would have found had Fortune favoured him with a fair return for his heroic endeavours.[6]

Impenetrable ice kept them away from Knox Land but soundings indicated that land was nearby. Further west still and south of Wilkes's Termination Land, already discredited by the *Challenger* and Drygalski, the *Aurora* encountered an ice tongue which Davis and Wild believed might have been the feature seen by Wilkes (and transferred the name accordingly), but it proved to be only the tip of a far larger structure, the Shackleton Ice Shelf. Time was running short, and not too much further west was the ice that had trapped the *Gauss*. Land to which the ice shelf was attached could be seen to the south, but unbroken floe ice separated it from the *Aurora*. Wild decided to take his chances. Davis landed the party by flying fox on the Shackleton Ice Shelf. There he left them, seventeen miles from land and a hundred feet up in the air.

At Cape Denison, where the first, eastern party had been landed, priority was given to erecting the prefabricated huts. When the main hut was finished, Mawson had a flagpole erected at its peak and, to the cheers of the party, the British and Australian flags were hoisted.[7] It was 14 March before the magnetic huts were completed, not least because 45 tons of rock had to be found to secure the magnetograph hut against katabatic winds of unprecedented duration. This was truly the home of the blizzard and the abysmal weather threw schedules into disarray. Little autumn sledging could be undertaken and the base settled early into winter routine. For Webb and his assistants, the daily struggle across the 350 yards separating the living quarters from the magnetograph hut, perilously close to the open sea, could be as dangerous as a polar dash of as many miles. Even during daylight hours touch was frequently the only sense available, when the drift, driven by 100 mph winds, obscured hands held at arm's length. Guide ropes were out of the question: they would have been buried in half an hour. In the worst weather Webb largely moved on his hands and knees, taking direction from the wind until he reached the ridge along which the magnetograph hut was placed, from where it was a matter of groping from one outcrop to the next, recognising them by feel. Brief everyday attendance to trim the lamp and change the photographic paper on the self-recorder was not too demanding, but Webb and an assistant frequently had to spend up to three hours in the absolute hut obtaining standard values against which the differential magnetograph record could be checked. On international term days the recording paper was 'quick run' to provide more detail over a given time. On one of these occasions Webb was fortunate enough, simultaneously with Scott's physicist at McMurdo, to record one of the largest magnetic storms either station had experienced.

Mawson refined his plans for the spring, carefully observing his colleagues and assessing their suitability for the sledging roles he had in mind. All five of the planned parties were to make magnetic observations as one of their routine tasks. His personal priority was eastward, to explore the coastal inland towards Cape Adare and to establish whether or not the discoveries of d'Urville, Wilkes and Ross joined to make, unequivocally, a continent. The magnetic pole itself beckoned but the expedition had been forced to set up quarters so far west that it was probably 400–500 miles distant. Even at a steady 15 miles a day a party would need at least 53 days of travelling weather. On the strength of the climate at Cape Denison it seemed unlikely they would be so blessed and the pole itself became a secondary objective; the far inland party's first task would be to investigate the nature and extent of the plateau to the south. Webb was an obvious choice to lead this main magnetic party, being expert, conscientious and cold-hardy, but he was also self-opinionated to the point of obnoxiousness. In May Mawson was so displeased with his 'perkiness' that he resolved to leave him off the sledging parties altogether if it were possible. In September, however, he gave the young man a dip circle and sent him on a nine-day reconnaissance along the magnetic meridian accompanied by 'Dad' McLean, the chief medical officer, and Stillwell, the geologist. When they returned Mawson obtained, in a roundabout way, their views about Webb

Mawson's magneticians and their instruments: clockwise from top left: Magnetometer;
Kennedy with Dip-circle; Webb in Magnetograph House; Webb reading Declinometer.

as a leader. The comments were less than flattering. This may have found its way back to Webb.

On 12 October, with Mawson chafing to get the sledging parties away, but with the weather still intractable, the expedition staged a burlesque opera (admission free, children half price). *The Washerwoman's Secret* told the story of Jemima, Princess of Adeliana, otherwise 'Theotherendofnowhere'. McLean played the princess, accompanied by Stillwell on the harmonium. The action included a duel fought between the Count and the Baron over which of them had given away the plot.

Nine days later Webb asked to speak to Mawson. He suggested that the other dip circle should be taken over by Bage immediately and 'worked at'. Puzzled, Mawson drew him out.

> . . . I find that he is disappointed with the Expedition. Thought everybody was a greater specialist in their line than they are. He thinks he is practically the only one on the Expedition who is properly fit. He says he has never seen me observe with a theodolite and doubts my accuracy. States that there was nobody on Shackleton's expedition capable of instrument work; at any rate it appears to be so and he was told so by certain people in New Zealand (evidently Farr and Skey).[8]

Mawson's guess about the identity of the 'certain people' was correct. In New Zealand they had made Webb privy to another secret of the other end of nowhere – that the prize of the South Magnetic Pole was still there to be claimed. Clinton Coleridge Farr, of Webb's alma mater, Canterbury University College and H. F. Skey, of the Christchurch Magnetic Observatory, had analysed Mawson's 1909 magnetic data and found it to be wanting. Indeed, in Mawson's absence they had asked David if there were other records, because those that they had been given showed that the David-Mawson party had *not* reached the magnetic pole's area of oscillation.[9] Did Webb now suspect that the ill report of Jemima McLean and his accompanist/accomplice Stillwell might be about to deny him the glory of leading the first party to the pole itself? Confirmation came quickly. Mawson decided that the young man had better go as second in command of the far inland party, under Bage, the assistant magnetician, with Hurley as the third member.

Not that the party had much chance of reaching the South Magnetic Pole. As in 1908–09, its needs were given a low priority. In spite of the fact that the gradual rise to the plateau from Cape Denison offered good going for dogs, these were reserved for Mawson's far eastern party. The approach to the pole would again be attempted by manhaul, but at least this attempt would have the benefit of a proper support party led by Murphy, the expedition's storeman. Bage's orders acknowledged the limitations he faced. He was to follow the compass south, along the magnetic meridian, while the direction it indicated was not far from true south. If there was much divergence it was left to him to decide whether to march magnetic or true. From 10 November, when Mawson's party cheered Bage's off from the Aladdin's Cave depot, five miles south of Cape Denison, there were 67 days available for the journey out and back, which made just 14 days allowance for bad weather. Mawson's ambition for Bage's party – that it should not merely reach the pole but make observations there for many days – was now hostage to the elements.

The far inland party's southern journey was neither easy nor uneventful, but it was set against an empty cyclorama rather than dramatic scenery. 'In the almost total absence of geographical features, our sole stimulus was the pursuit of the Magnetic Pole which, probably, was the more alluring because such a will o' the wisp'.[10] They blanked out the monotony, accepting that data systematically gathered along their way would be more important than any single observation at journey's turn, no matter where that might be. Bage hoped to do 400 miles before turning, a distance that Webb estimated would take them to the other side of the polar area, where reversal of the dip would help to define its extent. They took six days to haul the first 19 miles beyond Aladdin's Cave but by then they were at 3200 feet and, with the rise becoming more gradual, they could accelerate. Steering by sun compass, with a sledge meter to count off the miles and astronomical observation to fix position, they were seldom in doubt about where they were, but the ice was as featureless as the ocean.

> To either side the snow rolled away for miles; behind, perhaps a mile away, was the top of the last rise we had come up, while in front we made our first acquaintance with the accursed next ridge that is always ahead of you on the plateau. Generally we passed from one ridge to another so gradually that we could never say for certain just when we had topped one: still the next ridge was always there.[11]

Their support party left them on 21 November, after depositing its stores at what was named the Southern Cross depot, 67 miles out. Watching the three departing specks fading into the drift, Bage summed up his feelings in one word: 'Weird'. Bage's party also left as much equipment and stores at the depot as could

No peaks: the long, long ice slope behind Cape Denison

be done without: the all-important dip circle, a Kew land-pattern model, had been modified so that it could be mounted on the theodolite legs, as could Hurley's camera, to save weight.[12] The variation had swung from 10°W to 40°E and the dip had lessened rather than increased over the previous 20 miles. Clearly this was an area of considerable magnetic disturbance, which prompted Bage to consider the options Mawson had given him. On the basis that the plateau to the south-east was unlikely to be any less geographically boring than the plateau to the south, and with Webb urging that the best magnetic results would be obtained by continuing along the magnetic meridian, Bage decided they should go on as they were 'unless some special features cropped up'.

To earn some respite from the wind at night, they experimented by constructing a windbreak of snow blocks at their 76-mile camp. The innovation was so successful that thereafter Webb took approximate dip and variation readings each day in the lee of one, obtaining data on local disturbance against which the reliability of full observations taken at the main magnetic stations could be checked; 'also it gave us some vague idea as to the proper direction to the magnetic pole'. Bage found the windbreak equally as convenient for longitude observations with the theodolite. It also did wonders for confidence in the face of the elements:

> While we were lying half toggled into our sleeping bags writing our diaries, Hurley spent some time alternately imprecating the wind and invoking it for a calm next day. As he said, once behind a breakwind one could safely defy it, but on the trail one is much more humble.[13]

By late November the dip circle was consistently playing the same tricks they had come to expect from the compass. On the 28th it tried to persuade them that the inclination had increased by more than half a degree over the last twenty miles. They took the reading as confirmation that they were on track for the pole, 'though we were still distinctly doubtful as to the direction in which that track was running, for the declination had actually changed 80° in the last 10 miles'. Five days and forty miles later, the dip reading was little more than it had been sixty miles back. 'We consoled ourselves with the hope that a big sudden rise was being stored up for us along the way'.[14]

A snow storm on 7 December, when they were 174 miles out, forced them to camp for two days. Webb took the opportunity to make half-hourly observations of the declination over 24 hours and found that it ranged through five degrees of arc. Their detention, and slow going in the drifted snow when they resumed hauling, led Bage to decide on 12 December that it was time to establish a depot. They had come 200 miles. Half of their allotted time was gone. Even if they could count on making twice their outward speed when going back with a lighter sledge, of the 31 days now remaining (after allowing three for contingencies), only eight were available for reaching their furthest south.

> Up to our 174 mile camp, relying on improving weather and surface we had put down 400 miles as dimly possible, but with the snow fall there and the consequent delay and heavy going since, every day, had clipped a bit off this and now we saw we would be lucky if we could reach 300 miles. Moreover, the dip here was 89°11', practically what it had been ever since 150 miles – 65 miles before. '65 miles for nothing! How far for the 49' more that we needed for a vertical dip?' This problem depressed our state of mind. We had determined, however, to have a jolly good try for the 300 miles.[15]

The last day outbound, 20 December, yielded 15 miles. It was the only day going south on which they were able to achieve planned average mileage. On the following morning, of Midsummer Day, they made the now traditional dash with the sledge stripped down to dip circle, theodolite, tent and cooker. When the sledge meter showed 301 miles Webb set himself up behind a windbreak and took magnetic observations for four hours, in thin instrument gloves or with bare frozen hands. In the absence of horizontal force to indicate the magnetic meridian, dip readings were taken in two directions at right angles. Trigonometric calculation then revealed the true magnetic meridian and the true dip. The temperature was -12°F by the time he had finished. Bage took a longitude shot with the theodolite but, affected by snow blindness, had difficulty with the assortment of suns and cross-hairs that presented themselves. Webb prudently checked the longitude reading when he used the instrument. Bage boiled the hypsometer. Hurley photographed the camp. They were at 5830 feet in 70°36¹/₂'S and 148°10'E. The dip was 16.7' from the vertical. As it was their furthest south, they held a little ceremony.

> After lunch (taken at 6.30 pm) we hoisted our Union Jack and Commonwealth [of Australia] Ensign, giving three cheers for the King – willing, but rather lonesome away in here. We searched the horizon with our glasses but could see nothing but snow, undulating and sastrugi covered. To the south-east our horizon was limited by our old enemy 'the next ridge' only some 2 miles away. We wondered what could be beyond although we knew it was only the same endless repetition, for 175 miles on the same course would bring us to the spot where David, Mawson and Mackay stood in 1909.[16]

That night Bage admitted his disappointment to his diary. The uniform rate of increase in the dip since the 200-mile depot placed the South Magnetic Pole only 50–60 miles ahead of them, but that meant another week, a week they did not have. As it was they would find it difficult to get back on time, particularly as Webb wanted to take five more complete dip sets and each would cost half a day. Christmas dinner was deferred until they reached the 200-mile depot on 27 December. Hurley set the standard by cleaning out the cooker. The absence of reindeer hair (from the sleeping bags) and other accumulated detritus 'made all the concoctions taste quite strange'. The Christmas pudding was made of biscuit sawn up with a pocket tool and fat picked from pemmican rations, with raisins, glucose and sugar, all boiled in an old bag. The 'wine' was made from stewed raisins and priming alcohol from the cooker. This was not what Mawson

The last camp outbound: 301 miles from Cape Denison, on 20 December 1912, Hurley photographs Bage standing by the tent while Webb makes magnetic observations behind a windbreak.

had in mind when he had provided alcohol, which could be used as an emergency ration, in place of methylated spirit, which could not, and retribution was swift. After toasting the King in the vile concoction, it was some time before anyone could muster the courage to propose drinking to the Other Sledging Parties and Our Supporting Party.

With a following wind to fill the sail, hard snow and a downhill gradient, the party made a flying start from the 200-mile depot. On 29 December they did 41.6 miles, a manhaul record that still stands, over a stretch of country which had taken them 7½ days outbound. They congratulated themselves on being well ahead of schedule, with more than four days rations in excess of those needed to reach the Southern Cross depot. The satisfaction was premature. The sledge meter finally lost more spokes than it could spare and had to be abandoned. Bad light and snow reduced visibility, making it difficult to find the mounds that marked their outbound track. White-out brought on snow blindness for Bage and Hurley, incapacitating the former to such an extent that he had to ride on the sledge for the first two days of January. Webb had to be their eyes, although he found his own of little use:

The next 100 miles were marched practically in the dark . . . never had one more convincing demonstration that complete diffusion is equivalent to no light. Because [there was] no shadow, one could see neither the landscape, nor the surface at one's feet.[17]

On the 4th they were still eleven miles short of the depot and, not confident of finding it, reduced themselves to half rations. Altitudes of the sun taken on the 5th gave them a latitude only four miles south of the depot. The problem, as Bage complained, was to find longitude, because they had been unable regularly to check astronomically the rate [accuracy] of their sole half-chronometer:

When rates have been obtained over several sections of the journey, the longitude observations finally tell you quite accurately where you *have been*, but at the time they do not tell you where you *are*. The longitude obtained on this occasion from our latest known rate indicated that we were still several miles to the east of the depot so I concluded that our distances since the 90 mile [without the sledge meter] had been over-estimated and that we were probably to the south-east of it. Accordingly we moved off four miles to the north-west but by this time it had again clouded over and nothing could be seen. We camped for the night and on the 6th found it still overcast but at noon we checked our latitude by a lucky glimpse [of the sun] and moved on to the exact latitude of the depot. We walked east and west from the tent but it snowed all the afternoon and everything was invisible.[18]

On the following day the weather was unchanged. They moved camp four miles east 'and walked about without avail'. The unsuccessful search for the depot had cost them three whole days. They were down to one day's full ration plus a little pemmican, six lumps of sugar, nine raisins 'rather the worse for wear', two days' kerosene and a pint of alcohol. Bage found that the party was unanimous: 'There was only one thing for it now and that was to make a break for the coast'. It would be at least three days travelling, perhaps five, should finding the path down to the hut be difficult. The sledge was stripped of equipment:

We shed all the weight we dared, not sparing my beloved dip-circle, realizing that our lives and records were at stake; and set off under a heavy pall without a steering mark of any kind to be seen.[19]

The only superfluities tolerated were the aluminium prismatic compass that Mawson had carried in 1908–09 and Webb's precious dip circle needles, no more than a few ounces all up. They did their twenty hungry miles on 8 January but the weather on the 9th was the worst experienced on the entire journey. A 60 mph gale from the south-east, across their course, blinded them with falling snow and lashed them with the drift. The direction of the blow was their only navigational reference until 4 pm, when a glimpse of the sun disclosed that the wind had shifted to south by east, 'so for possibly several hours we had been doing Heaven knows how many times the amount of work necessary', into the wind and three points off course. They found the going easier downwind, and at midnight agreed that they had put their twenty behind them. They camped on blue ice, which was thought to extend no more than thirteen miles from the hut. They assumed that they must have been working east of their course during the 9th and so, on the morning of the 10th, veered west, looking for snow bridges across the crevasses. It was only when the islets off Cape Denison came into view that it became apparent that they had done 54 miles over the two preceding days and were now only three miles west of Aladdin's Cave. At the cave an open tin of dog biscuits was quickly disposed of, followed by a week's supply of chocolate as soon as a food tank could be dug out. On the 11th, with the best part of five days to spare, they descended the last few miles to the hut at their leisure. At twenty miles a day those five days might have taken them to the pole, although the lost opportunity was the furthest thing from Webb's mind.

> As for getting in on our own resources, I dimly thought with the greatest luck we might get in on hands and knees. The facts only go to show what men can do in straits and that we must be pretty tough. The marvel is that, beyond being very tired, we are all physically fit . . . Looking back, I don't know how on earth we did it. When I think of those two blank, dark, dark days, when we fell or scrambled along to we knew not what end, it seems incredible that it's really over. The strain came less in what we have actually passed through than in what we reasonably supposed we might.[20]

Only one of the other parties was back, but five days later Madigan's eastern coastal party came in. They had marched forty miles out onto the sea ice looking for Wilkes's Cape Hudson but, finding nothing, had returned to the coast. There, beyond the Ninnis Glacier Tongue, they discovered a line of ice cliffs and 1200-foot dolerite columns which bore 'no analogy' to Wilkes's coastline. These columns, Horn Bluff, were the party's outward limit, but thirty miles further east they saw a well-defined cape, subsequently named Cape Freshfield. By the 18th only Mawson's party was unaccounted for. Davis, who had returned in the *Aurora* after wintering in Australia, waited while search parties were despatched. Anxiety mounted. By 8 February, after a week that included the worst squalls he had ever experienced, Davis felt that any further delay would prejudice his chances of reaching Wild at the western base. The *Aurora* started west, leaving behind a six-man relief party, including Bage, to wait for Mawson. Few of those six believed that Mawson, Mertz and Ninnis would be seen again.

Shortly after the *Aurora* quitted Commonwealth Bay Davis received a wireless message calling him back. Mawson was there. He had walked in, alone, to tell an astonishing tale. On 14 December, eight weeks earlier and 311 miles east of winter quarters, the sledge carrying nearly all of his party's food, its tent and most of its equipment had vanished into a crevasse, killing Ninnis and the best dog team. Mawson and Mertz were left with one-and-a-half weeks' food for themselves and none for the six remaining dogs. On the all-but-hopeless return trek the dogs were eaten one by one, but there was little nutrition in their emaciated flesh and no marrow in their bones. Worse, because it was unsuspected, the men were slowly being poisoned by the amount of vitamin A concentrated in the dogs' livers. Mertz succumbed on 8 January. Mawson sawed the sledge in half and staggered on alone. Although he was in appalling condition, he believed that he might have just about enough food to make it back when, on 29 January, 21 miles from the Aladdin's Cave depot, he came upon a cache left for him by the relief party that very morning. He would have arrived at winter quarters by 3 February had not the same blizzard that was causing Davis so much concern detained him at Aladdin's Cave for a whole week.

The gale prevented Davis from taking Mawson on board so he continued west to pick up Wild. On 22 February the party at Cape Denison heard by wireless of the death of Scott and his companions a year earlier.

Scott's Last Journey

Scott began the race to the South Pole with three handicaps: he started five days later than Amundsen; his starting point at McMurdo Sound was 60 miles further from the pole than Amundsen's on the Ross Ice Shelf;

and, for the greater part of the journey, his party had to manhaul their sledges. The Norwegian used dogs – four-legged tractors which could be killed to provide fuel for the others as the consumption of stores progressively reduced the load they had to pull. When Scott reached the Pole on 17 January 1912 he found that his rival had beaten him by a month.

Already struggling and denied the boost to morale a win would have brought, Scott and his four companions began the 800-mile return journey. Petty Officer Evans fell heavily and subsequently succumbed to a concussion of the brain. At 80°S, Captain Oates, unable to continue on frostbitten, gangrenous feet, told the others that he would be absent from the tent for some time and walked out into the blizzard. Scott, Wilson and Bowers struggled on. By 19 March they were within three days' haul of their One Ton Depot, 150 miles from McMurdo Sound, but with only two days' rations left. Then a blizzard confined them to the tent for ten days. As the food and fuel dwindled to nothing, it became obvious to them that they would be too weak to continue the march even if the weather improved.

Their bodies were found in the tent eight months later, just 11 miles from the One Ton Depot, which contained enough of everything to have restored them for the last lap. Scott had originally planned to place that depot closer to the pole, at 80°S, where it might have saved Oates as well as the last three.

Having missed the boat, Mawson was stranded in the Antarctic for another year, which gave him time to recuperate and to write his account of the expedition. His preparation for the task included rereading the accounts of his predecessors, and in that of Wilkes he found 'less truth . . . than ever'.[21] The strain of study unnerved him and he began to fear for his sanity. He later believed that he would have died at sea had the *Aurora* been able to evacuate him immediately, so desperate was his physical and mental condition. By the time he was able to return to Australia, in February 1914, he had finished only seven chapters. All who knew him noticed a great change. To Webb he was a superman, sustained by faith and determination when youth and vigour had been exhausted. It was as though the man had been rendered down to his essence, purged of the demands of flesh until all that remained was will and an inner light. Webb had changed as well. In later life he acknowledged that Bage and

Hurley had completed his education: 'they rounded off that process of school and University which had left me unduly priggish, and which many years of civil life might have failed to correct'.[22]

In his wireless report to Australia, Mawson referred to magnetic data obtained 'in close proximity to the magnetic pole'.[23] In his book, *The Home of the Blizzard*, he published Bage's account without comment. In the popular edition issued fifteen years later, he emphasised geographical achievement, not magnetical, asserting that the far inland party had proved that Adelie Land was continuous with Victoria Land and 'part of the great Antarctic Continent'. This was the discovery that he had hoped would have been made by his own far eastern party.[24] In the original edition he had variously described himself as a member of the 1908–09 party 'which reached the South Magnetic Pole', or, less precisely, the South Magnetic Pole 'Area'.

What he appears to have been unaware of for some time was that David, as early as 1913, had blurted out the secret of the other end of nowhere – that the pole had not been reached in 1909. As soon as Webb had prepared a pre-liminary report, and before Mawson's return from the Antarctic, David had sent it off to *Nature* with a commentary comparing the 1908–09 and 1912–13 results, saying that he had 'just received by wireless' some additional Mawson dips not published in Shackleton's 1909 book. He reported that Mawson's plateau observations were of only 'approximate accuracy' and that, in the light of Webb's observations:

> it is possible that at our furthest point north-west we may have been on the edge of either a local pole, an 'outlier' of the main magnetic south pole area, or on a local lobe of the magnetic pole area, or may even have been just outside an area of absolute verticity altogether.[25]

Or, more bluntly put, that Mawson had got it wrong and they had not reached the pole. By 1925, when publication of Webb's final results again brought the issue to public notice, Mawson's relations with David were at a low ebb: the Prof had declined to support Mawson to succeed him in the geology chair at Sydney University.

CHAPTER 14

Frozen Frontiers

In Australia Mawson found himself confronted by a mountain of expedition debt. Public interest in matters Antarctic was still focused on the fate of Scott, but that too was soon overshadowed more generally by the prospect of war in Europe. Within a year of Mawson's return, many of the associates who would have helped him prepare the results of the expedition for publication were in uniform. Bage contributed his narrative before embarking for the Gallipoli campaign, which he did not survive. Prior to enlistment in 1915, Webb scaled his curves and prepared his data for reduction, but he left much to be done in his absence. As in many other matters during those years, women filled the gap: Farr and Skey used twelve women students – the 'magnetic ladies' of the 'Mawson Club' – to reduce the magnetograph curves. Hurley, of whose cine film much was expected in the way of revenue, had already signed on for Shackleton's forthcoming Imperial Transantarctic Expedition. Mawson edited the film himself and a contract for sale of the rights was due to be signed on the very day war broke out. The purchasers declined to proceed.

With 'Dad' McLean's help *The Home of the Blizzard* was completed in London in the summer of 1914, and during that last glow of peace Mawson was knighted. When the book appeared, in early 1915, sales were adversely affected by the war. The award by the Royal Geographical Society of its Founders' Medal was honour without profit. Mawson took to the paid lecture circuit. In North

America at the beginning of 1915, one of his invitations to speak came from William Herbert Hobbs, professor of geology at the University of Michigan. They had previously corresponded on glaciology and now, face to face, Hobbs was so taken with Mawson that he is believed to have offered the Australian a university appointment. There was strong personal rapport, at least on Hobbs's part. In a letter to Mawson he wrote:

> You seem . . . to have cast a spell over those who met you socially. Speaking of myself I can say that I have never been so drawn to anyone whom I have met for so short a time.[1]

In 1916 Mawson also joined the war effort, and the publications program made little progress in his absence. Not until 1925 did Webb's report on terrestrial magnetism appear. In it he published for the first time the results of the magnetic observations made by Mawson on the polar journey of 1908–09. He paid close attention to the observations made at the two recording stations of the last day outbound, 15 January 1909, and noted that they had been described as hurried.

> Furthermore, these latter hasty readings were made after the instrument had become invaded with drift snow as a result of a blizzard a few days previously, and there was some uncertainty as to how completely all the ice had been removed from the parts. It should, therefore, be understood that the [15 January] determinations . . . are to be accepted as indications only . . .[2]

The availability of Mawson's 1908–09 data had 'tempted' Webb, as he put it in his 1925 report, to discuss at length the location of the South Magnetic Pole. Using data gathered by the two Scott expeditions at McMurdo Sound and Cape Adare as well as his own, he calculated that the pole had moved about 35 miles in a north-westerly direction between 1908 and 1912. From the approximate mean ranges of variation and horizontal force at Cape Denison he concluded that the polar area, defined as the area of 'diurnal peregrination', was 23 miles along its NW–SE axis and 15 miles NE–SW. The values for Mawson's last two stations he dismissed as being of no weight in fixing the pole's position:

> The observer's note states that one end of the needle only was read hurriedly, and polarity was not reversed. In addition, it is generally accepted by competent observers that a Lloyd-Creak circle tends to give high dips and is a

difficult instrument from which to obtain good results under the best conditions. Hence, the possibility of error in each case is so large that little importance can be attached to the values read.[3]

Webb concluded by publishing to the world what he had hinted to Mawson in their interview at Cape Denison thirteen years earlier: David's party had in all probability not reached even the fringe of the polar area. Webb conceded that his own estimated position for the pole was not compatible with that calculated by Chetwynd for epoch 1903. The difference between the two was 167 miles, whereas it should have been in the range 68–90 miles. In his view, Chetwynd had relied too much on declination and intensity values drawn from observations on one side only of the pole. It would have been of little consolation to

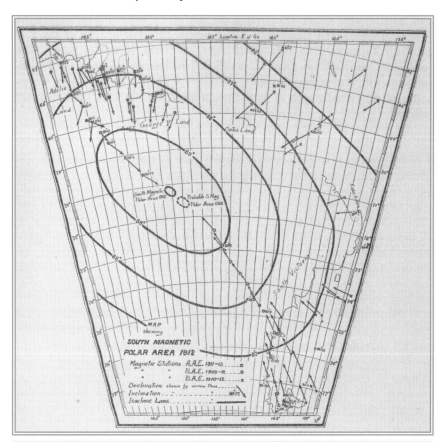

Falling short: Webb's 1925 map shows that neither David's party nor Bage's reached even the magnetic polar area, much less the pole itself.

Mawson to learn that while on the march in 1908 he had correctly identified the anomaly between Chetwynd's reduction and Sabine's.

Webb recognised that his would not be the last word. He cautioned that exact location of the pole by intersection of magnetic meridians would require a large number of determinations on at least three sides of the polar area. No proximate observations had been obtained anywhere to the west. Mawson was less restrained. In his desire to gain full credit for his 1911–14 expedition, he was determined not only to overlook the implicit criticism of his own shortcomings as a magnetic observer in 1909, but to ignore Webb's caveat. In his editorial preface to the report he declared that Webb's work left 'no further doubt as to the exact location of the South Magnetic Pole, a quest that figured prominently in the scientific programme of this Australasian Antarctic Expedition'.[4]

Glory enough for all, it would seem. In his most considered statement on the matter, made some years later, Mawson was careful not to claim too much for the 1908–09 journey: the party had proved that the pole lay to the north-west of the position indicated by Chetwynd, and it had more accurately located the pole's position, but without exactitude. By the mid-1920s Mawson believed that future magnetic work in Antarctica should concentrate on collecting data from chains of stations, including old ones reoccupied, and studying the aurora. Neither was a high priority.

The magnetic agenda were changing. The gyroscopic compass had made a tardy but auspicious debut during the First World War, and looked to be the future for direction-finding at sea, at least for large vessels. The radio compass had been invented in 1913. New theories were emerging. Verne had his Sphinx derive its magnetic power from surplus electricity in the ether, an idea suggested to him by James Clerk Maxwell's work in the 1860s on electromagnetic lines of force. Maxwell had later pointed out that the magnetic elements in magnetic iron substances have angular momentum and therefore act gyroscopically on rotation; now, in 1919, Joseph Lamor was suggesting that the Earth might be a self-exciting dynamo in which a solid iron inner core rotated and a fluid outer core acted like the rotating field of an electric motor's stator. If so, here might be an explanation of Hansteen's foci and the non-dipole field. An outer core capable of generating magnetic storms within the planet, analogous to sunspots, could conceivably produce phenomena independent of the dipole.

The paper Mawson contributed to the American Geographical Society's 1928 symposium on *Problems of Polar Research* dealt with magnetic research only in passing. It focused on establishing the continental nature of the Antarctic land mass. In discussing the contribution of Wilkes 'who ... had reported distant land at intervals in the Australasian sector', Mawson noted that, although the *Aurora* had not found land in some of his assigned locations, soundings indicated that it would be found not far to the south. However, the existence of Wilkes's Knox Land at least could no longer be doubted. This seemed rather dismissive to Isaiah Bowman, the symposium's American editor, who tartly footnoted that 'it is indisputable that [Wilkes] first outlined in their continuity, and recognised as such, the phenomena of a continental margin for a distance of 1800 miles'.[5]

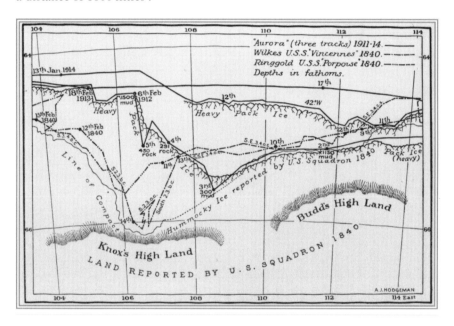

From the *Aurora*, Davis was able to confirm Wilkes's discovery of Knox Land.

Mawson might not have known it, but he was treading an icy slope. In 1927 Hobbs had again invited him to speak at the University of Michigan during another American lecture tour undertaken primarily to raise funds for the publication program. If Bowman was a mild defender of his countryman's reputation, Hobbs had long been the fiercest of American partisans, and it can only be assumed that Mawson had not questioned the discoveries of Wilkes in either his 1915 or 1927 lectures. Just how sensitive this issue was with some Americans Mawson did not learn until after his return in 1931 from his third Antarctic expedition, a British, Australian and New Zealand effort known from its initials as BANZARE.

The R stood for Research but, useful though the expedition's oceanographic work was, the main objectives were territorial. Mawson was ambivalent about this. He had often played the nationalist card when soliciting for financial support in the past, and with him the sentiment was genuine, but science always came first. His problem was that by the 1920s the issue of sovereignty over Antarctica was no longer academic. As early as 1912, the French, in reaction to Britain's 1908 declaration of the Falklands Islands Dependency and the Mawson expedition, had revived their interest in Adelie Land. In 1924 they formally declared sovereignty over d'Urville's discovery, again in reaction to a British declaration, that of the Ross Sea Dependency centred on McMurdo Sound. These developments excited American interest. A Republican Party official wrote to the Secretary of State, Charles Hughes, asking what objections there might be to annexing Wilkes's discoveries. In reply he got what came to be known as the Hughes Doctrine.

> . . . the discovery of lands unknown to civilization, even when coupled with a
> formal taking of possession, does not support a valid claim of sovereignty
> unless the discovery is followed by an actual settlement of the discovered
> country. In the absence of an Act of Congress assertive . . . of dominion over
> Wilkes Land this Department would be reluctant to declare that the United
> States possessed a right of sovereignty over that territory.[6]

In other words, the United States made no claims and declined to recognise those of others that were unsupported by occupancy. This was in keeping with the so-called Open Door policy whereby the United States resisted the efforts of other imperial powers to exclude American business from the markets and resources of their spheres of influence. Hobbs was not the only American who regarded the Hughes Doctrine as pusillanimous. In any event, the doctrine did not deter Mawson and others from urging the Australian Government to resist the French claim and seek British help to obtain for Australia territorial control of Antarctica from 90°E to 160°E.

An Imperial Conference in 1926 agreed that British exploration up to that time might support claims to Enderby Land (45–53°E), Kemp Land (58°30'–60°E), Queen Mary Land (86–101°E, which included Kaiser Wilhelm II Land), Wilkes Land (131–135°30'E), King George V Land (150–153°E) and Oates Land (157–160°E), but no action was taken. The question of the gaps (53–58°30', 60–86°, 101–131°, 135°30'–150° [containing Adelie Land] and 153–157°E) was not addressed. The Australian Government considered how it might at least take possession of those areas not claimed at the time of their discovery. Its motives were, as Hughes would have understood, partly commercial: there was money to be made in the licensing of whaling, and control could also ensure conservation of the asset.

Not until 1928, however, was Mawson asked to take Scott's *Discovery*, lent by the British and commanded by J. K. Davis, south again. He was now 44 and his old organisational flair seemed to have deserted him. Most of the London work to obtain the ship and fit her out was undertaken by the Australian Government's liaison officer in Whitehall, Richard Casey. He found Mawson to be lacking 'the gift of clearness of thought or expression which a scientific training usually engenders', but pleasant enough on acquaintance.[7] The ship carried a Gypsy Moth aircraft for aerial observation but no land-based activity was contemplated. Mawson was authorised by Royal Commission:

> . . . to take possession in Our name . . . of such territories now unknown as may be discovered in the course of the aforesaid expedition, and further of certain territories not under the sovereignty of any other State which have been discovered in the past by subjects of Our Royal Predecessors or of Ourself, to wit . . .[8]

Adelie Land, claimed by Britain's recent ally, France, was out of bounds, but Kaiser Wilhelm II Land, the discovery of Britain's recent enemy, Germany, was available. Mawson thought that Drygalski's work was a far better basis for a claim than d'Urville's, but the Peace Settlement had put paid to such ambitions for the defeated power. In truth though, the spur to do something about Antarctic sovereignty south of Australia was coming from another quarter. Both the Falklands and the Ross Sea Dependencies had been proclaimed to control the activities of Norwegian whalers. Lars Christensen, a leading owner, decided that the only way to avoid the restrictions imposed by foreign powers was for Norway to claim part of Antarctica for itself. In 1929 he sent the *Norvegia* south under Hjalmar Riiser-Larsen.

Although Norway had agreed to accept British territorial rights as discussed at the 1926 Imperial Conference, no one had bothered to tell Riiser-Larsen and it became clear that his objective was Enderby Land. To counter the perceived threat to Britain's interests in the sector where her claims were weakest, Mawson's suggestion that the *Discovery* should start from the western end of the Australian claim was adopted. The 'race', as Mawson disparagingly described it to the *Cape Times*, was won by the Norwegians, who on 22 December 1929 landed a seaplane near what they took to be Biscoe's Cape Ann and raised the national flag on an ice hummock which may or may not have been covering an offshore rock. When Mawson received a vague report by wireless he assumed that the area so claimed was west of Enderby Land. He was clearly some way behind, but no damage appeared to have been done. On 26 December 1929 the *Discovery* met with floe ice in 66°57'S and 71°57'E. Mawson suspected that it was fixed to land to the west or south.

> The wind died down considerably in the early evening hours, and mirage brought above the south-western horizon what appeared to be the undulating surface of snow-covered land . . . Our considered opinion at the time was that we had seen land very far distant, evidently below the horizon from the masthead during the warmest hours of the day, but brought into view as the sun descended low into the horizon and a cool flow of air from the highland spread over the sea-ice.[9]

The mirage did not reappear but, five days later and seven degrees further west, aerial reconnaissance reported appearances of land to the south. On 5 January 1930 Mawson and his pilot, Flight Lieutenant Stewart Campbell, flew 30 miles south of the ship, which was in 61°E and on the Antarctic Circle. He reported peaks 80–90 miles to the west, with the coast trending northwards. Attempts to work the ship further south were frustrated by ice, but a westerly course gradually brought the coast to them. Mawson was preparing to land when on 9 January 1930 a wireless message told him that Riiser-Larsen's reported flight had been *not* been west of Enderby Land but to the land itself, along the very stretch of coast which the *Discovery* was now poised to claim. It was Wilkes and Ross, Amundsen and Scott all over again. Mawson was not amused.

> This is most exasperating, for they have evidently made a direct voyage here to raise their flag, and they knew this was in our itinerary. This sort of thing is not helpful to science, for it means [that] to compete with such 'explorers' an expedition should not arrange any organized programme of scientific work but just rush to most likely points of coast to make landings and raise flags . . . It is remarkable that this news of the Norwegian discovery and claim should reach me today when I had intended making a proclamation regarding the British territories here. The draft was prepared yesterday, and I was to have had ceremony at noon today. Now shall defer same.[10]

Mawson had been caught napping. He had taken his time doing sub-Antarctic research before proceeding south and had paid the price. To protest then that the Norwegians had done what the Australian Government expected him to do seems rather hollow. He landed on 13 January. Proclamation Island was only connected to the mainland by ice but from this toehold the mighty edifice of a claim to all Antarctic land from 47°E to 73°E was held aloft. The ship then hurried on 'without delay, as Norwegians may be busy W of us'. Indeed they were: two days later a small ship was sighted. She turned towards *Discovery* and, as USS *Porpoise* had ninety years earlier, *Norvegia* closed to salute her rival. Mawson did not forget his manners; *Discovery* dipped her ensign in reply and signalled 'wish you a pleasant voyage'. 'Thank you' came back, followed by a megaphoned request for permission to come aboard.

Face to face, each of the expedition leaders found the other to be a fine fellow, but both had responsibilities. Their meeting could have been mistaken for a friendly game of poker, with the amiability of the play concealing the size of the stakes. Riiser-Larsen described his landing in general terms and re-marked that he had been warned from Norway that there were 'acts' – which he did not specify – that would be resented in Britain. Mawson, anxious to avoid acknowledging the landing, did not press him about the 'acts' and so did not learn that on 10 January the Norwegian had been told by wireless that his claim to Enderby Land had been repudiated by his government and that he could only claim between 45°E and 15°W.

Mawson, for his part, gave the impression that little remained to be discovered to the east, although of the huge tract between Kemp Land and Queen Mary Land he had in fact seen only a portion, by mirage or from the air at a great distance. This he had named Mac. Robertson Land, after the con-fectioner who was the expedition's major private donor. To the west, Mawson said, 45°E could be considered the limit of Enderby Land and the extension of his cruise five degrees beyond that would be considered only if conditions were propitious.[11] He expected to be returning east in a day or two. Riiser-Larsen agreed that overlapping was wasteful and said he would seek approval to operate in the unknown regions further west. In a double bluff the *Discovery* departed to the west and the *Norvegia* to the east. There was probably relief aboard both ships when they crossed again two days later, each then heading in its direction of declared interest.

On 25 January Mawson flew inland over Proclamation Island and solemnly intoned his proclamation again over the ice cap, this time extending the claim as far as 45°E. Campbell throttled back so that the words would not be lost in engine noise and they dropped a flag. With the ship low on coal and Davis low on patience with 'this bloody flag-raising business', *Discovery* left the Antarctic on 26 January with only a part of her claim-staking mission accomplished.

The remainder would have to wait for the following summer, but the interval gave Mawson time to publish an abridged edition of *Home of the Blizzard*. A new footnote retrospectively foreshadowed how he would deal with the vexed question of nomenclature along the coast of Wilkes Land.

> On some charts the name of Wilkes's Land has been applied to prospective Antarctic coast extending over a couple of thousand miles in length in the region visited by Wilkes. In view of the fact that d'Urville was actually the first to sight land in that sector, I propose to describe the land in general as the Antarctic Continent, but to retain the names adopted by individual discoverers for the stretches of coast actually seen by them. Though Wilkes fixed such names as Knox Land, North's High Land, etc., to coasts reported to have been seen by him, it has been left for us to commemorate his own name in like manner by attaching it to this new [in 1912] stretch of coast [131°–135°30'E].[12]

This was too clever by half. The whole would retain the name that Wilkes coined for it, the Antarctic Continent, but the names he gave to its parts would disappear next summer should Mawson find that they were not 'actually seen' by him. In the end, Wilkes's own name might be the only American one left on the map, graciously attached to an Australasian discovery.

The Wilkes end of Australia's sphere of interest, neglected during the 1929–30 season, was the primary objective for 1930–31. *Discovery* sailed again on 22 November 1930, this time without the disgruntled ('bloody flag raising') Davis and under the command of K. N. MacKenzie, formerly her First Officer. On her way south the ship was twice able to take on coal from whaleships. The meeting with the *Sir James Clark Ross* was prearranged. The other, with the *Kosmos*, was fortuitous, evidence that the Antarctic was no longer a place of rare encounters. Indeed, it was estimated that the 40 floating whale factories and their 240 catchers in the Antarctic in 1931 would have girdled the globe if stationed fifty miles apart along the Antarctic Circle. On 5 January 1931 the *Discovery* effected a landing at the former Australasian Antarctic Expedition base at Cape Denison. It took several hours of chipping to clear Webb's magnetic hut of ice before A. L. Kennedy, who had been the magnetician with Wild's western party in 1912–13, could take observations. He concluded that the pole had continued to move north-west since 1914 and was now probably not more than 250 miles distant. Again, however, the purpose of landing was to raise the flag, not to seek the pole. Any deficiency there might have been in Mawson's 1912 wording was rectified by burying a copy of the new proclamation at the foot of the flagpole. The claim was 142°E to 160°E, from Adelie Land to the Ross Sea Dependency.

As the ship pushed west along the margin of the ice, Mawson sent the Gypsy Moth aloft whenever sea and sky permitted. He confirmed that the Clarie Coast seen by d'Urville and Wilkes must have been an immense tabular berg aground on the outer edge of a shoal, although the irregular bottom indicated by soundings did not preclude the presence of islands. Off Wilkes Land an excessive mirage effect was seen fifteen miles to the west, with objects appearing and disappearing.[13] Beyond Wilkes Land, flights south of the ice edge on 15 and 16 January located a continuation of the coast: Mawson named it Banzare Land. The ship sailed over Balleny's supposed Sabrina Land. Two days later Mawson went aloft himself and thought he saw ice-covered low land to the south-south-west which, if confirmed, he proposed to name Sabrina Land in commemoration of Balleny's effort. By 24 January the ship was close to the position Wilkes had charted for Budd's Land. Next day there was an appearance of land bearing 117°–236° from the ship, but at a great distance to the south. For three days they loitered along, hoping that the weather would permit a flight before they passed the charted position of Knox Land. A falling barometer on the 27th indicated that it was then or never and, in a rising sea, Mawson and his pilot, Flying Officer Eric Douglas, attempted to get their tiny seaplane airborne.

As they taxied downwind, the plane's floats kept burying in the swell. Douglas turned upwind, towards the pack ice, and opened the throttle. It was touch and go, for as the plane picked up speed it began smashing from one crest to the next in a smother of spray. Half a dozen times it was thrown into the air without sufficient speed to stay airborne. It was all Douglas could do to keep the nose up without stalling. The ice was only a hundred yards away by the time the Gypsy Moth finally lifted off. It climbed above the clouds but, even from there, all was obscured except, at a great distance, the far southern horizon. There, in the direction of Knox Land, 'the sun was shining brightly on what appeared to be undulating land-ice'. Mawson computed the distance. Land seen on the horizon from 4500 feet is 71 miles away. Assuming that the horizon line is at an elevation of 1500 feet, add 41 miles, then subtract 20 to allow for the rise from the coast to the 1500 foot contour. The maximum distance, ship to coast, should be 92 miles, which would place the latter about

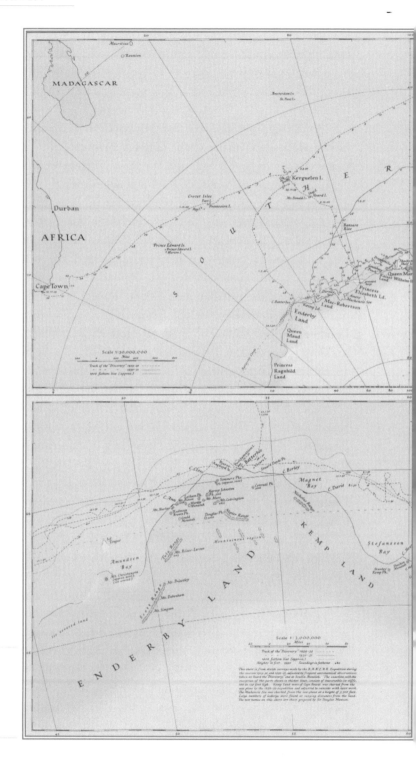

BANZARE
reached out
to claim a
third of
Antarctica.

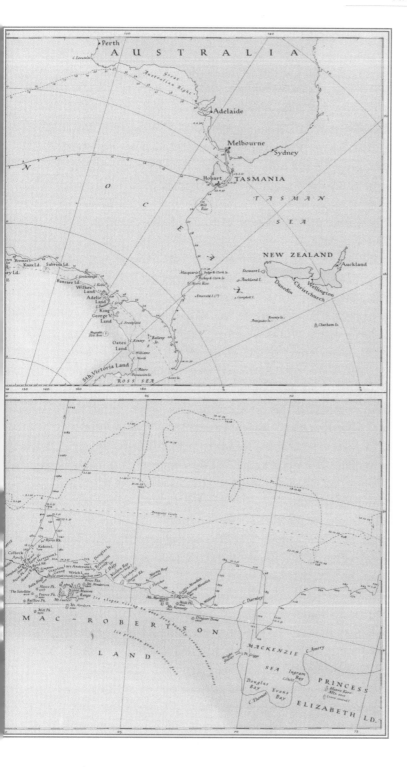

20 miles south of the eastern end of Wilkes's 'high land'. Near enough to give Wilkes the benefit of the doubt?

Mawson's calculation was almost lost to the world when the plane was being hoisted aboard after landing. A roll of the ship dipped one float under, tilting the plane into the side of the ship. The plane jerked onto its lifting bolts and one gave way, dropping the starboard wing into the sea. The machine then began slipping backwards out of the sling until it was suspended upside down with its tail submerged, propeller still turning. Mawson found himself hanging underneath, feet in the water. The sling parted, setting the plane adrift but somehow Mawson and Douglas scrambled onto the forepart of the floats to be rescued with no more injury than wet feet. The plane looked a wreck but was soon repaired and flying again.

Two days later the weather had turned as nasty as the barometer had predicted, with a force 9 blow pushing them west towards the Termination Ice Tongue. Mackenzie began to fear that the ship would run onto this lee shore, but when the dirty weather cleared, on the 30th, they were presented with the greatest surprise of the cruise. The Ice Tongue had vanished, as had the north end of the Shackleton Ice Shelf to which it had been attached. In spite of instructions that he was not to proceed west of Queen Mary Land without raising the flag ashore, the inaccessibility of the land pushed Mawson ever further west and he contacted his government by wireless for advice. The reply was cautious: *Norvegia* had completed a circumnavigation and was now in 5°E; it was to be expected that she would attempt new discoveries from the air and take possession for Norway. On the 29th the *Discovery* encountered the whaler *Nielsen Alonso*, and for some time thereafter hardly a day went by without the barque meeting a floating factory or its catchers. It must have been galling for alleged explorers to be informed of ice conditions further south by seamen for whom they were just another fact of everyday occupational life. It was also difficult to feel hardy and heroic in the presence of stewardesses being carried by two of the factories, *Lestris* and *Falk*.

Falk had unwelcome news. Lars Christensen's newest factory ship, *Thorshammer*, had discovered land in 75°E, two degrees to the east of Mac. Robertson Land as claimed by Mawson the previous summer. It was noted in *Discovery*'s log, incorrectly as it turned out, that this gap between Mac. Robertson Land and Queen Mary Land had been claimed for Norway. On 8 February *Thorshammer* was sighted. The captain of one of her catchers came aboard, gave Mawson the *Norvegia*'s position and showed him their chart. *Norvegia* had filled in the Atlantic sector gap between Enderby Land

and the Weddell Sea. Mawson was becoming desperate. He was beyond Queen Mary Land and no nearer a landing. On the following day he and his other pilot, Stewart Campbell, ascended in the patched-up Moth. From 5700 feet in 76°57'E, just south of the Antarctic Circle, they could see an ice 'jumble' stretching SEbyE to ESE, solid pack to the south and a belt of 'slack pack' west of south. Behind the ice a low light-blue line on the horizon suggested land from ESE to SSW.[14]

The ship's log estimated the distance to this appearance of land as about 90 miles, which closely accords with Mawson's calculation of his distance from Knox Land eleven days earlier. On the strength of this appearance Mawson claimed discovery of what he placed on the map as Princess Elizabeth Land, named for the present queen. His map shows the coast tracking more or less parallel with the *Discovery*'s WSW course. In fact, the coastline here falls away to the south-west until it meets the north-west face of the Amery Ice Shelf in 76°E to form Prydz Bay. On 9 February, the day Mawson and Campbell had gone aloft, *Discovery* had been more than 200 miles from the nearest land and 230 miles from the Munro Kerr Mountains, due south at the head of the bay. Like Wilkes, Mawson had been guilty of willing land into existence.

From Prydz Bay west they were on the edge of Mac. Robertson Land but still there had been no landing. On 11 February snow-covered land was seen to the west of the Amery Ice Shelf. At great personal risk Campbell managed to get airborne, with zero wind assistance, by dodging through brash ice. He succeeded in dropping a flag onto the land. Two days later there was an opportunity to land near a nunatak which was given the name Murray Monolith. As described by Mawson, the attempt was more reminiscent of Laurel and Hardy than Shackleton and David.

> Swell bad and no shelter, sea breaking . . . We touch rock with oar and then throw cylinder with proclamation amongst boulders above beach – after reading – then throw wood plate with copper inscription – it strikes rocks and tumbles into sea. Matheson throws flag on pole – it strikes rock and falls into sea . . .[15]

But the land could not reject their tokens indefinitely. Before lunch on that same day, 13 February, Mawson and a party were ashore at the next nunatak along, Scullin Monolith, and there repeated the ceremony of possession. Simmers, the meteorologist, was 'rather staggered' by the extent of land claimed: from Adelie Land to Mac. Robertson Land, 60–138°E and south from 64° to the South

Pole. Five days and 160 miles further west, in sight of the mountains seen from the air on the previous cruise, but now found to lie much further south, another landing was made. As Simmers saw it, Mawson was determined to get the proclamation right:

> ... at last we were in a position to make a legal, complete and entire observance of claiming land ... In all other attempts (except, of course, that at Cape Denison) there has been some little thing wrong: – 'Proclamation' was only an island; the first proclamation on the 13th floated out to sea and the second ... had no board or proclamation, but this time things have been done properly – mainland, cairn, board, proclamation, several people, lusty singing ... The ceremony over it was made doubly correct by the pouring of a little champagne over the cairn – only a little as we wanted to (and did) drink the rest ... [16]

The Bordeaux quaffers of d'Urville's expedition would have approved. They had found that the coast was forty miles further south than it had appeared from the air in 1930. Another day's steaming would join up the accurate ship-based surveys of the two cruises, but by now MacKenzie was even more concerned about coal reserves than Davis had been the year before and, in spite of Mawson's conviction that the captain was being unnecessarily cautious, the ship turned north for Hobart on 18 February 1931. BANZARE was over. In February 1933 a British Order in Council affirmed that King George V had sovereign rights over Antarctica between 45°E and 160°E (excepting Adelie Land) and would place this territory under the authority of Australia as soon as the Commonwealth Parliament legislated for acceptance. That it did in May 1933.

Mawson's first scientific report on the expedition was placed before the Royal Geographical Society on 7 March 1932. In the absence of the author it was read by Frank Debenham, Director of the Scott Polar Research Institute at Cambridge and himself an Australian veteran of Scott's last expedition. It was Mawson's view that BANZARE's addition of hundreds of miles of coast to the map was a significant contribution to geographical knowledge, but beyond that:

> ... the approximate location of so much of the remainder of the margin of the land throughout this [Adelie Land to Enderby Land] arc has been indicated that the existence of an Antarctic land mass of continental proportions is now very much more definite than formerly. [17]

At the same time he had to acknowledge that the Mac. Robertson Land coast which he had 'seen only at a distance and . . . but approximately located' in 1930 had been found in 1931 to lie much further south. He attributed the mistake to the clarity of the atmosphere in fine weather, which gave 'a wonderful degree of visibility, easily misleading in regard to distance'. Having experienced for the first time the unrealised hopes and all too real disappointments that ice navigation could inflict upon a ship-based expedition, even one with the advantage of aerial observation, Mawson also seemed prepared to take a more generous view of the difficulties experienced by Wilkes:

> Once again operating throughout the sphere of Wilkes's voyage executed ninety years previously, I was again struck with the merit of his excellent performance conducted with ships provided only with sail, and but poorly constituted and equipped for operations in the polar regions. The Wilkes Expedition certainly deserves more credit than has usually been accorded to that superhuman effort. Not only did they independently discover d'Urville's Adelie land, but they also sighted new land elsewhere within that region then entirely unknown.[18]

For new land read Knox Land, and perhaps Budd Land. It was nonetheless a handsome acknowledgment, even if more for the effort than the achievement. Isaiah Bowman of the American Geographical Society, for whom Mawson had named an island off Knox Land, might be mollified; William Herbert Hobbs would not, in spite of the cape that Mawson named for him in Kemp Land.

If Australia hoped that BANZARE would establish its Antarctic claims to the exclusion of other nations it was soon disappointed. Continuing Norwegian exploration along the coasts of the Australian Antarctic Territory gave rise to fears of a counter claim, particularly to Princess Elizabeth Land, which were not allayed until January 1939, when Norway settled for the hitherto unclaimed area between 20°W and 45°E. A wealthy American, Lincoln Ellsworth, introduced an additional complication. During an unsuccessful attempt in January 1939 to fly across Antarctica from Princess Elizabeth Land to the Ross Sea, he dropped a cylinder over what he called the American Highland, about 200 miles inland from his start point. On the strength of overflight alone, he claimed from 70°S to 72°S, and to the horizon 150 miles further south, for the United States by virtue of exploration. This was not a 'pie slice' sector but a large and measured bite out of what Australia asserted was its sovereign territory.

Fortunately Ellsworth was a private citizen and the Australian Government was quick to point out that his claim had not been publicly supported by the United States. It was just as well, for Australia had introduced this practice of claiming from the air and was in no position to protest when others did so.

The Norwegians found themselves similarly challenged. In that same eventful January a German expedition conducted aerial photography of the hinterland behind the Princess Martha and Princess Astrid coasts. It displayed the swastika, named the area Neu-Schwabenland and claimed 350,000 square miles for Germany. Alarmed, the Australian Government purchased Ellsworth's two aircraft and their tender, the *Wyatt Earp*, and announced that the ship would be used to show the flag in Australian Antarctica.

CHAPTER 15

'Hazy, Indistinct and Movable'

Within two months of the publication of Mawson's Royal Geographical Society paper, Hobbs was in print with an article entitled 'Wilkes Land Rediscovered'. By the 1930s he was a polar explorer in his own right, having led three University of Michigan summer expeditions to Greenland. He had also embarked on a personal crusade to vindicate and gain recognition for America's Antarctic explorers. He was by no means the first to do so, but not since Wilkes himself had there been an American with such a gift for Antarctic controversy. Mawson was his friend, but Mawson was yet another in a long list of 'British' who, in Hobbs's view, had not given Wilkes his due. Ross was the first of these and Markham and Scott had hunted with the same pack. Their national bias was obvious. On finding Wilkes's eastern landfalls to be 'unsubstantial', Scott had been ready enough to imply that the American might have 'wilfully perverted the truth', but there had been no reflections on bad navigation or falsification of records when Ross's Parry Mountains had failed to materialise.

In Hobbs's eyes Mawson's offence was less serious. His attempts to discredit Wilkes, on the grounds that the American's charted positions were incorrect, were contradicted by his own work which, said Hobbs, confirmed three-quarters of them. Only in the 'easternmost fifth' and the 'remaining extreme west' did Wilkes's landfalls appear to be erroneous, 'at least in the positions he assigned to them'. It was true that Mawson was the only explorer personally familiar with the whole extent of Wilkes's discoveries, but he was possibly guilty of taking 'a rather narrow view of the question' in relation to the eastern landfalls. Hobbs recited the difficulties of estimating distance in conditions of exceptional visibility, and could not resist pointing out how Mawson himself had erred in estimating Mac. Robertson Land to be up to seventy miles north of its subsequently surveyed position.[1]

The main concerns of Hobbs were to establish Wilkes's priority of discovery over d'Urville and to restore the name Wilkes Land over its former extent of territory. To accomplish the first, he had to rehabilitate at least one of Wilkes's eastern landfalls, as there was no denying that d'Urville had been first to Adelie Land. Ringgold's Knoll was a possible candidate but Cape Hudson was better: Wilkes had been definite that it was mainland. If Cape Hudson could be shown to exist, even if it was not quite where Wilkes had placed it, priority would be his, albeit by the finest of margins, because it had been seen some hours before d'Urville had discovered Adelie Land 300 miles further west. And Hobbs had witnesses, although of a strange sort. He called on the evidence of a group of people who believed they had *not* seen the cape. In 1915 the *Aurora*, then serving as an element of Shackleton's disastrous Transantarctic Expedition, had been trapped in the pack ice of the Ross Sea for nearly eleven months and had drifted west of the Balleny Islands. By late November 1915 they were only 27 miles short of the position from which Cape Hudson had been sketched from the *Peacock*. The ship's captain, Stenhouse, recorded a strange phenomenon.

> November 23. At 3 am Young Island, Balleny Group, was seen bearing north 54° east (true). The island, which showed up clearly on the horizon, under a heavy stratus-covered sky, appeared to be very far distant. By latitude at noon we are in 66°26'S. As this is the charted latitude of Peak Foreman, Young Island, the bearing does not agree [ie. 36° out]. Land was seen at 8 am bearing south 60° west (true). This, which would appear to be Cape Hudson, loomed up through the mists in the form of a high, bold headland, with low undulating land stretching away to the south-southeast and to the westward of it. The appearance of this headland has been foretold for the last two days by masses of black fog, but it seems strange that land so high should not have been seen before, as there is little change in the atmospheric conditions.

November 24. Overcast and hazy in the forenoon. Cloudy, clear and fine in afternoon and evening. Not a vestige of land can be seen, so Cape Hudson is really 'Cape Flyaway'. This is most weird. All hands saw the headland to the south-west, and some of us sketched it. Now (afternoon), although the sky is beautifully clear to the south-west, nothing can be seen. We cannot have drifted far from yesterday's position. No wonder Wilkes reported land. 9 pm – a low fringe of land appears on the horizon bearing south-west, but in no way resembles our Cape of yesterday . . .[2]

In 1932, when Hobbs first came across the reference to this incident, he immediately followed up its possibilities for vindicating Wilkes. If Commander Stenhouse on the *Aurora* had been able to see the Balleny Islands 160 miles or more to the east, there was no reason why the Ex Ex, from almost the same position, could not have seen the land charted by Mawson in 1912, which was only 130 miles to the south. The distances were great, 'but in the clear air occasionally met with in such regions' and with 'the mirage so common there', Hobbs's Greenland experience suggested to him that the Wilkes sighting was within the bounds of probability. He would have preferred to rely on faulty estimation alone to explain Wilkes's errors, but the curvature of the earth precluded direct observation of a 2000-foot peak from a 120-foot masthead over such a distance. Mirage would have to assist. Hobbs sought the *Aurora* sketches, but those made by Stenhouse had been lost sometime during the war.

As Far As The Eye Can See

Refraction and air clarity are the great deceivers when it comes to estimating distance in the polar regions. They were, and are, capable of misleading someone as experienced and cautious as James Clark Ross.

Refraction is caused by temperature inversion. When warmer upper air overlays colder ground air, a common occurrence in the polar regions, light curves downwards. The result is a superior mirage, in which the object appears above its actual position without being distorted in form or size. The effect of this *looming* is to bring into view objects that would otherwise be below the horizon. Off Cape Horn Wilkes sketched a more complex example of the phenomenon, a three-part superior mirage. The presence of three layers of air – cold, warm, cold – caused the light rays to cross, producing two erect images and one inverted.

The taller the object, the further its mirage will be seen. If, as seemed likely to Hobbs, Ross's Parry Mountains included Mount Hamilton, it was being seen at a distance of 245 nautical miles. Without the aid of refraction, a lookout on the *Erebus* would have needed a masthead as high as the mountain to see it over the curvature of the earth.

The main topgallant cross-tree on the *Vincennes*, her highest regular lookout point, was about 120 feet above sea level. From that height a lookout's sea horizon would have been 12½ nautical miles. Beyond that horizon, the top of an object 3600 feet high could be seen directly if it was no more than 69 miles further off. In other words, a land horizon at that elevation could theoretically be seen from the *Vincennes* at a distance of 81½ miles.

But it could have appeared much closer. The absence of dust in the polar atmosphere means that, when the light is good, objects are seen with a clarity rarely experienced elsewhere. Two of Scott's officers discussed the prospects of a day's excursion to the top of Mount Erebus, so clear and near did it stand. The round trip would have been 30 kilometres with a 4000-metre climb. Scott gave other examples in which estimates were grossly short of actual distances. W. G. Rees has pointed out that the common value of magnification in these examples is approximately four-fold. Few escaped error: Wilkes, Ross and Mawson were all victims at one time or another.

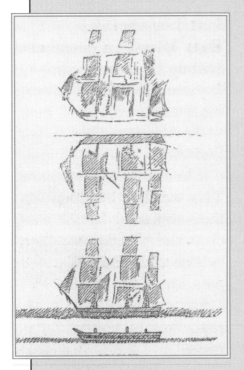

Wilkes's mirage.

Frank Debenham reviewed Hobbs's 'Wilkes' Land Rediscovered', which he described as 'able'. The tone was conciliatory, with Debenham going as far as to apologise for Ross's temper and remarks that 'exceeded the limits of courtesy', but he drew a line at Cape Hudson. In Debenham's view there were three possible explanations for the Wilkes errors: faulty navigation; excessive mirage combined with faulty judgment of distance; and a tendency to accept clouds or icebergs as land. Faulty navigation he dismissed out of hand. He considered mirage and distance carefully, but found it difficult to accept that 140 miles and more could be mistaken for 20. Most telling, in his opinion, was Wilkes's statement that land was most distinct to the SSE. The nearest land in that direction was Oates Land and it was at least 200 miles away: 'now errors of distance must be forgiven in so deceptive an atmosphere, but errors of direction simply cannot occur with navigators of his calibre'. That aside, Debenham's main difficulty lay with Wilkes's description and sketches of the cape. In 1912 Mawson had traversed this coast from the land and Madigan from the sea ice. Ice cliffs and dolerite columns rose from the sea, capped with an ice slope that gradually ramped upwards to the south. No peaks, no ranges. Wilkes, like Stenhouse, must have been observing a curious cloud effect; unlike Stenhouse, he had been denied a reality check on the following day. Debenham concluded by offering an olive branch. It seemed only fair to him that the name Wilkes Land should apply in its full extent on the basis of, as the American Geographical Society put it, 'Wilkes's recognition of the existence of the continent'. The lands within it, however, should be redesignated as coasts, so Wilkes Land would include a Knox Coast, for example.[3]

Hobbs was disinclined to let the matter rest. Debenham was 'very able', but he had been misled by what was obviously a misprint in the Wilkes narrative. Wilkes's statement that the clearest view of the land was to the SSE was incompatible with the *Peacock* sketches that showed Cape Hudson, the most prominent feature of the coast, bearing south-west. Wilkes's chart made the bearing S20°W. Clearly, SSE should be read as SSW, 'an error easily made at any time in proof-reading, and especially so before typewriters were invented'.[4] As to the form of the coast, the upward refraction necessary to bring the hinterland into view at such a distance would have eclipsed the ice cliffs and dolerite. The hinterland peaks might yet exist; who could tell what would be found between Bage's furthest south at 5900 feet and David's furthest north at 7200 feet? With regard to Stenhouse's experience, the explanation was simple: he had reversed the sequence of image and reality. He really had seen Cape Hudson on the 23rd, and its disappearance on the 24th could be 'easily explained by the stepping-up of the down-slope wind over the ice-cap, which by raising the fine snow high in the air would blot out all features and transform the entire landscape into a grey haze'.[5]

Hobbs simply ignored the beautifully clear afternoon sky that Stenhouse had said replaced the morning haze on the 24th. From London there was a puzzled silence. Why was such brazen misrepresentation needed? It was surely sufficient for Hobbs's purpose that a mirage seen one day had failed to reappear the next. Sufficient, that is, unless it were hoped that the landscape obscured by grey haze was not a miraged one, but actually there. Hobbs still hoped that he could salvage all of Wilkes's eastern landfalls without having to plead refraction.

> It is highly probable, though by no means to be assumed, that the rounded crests (Ringgold's Knoll and Eld and Reynold's peaks) seen from the *Porpoise* on January 16 and located on Wilkes's chart, were snow-covered crests of the Antarctic hinterland; since the lines of sight extended over them correspond in direction fairly closely with the western salient of Oates Land, an apparent eastern salient of King George V Land, and that of the same land behind Cape Freshfield, toward which the line of Cape Hudson points. It is a characteristic of the inland-ice of both Greenland and the Antarctic that it rises generally higher behind such salients, and Mawson's contours indicate this to be true for the salient behind Cape Freshfield.[6]

Hobbs welcomed Debenham's suggestion about the one land of many coasts, but he was not about to quit just because he thought he was ahead. He again sought the sketches. Stenhouse's were still missing, but the commander had tracked down those made by A. H. Ninnis, one of the other expeditioners. There was no denying a remarkable similarity between one of the Ninnis sketches and those published by Wilkes ninety years earlier. In triumph, Hobbs rushed back into print. The features, he wrote, 'might well have been drawn by two competent draftsman working at the same time'. But he had to concede that Ninnis's sketch carried the hallmark of a mirage in its horizontal lines.[7]

Hobbs had won a battle but only at the cost of conceding the campaign. Mirage would suffice to redeem Wilkes's honour, but only proof of direct observation, which Hobbs had been unable to find, would have reinstated him as a first discoverer. A mirage, after all, is but the appearance of land and if land cannot subsequently be found in the location specified, there has been no discovery. Mawson, who had listened to the shot whistling overhead, felt that the time had come to give his own considered account of Wilkes's Antarctic landfalls. His stated purpose was to respond to criticism of the way he had dealt with Wilkes in the 1930 edition of *Home of the Blizzard*, which he excused as a 'popular account of our adventures'. It had been his intention, he said, to deal with the whole question in the scientific reports of the 1911–14

Hobbs's 'confirmation' of Wilkes's Cape Hudson.

expedition, but as these were so slow to appear, and as there was renewed American interest, he felt that the time had come to make his position clear.

> I am sure that all those who, at sea in more modern vessels, have weathered out an Adelie Land hurricane, will be ready to assist in securing for Wilkes in his Antarctic achievement, the fullest possible credit. At the same time, it would be a dis-service to science should we, in our investigations, go beyond the limit of the horizon of the floodlight of fact and possibility.[8]

Mawson dealt with each landfall in turn, and specifically with Hobbs's identification of Cape Hudson with Cape Freshfield in spite of the difference in their outlines. This difference, like the exceptional distances involved, Hobbs had put down to mirage distortion. Mawson drew attention to differences in the morning and afternoon views of the cape as sketched from the *Peacock*. The substantial change in form, given the short distance traversed by the *Peacock* in the interval, argued that the object was comparatively near, certainly not 150 miles away. The resemblance between the *Peacock* and *Aurora* sketches was not evidence for Cape Hudson as Cape Freshfield because the former's bearing, S60°W from the *Aurora*, intersected the coast at Cape Webb, 230 miles from the ship.

> Consequently, even though we invoke every miracle that may be ascribed to mirage, the objects seen and sketched cannot be referred to Cape Freshfield. If it does not refer to Cape Freshfield, it cannot support the argument that Wilkes's Cape Hudson is Cape Freshfield.[9]

As for Stenhouse's sighting of the Balleny Islands on the same day, Mawson would not even admit the possibility of mirage. The discrepancy of bearing alone precluded Young Island and, at 225 miles, this island of no great height could not have been seen. In all probability it was an ice mass much closer to the *Aurora*. The other landfalls were subjected to the same rigorous treatment and then categorised: Mawson was satisfied that Wilkes had definitely seen Adelie Land (136–142°E) and Knox Land (104°30'–108°30'E), and may have seen Budd's High Land (110°30'–112°30'E) and part of North's High Land (Cape Goodenough). He was unlikely to have seen Point Case, his western arm of Disappointment Bay. He definitely could not have seen anything else east of Adelie Land, nor Cape Carr, the western part of North's High Land, Totten's High Land or Termination Land. Hobbs's explanations he found 'characteristically ingenious', but:

> ... in my opinion he goes beyond all reasonable expectation and deduction. Evidently Hobbs cannot agree that Wilkes was human and subject to the same misinterpretation of cloud and ice formations as other mortals.[10]

Nor could Hobbs expect that further exploration might reveal peaks or irregularities in the hinterland of Cape Freshfield. Mawson could personally testify, on the basis of information that he regarded as adequate, that there were no features large enough to disturb his deductions. He foreshadowed a fuller discussion of the question, which was presumably a reference to *Frozen Frontiers*, an account of the 1929–31 voyages which he never got around to writing, but Mawson's most telling blow against giving undue weight to isolated sightings of land, as Wilkes had done, was indirect. The BANZARE landfalls might have been more definite than those of Wilkes but they were still only dots more or less submerged in an ocean of ice. More important were the rocks retrieved and the continuous echo sounding conducted along the margin of the ice. The rocks were more siliceous and aluminous than those in the deeper crust of the earth or in the ocean basins.

> This is one of the principal facts which give much confidence in maintaining the existence under the ice cap of a real continent. The other factor which we believe to be conclusive in this contention is that the delineation of the sea floor over a vast stretch in Antarctica, recently consummated by us, shows that everywhere marginal to the coast of our postulated Antarctic continent the deep floor of the Southern Ocean rises to shallow depths. Thus a continental shelf has been established even where the land itself is hidden by ice.[11]

It seemed unlikely that there would be a continental shelf without a continent. With these findings as the cornerstones of BANZARE scientific contribution, Mawson was in no mood to entertain the assertion by Hobbs that, not only had Wilkes seen a continent, but that he had gathered rocks of a continental nature from icebergs and 'was able further to prove that a continental shelf lay along its front' by making soundings. So he did, said Mawson, but he found bottom in just two localities and rock-laden icebergs in one. This was harsh. A disinterested commentator might have congratulated Wilkes for correct deduction from limited data. Mawson was also less than generous to Wilkes when he summarised the achievements of BANZARE, whereby:

> ... the presence of a real continent within the ice has been finally established, with its main bulk towards the Indian Ocean, as prognosticated by Captain James Cook 160 years ago.[12]

Had not Wilkes similarly prognosticated? No, according to Mawson. Cook, he said, had legitimately inferred, while Wilkes had been over-ready to take appearances for facts and on them 'to conjure up a continent'. The American's loose use of the word 'continent' indicated either, that he was not aware what it meant, or had already made up his mind to find one. Anyway, it was premature. For all that, and in spite of American criticism for the 'negative compliment' of naming Wilkes Land, Mawson protested that he was still prepared to acknowledge Wilkes if it could be done appropriately.

> My view-point has been, firstly, that evidence is conclusive that Wilkes did not sight the coast we charted as Wilkes Land [i.e. as discoverer Mawson could name it for whomever he pleased]. Secondly, the appearance of the words

'Land reported by Wilkes' or in other cases 'Wilkes Land' over the wider areas in some maps was intended to convey the fact that there was the sector through which Wilkes believed continuous land to exist within the pack-ice. As, however, the record of his cruise in no way definitely established the continuity of land through that sector, and as a portion of it already had the prior title Adelie Land, it had not appealed to me that the application of the title Wilkes Land as a geographical term could be correctly applied thereto. I should still like to honour Wilkes if I may.[13]

Hobbs appeared to fall silent, but in fact his attention had shifted elsewhere. If Mawson and the British thought that they had been embroiled in a controversy over Wilkes, it was as nothing compared with Hobbs's next project. He had undertaken to prove that an American sealer, Nathaniel Palmer, was the first discoverer of the Antarctic Peninsula and therefore of Antarctica. This required demolition of the claims of priority made on behalf of two Englishmen, Smith and Bransfield. The air became thick with allegations of hoax, forgery and con-spiracy, directed at such venerable institutions as the British Admiralty and the Royal Geographical Society. It did not do to excite Professor Hobbs, nor to expect that he would be denied the last word.

Even as he directed this second fusillade against the British geographical establishment, an Ex Ex centenary symposium held by the American Philo-sophical Society in 1940 gave him an opportunity to refine his interpretation of the Stenhouse evidence about what Wilkes might or might not have seen off Cape Freshfield. The *Aurora*'s compass bearing to Young Island (N54°E) must have been wrong, he wrote. Now Stenhouse had simply noted that the bearing did not agree with his latitude, implying that the island may have been incorrectly charted. Hobbs averred that because astronomical observation had placed ship and island in the same latitude (that is, island due east of the ship), it 'supplied a correction to the compasses'. If the bearing towards Cape Hudson were adjusted accordingly, the line of vision from both *Peacock* and *Aurora* would be seen to intersect the high land above Cape Freshfield. The evidence, he declared, was complete. The Cape Hudson seen by Wilkes in 1840 was the salient of Cape Freshfield as mapped by Mawson. The distance was about 230 statute miles, instead of about 30 as Wilkes had believed.[14] Furthermore, it was likely, although not proven, that Wilkes's earlier sightings of land were explainable in the same way. Other than these, and his mistaking shelf-ice for 'the land behind it' to the west of 100°E, the discoveries of Wilkes could now be regarded as confirmed.[15]

Surprisingly, Hobbs conceded the non-existence of Cape Carr, although Mawson seems to have thought that it could have been a mirage of Cape Goodenough much further west. The American attributed no significance to Mawson's topography and bearing for the Cape Carr coast and merely noted his 'correction of its position'. The explanation for this is probably that Hobbs now realised that Wilkes's descriptions of land in this sector were suspect and it was safer to point to how closely his chart approximated those of his successors who had the advantage of developments such as wireless time signals for chronometer checks. Hobbs was also able to note partial success in his campaign for the name Wilkes Land. The Debenham compromise had been accepted by the Australian Government. As gazetted among the lands of the Australian Antarctic Territory, Wilkes Land extended from 102°E, the eastern boundary of Queen Mary Land, to 136°E, the western boundary of Adelie Land, subsuming as coasts not only Mawson's Wilkes Land but Banzare, Sabrina and Knox lands as well.

While the geopoliticians were posturing, preparation of the scientific results of BANZARE had quietly been going forward. As with the 1911–14 expedition, war and lack of finance would play havoc with the publishing schedules, but the report on magnetism appeared in 1944. Farr, Webb's New Zealand interlocutor about Mawson's 1908–09 observations, but long since retired from his academic post, had reduced the BANZARE data and written a substantial section on the location of the South Magnetic Pole, from Duperrey and Gauss onwards. It was his last project, undertaken with the assistance of his old colleague Skey, and a fitting conclusion to a 40-year engagement with the magnetic exploration of Antarctica. To Mawson's regret, the New Zealander died the year before his work was published.

Mawson read the drafts of Farr's magnetic report while in the throes of his debate with Hobbs. Where determination was by dip circle, wrote Farr, the pole would probably be a 'hazy, indistinct and movable area' rather than a point. Much the same with coastal topography, Mawson must have thought. Kennedy's magnetic observations at Cape Denison in 1931 had been too few and too sketchy for the derivation of a new and independent polar position, but comparison with Webb's well-determined 1912 position for the pole allowed Farr to place it, epoch 1939, in 70°20'S and 149°E, about 170 miles due south of Cape Wild. He was more interested in its direction and speed of movement than its position. The dip had increased at an average rate of 2.3' a year but the variation hardly at all. This translated into continued movement to the north-west at a rate of approximately four miles a year.

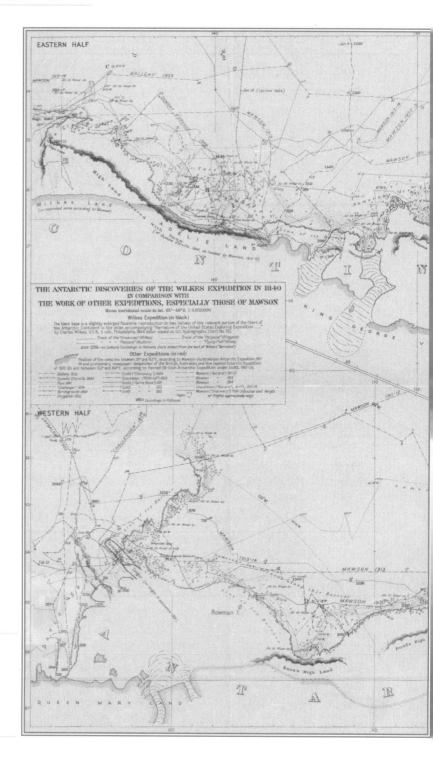

Hobbs maintained that the 'essential accuracy' of Wilkes's work had been demonstrated by Mawson.

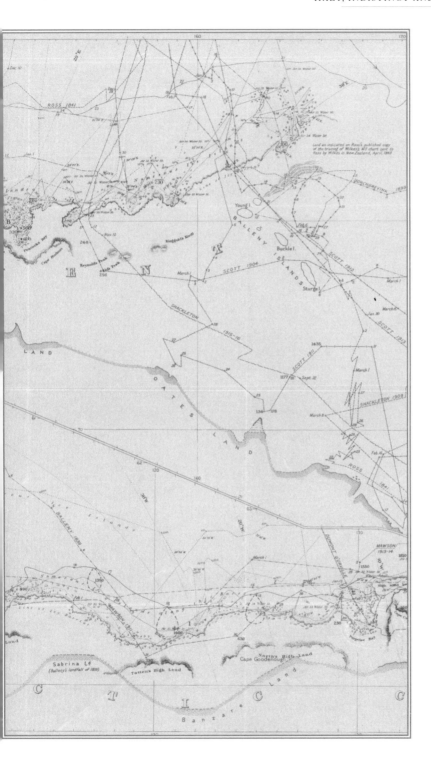

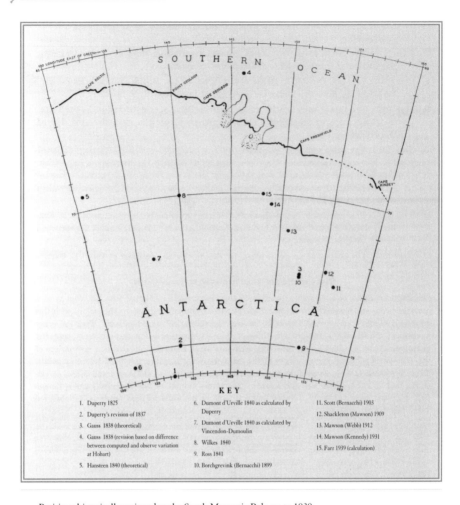

Positions historically assigned to the South Magnetic Pole up to 1939

Mawson did his sums. By 1950 the pole would be within 120 miles of Cape Freshfield, one more argument in favour of the cape as a base for further exploration. Looking further ahead, by the turn of the century the pole would be in the sea area to the west of the Mertz Glacier Tongue, on the doorstop of Cape Denison. The field magneticians of the heroic era had sought the pole far from their bases, with instruments ill-suited to the conditions, condemning them to what Farr described as 'sometimes very painful work'. Their successors could look forward to an era in which the pole would conveniently present itself for further examination, offering opportunities to delve into its still extensive mysteries with less hazard to life and fingers.

Mawson agitated for occupation of Cape Freshfield. From there a scientific station could be constructed at the South Magnetic Pole when it became accessible. A reconnaissance to find a route through the pack ice was planned for 1940 but it was too late. The exigencies of war had found another use even for a tiny, wooden auxiliary steamer. The *Wyatt Earp* had been commissioned as a munitions ship, the first and only of His Majesty's Australian ships to carry the name of an American gunfighter.

CHAPTER 16

Pax Antarctica

The Second World War was as disruptive of Antarctic exploration and science as the first had been, but there was a huge bonus at its end. In 1946 the United States Navy was keen to find employment for the immense material resources left on its hands at the end of hostilities. Thirteen ships, including two seaplane tenders, an aircraft carrier and a submarine, were assembled for Operation Highjump. Its main objective was to train personnel and to test equipment under Antarctic conditions, but while doing so it would consolidate and extend the basis for American claims in Antarctica against the possibility of claims subsequently being made. An insurance policy was being taken out for the Hughes Doctrine. The 4700 personnel deployed made Highjump the largest single expedition ever sent to Antarctica, a distinction it still retains.

After Wilkes, American interest had shifted to the Antarctic Peninsula and the Pacific-facing coast, the area known as West or Lesser Antarctica. The US Antarctic Service, in the two years following its creation in 1939, had mounted an extensive expedition in the area to follow up the private efforts of Byrd, Wilkins and Ellsworth, who between them had overflown much of it during the 1930s. The expedition had been given a secondary and out-of-area objective by President Roosevelt himself. He wanted it, if possible, to make an aerial investigation in the vicinity of the South Magnetic Pole. In this can be seen the influence of Hobbs: perhaps the aircraft might discover the peaks that Wilkes had depicted as Cape Hudson. In the event, the mission was not flown.

Operation Highjump put most of its resources into West Antarctica but in 1946, for the first time since Wilkes, the US Navy also went back to his 'Antarctic Continent'. The force was divided into three task groups, of which the Western Group conducted operations along the coast of East or Greater Antarctica from the Balleny Islands westwards as far as Princess Astrid Coast in the Norwegian sector, around nearly half the circumference of the conti-nent. Aerial photographs were taken of most of the coast and its immediate hinterland. The absence of ground reference points limited the use of the photographs for map-making purposes, but radar tracking of the aircraft by the ships sometimes made it possible to plot the coast. The deepest penetration inland, in effect the mission sought by President Roosevelt eight years earlier, was achieved on 22 January 1947.

Lieutenant Commander William Rogers took a Martin Mariner flying boat south over the Adelie coast along the meridian 135°E. The shoreline was indeterminate, the continental slope gradual and featureless. At 380 miles inland the ice had reached an elevation of 9500 feet and was still rising. The horizon continued to unroll endlessly away to the south. Hobbs's longed-for peaks did not appear; the Mariner's horizon was merely Bage's 'next ridge' writ large. Similar inland flights were made over Oates Land, Cape Carr, North's High Land, Totten's High Land, Budd's High Land and Ellsworth's American Highland. Most of the hinterland was seen to be similarly feature-less to a distance of 300 miles or more. Only in the vicinity of Budd's High Land did it assume the rounded appearance recorded by Wilkes. No attempt appears to have been made to overfly the South Magnetic Pole itself, although one of the expedition's many items of military equipment adapted for peaceful purposes was the magnetic anomaly detector, designed for submarine-hunting. It was, in effect, Verne's Sphinx in miniature. It rotated a closed coil of wire in the Earth's magnetic field to induce an electrical current, which was at a maximum when the axis of the coil was aligned with the field. When the axis of the coil was at right angles to the field, thus aligning the axis of rotation to it, the current ceased, indicating the field's direction. Anything submerged which caused an anomaly in the magnetic flux while the aircraft was on the hunt was in for a nasty surprise. In the hands of Highjump operators the device was used to identify rocks from the air by their magnetic signature.

Ground reference points for the aerial photographs taken in 1946–47 were provided by Operation Windmill, more officially the Second Antarctic

Developments Project of 1947–48. Its icebreakers used helicopters to land parties which conducted short-term explorations to produce the necessary ground tie-ins. Fifteen geodetic stations were established between the Budd Coast and Kaiser Wilhelm II Coast, which made it possible for the first time to produce medium-scale maps of the region. No permanent American presence followed this extensive reconnaissance, but one site became Wilkes station and three were occupied by other nations during the International Geophysical Year 1957–58.

With only two icebreakers and 500 men, Windmill was the merest shadow of Highjump, but even it appeared lavish compared with the Australian expedition which also sailed in the 1947–48 season. The Australian Government had become anxious that, without continuity of occupation, its claims to sovereignty could be challenged. Mawson was consulted. He again advocated Cape Freshfield, mainly for its proximity to the South Magnetic Pole, but could not guarantee that it would be possible to find a suitable building site. It was agreed that the *Wyatt Earp*, refitted for the purpose, would reconnoitre the coast to find an alternative location (Mawson could not bring himself to wish the winds of Cape Denison on his successors), while an amphibious landing ship would convey wintering parties of scientists to Heard and Macquarie islands in the sub-Antarctic. In the event the *Wyatt Earp* nearly broke down, returned to Melbourne for repairs and sailed again too late to penetrate the ice. The senior scientific officer, Phillip Law, was bitterly disappointed that he was unable to land at Cape Denison to make magnetic observations. In 1950 Cabinet approved a continental base but it was 1953 before Richard Casey, by then Minister for External Affairs, was able to get the necessary funding and only then by trading off the Heard Island station.

One of the factors influencing this decision was the reappearance of the French. In 1948–49 the French Polar Expeditions ship *Commandant Charcot* had failed to penetrate the ice, but in the following season she succeeded in landing a wintering party at Port Martin, near Cape Discovery. The main purpose was scientific, but the leader of the expedition, André-Frank Liotard, was also appointed representative of the French Government of Adelie Land. This demonstration of sovereignty was underlined by the establishment of a notional post office which 'issued' a Madagascar stamp specially overprinted. The magnetic program included a visit to Cape Denison in October 1951 to repeat Webb's observations of 38 years earlier. In the following month the French began laying depots for a journey to the west using Weasels, American-made tracked vehicles that had been adapted for over-snow use.

They were soon defeated by sastrugi which strained their suspensions and so put paid to a secondary objective, the South Magnetic Pole. Observations made en route, however, suggested that the pole was now less than 150 kilometres south of Port Martin. The work of the expedition was brought to a sudden conclusion early in the morning of 23 January 1952 when a fire, fanned by hurricane winds, reduced the station to charred ruins in half an hour. Fortunately it was summer and the relief vessel was at hand, but there was no option other than to abandon the base. A party of seven stayed on to winter at Point Geology.

In the protracted debate about where to locate an Australian station on the mainland, the need to reinforce the BANZARE claims at the western limit in the face of subsequent Norwegian and American exploration weighed heavily, as did having Highjump photography of the area available as an aid to site selection. In the end Mawson supported the preference of Phillip Law, now the Director of Australian National Antarctic Research Expeditions (ANARE), for a horseshoe-shaped harbour on the Mac. Robertson Land coast. Mawson had expected that Law, as a physicist, would have been drawn to the magnetic pole, but no. He and the other physicists of the ANARE considered that the auroral zone (a belt of maximum auroral display surrounding the pole) was a more interesting phenomenon than the pole itself, and the zone intersected the coast of Mac. Robertson Land.[1]

Aurora Polaris

Jules Verne had not been too wide of the mark when he speculated, in the light of Birkeland's experiments, that the aurora was caused by the same 'surplus' atmospheric electricity that accumulated at the poles and magnetised his Sphinx. Mawson had noted that brilliant auroral displays appeared to affect telegraph services in Australia, and he too was of the opinion that they could be related to electric currents in the upper atmosphere.

In 1951 Ludwig Biermann advanced the concept of a solar wind to explain the tails always presented by comets on their sides furthest from the sun. The wind is a plasma, atoms without electrons and electrons without atoms. When it flows around the earth, it compresses the geomagnetic field upwind and stretches it downwind to give the planet its own invisible tail. It is electrically neutral but can conduct electric currents.

Sydney Chapman subsequently proposed that the tidal movements he had detected in the atmosphere might be capable of generating such currents by moving electrically charged particles through the earth's magnetic field. Most of the plasma is prevented from reaching the earth by a boundary layer called the magnetopause, but cusps in the layer allow some plasma deep into the atmosphere above each magnetic pole. The magnetic field lines in the magnetosphere become transmission lines for the charged particles of plasma, which excite into luminosity the oxygen molecules encountered in the atmosphere over the poles. So prosaic an explanation for one of nature's most beautiful phenomena.

Mawson would not have been too disappointed, as auroral studies had been one of his Antarctic priorities since the 1920s. Geomagnetic science was looking from the earth to the heavens, trying to account for the portion of terrestrial magnetism that could not be related to the earth's internal field. Mawson Station was established in the early months of 1954 at Horseshoe Harbour. Law himself helped to determine the elements of the earth's magnetic field at the station, observations subsequently used to revise the magnetic variation shown on sailing charts of the southern Indian Ocean. Like Mawson, Law understood the importance of appeasing the 'practical men' among his political masters. Even those politicians who considered expenditure on science unnecessary could appreciate the continuing value of magnetic observation because, contrary to expectations, the magnetic compass was still in use. Indeed, the gyroscope had become its handmaiden: one of the most widely used navigational instruments of the day was the gyromagnetic compass, which combined the reliability and sensitivity of the magnetic needle with the stabilising qualities of gyroscopic mounting. Sadly, the pure gyrocompass had not lived up to its theoretical perfection as designers had been unable to eliminate completely the friction-generated torque which disturbed its directional qualities.

The ten men left behind by Law to overwinter at Mawson Station in 1954 comprised the entire population of Greater Antarctica at that time. It was the beginning of a permanent Australian presence in Antarctica, with exploration and resupply each year during the summer months. Three years later, in International Geophysical Year (IGY), there were fifteen stations and hundreds of scientists – American, Russian, Australian, French, Norwegian, Belgian and Japanese. Originally conceived as a third International Polar Year (following 1882–83 and 1932–33, which had mainly looked to the Arctic),

IGY was the great leap forward for Antarctic earth science of all kinds, including geomagnetism.

The main theatre for this science, as foreshadowed by Law, was the upper atmosphere, where observation and experiment (including nuclear explosions) revealed the existence of the Van Allen belts of ionising radiation, evidence of interplay between the solar wind and the earth's magnetic field which linked such disparate phenomena as sunspot activity and the aurora. The year was selected to coincide with a predicted peak in the cycle of solar activity, and nature did not disappoint. The magneticians found themselves observing perhaps the most intense burst of activity since Galileo first recorded sunspots in 1610. Mawson's dream of obtaining extended observations close to the South Magnetic Pole was realised by the French, who established Charcot station 318 kilometres inland at 69°22.5'S and 139°01'E. Although regarded as no more important than any other, this temporary station provided some of the most interesting terrestrial magnetic data of the IGY. It was west of the magnetic pole area rather than east, thus becoming the first station to observe at close quarters from the Other Side of Nowhere, and was between the South Magnetic Pole and the South Geomagnetic Pole. The diurnal variation in summer at Charcot seemed to have rules of its own. Two days that elsewhere met the criteria for classification as International Disturbed Days were among the quietest days recorded at Charcot. Overall, Charcot in summer was quiet when it should have been disturbed, something like the eye of a hurricane. Farr would not have been surprised: the more one learned about magnetism, it seemed, the less one knew.

IGY also consolidated another major player in the claim game. Soon after the outbreak of the Cold War the Soviet Union had dusted off Bellingshausen and was prepared to argue with a straight face that, if discovery was a precondition for sovereignty, it had a good claim to the entire continent. More realistically, it adopted a position of declining to accept the claims of others even where there was effective occupation. Both superpowers were in effect signalling that there could be no international settlement in the Antarctic without their participation. There were now two whales swimming alongside minnow Australia. The United States had a subtle message for everyone: their Amundsen-Scott base at the geographic pole put the tip of an American finger in every slice of the Antarctic pie. Knowing that the Soviet Union intended to establish IGY stations in its Antarctic territory anyway, Australia sent an invitation. It was not acknowledged. Nor were the Russians to be outdone by the Americans in defying the inhospitability of the Antarctic: they constructed a station at the geomagnetic pole (Vostok, 900 miles inland at 78°27'S and 106°52'E) and journeyed to the so-called Pole of Inaccessibility, 1300 miles inland. The seismic soundings made during this great traverse convinced them that Wilkes and Mawson had been right: East Antarctica was a continent, with most of its sub-ice surface above sea level. Were the ice to be removed, isostatic rebound would raise the land even further.

The main Australian initiative was the development a second mainland station, Davis, at Prydz Bay. A third was added when the United States, after IGY, transferred its Wilkes Station on the Budd Coast to ANARE. But even in the intensely competitive (as well as cooperative) atmosphere of IGY, the Australian effort at the eastern extremity of its national claim, Oates Land, was limited to what Law called 'hit and run exploration' during the summer resupply season. On 16 January 1958 Flying Officer William Wilson flew Law in a ship-based Beaver floatplane from Horn Bluff eastwards towards Cape Freshfield. Where the elongated tip of Cape Freshfield should have been, there was only a corner as the ice cliffs curved south to form Cook Bay. The place where Mawson had wanted to see a station placed, and which Hobbs had been sure was Wilkes's Cape Hudson, had been ice, which sometime after 1912 had broken off and floated away.

Law's party was unable to land in 1958, and so in the following year he returned to the area aboard the resupply ship *Magga Dan*. On 20 February, this time in an Auster piloted by Squadron Leader Douglas Leckie, he again took to the air. With its floats and an unwieldy F24 hand-held camera, the Auster was 360 pounds overweight and the large sheet of open water from which it took off was barely large enough. They were seven degrees further east than Law had been the previous year. The coastal features below, the Wilson Hills, had been discovered by Pennell in 1911 and visited by air from the Soviet research ship *Ob* in 1958. Law's determination to squeeze every available moment and photograph out of the flight left Leckie with little fuel in reserve when they turned back. It was then that the ship reported that the ice had closed up their landing pool. This would have been of more immediate concern to the aviators had they known where the ship and the erstwhile pool were, for ice shift had rearranged the seamarks. 'Can the ship make smoke?', radioed Law. 'Not with diesel', came the reply. Well then, said Law:

> Get every pair of binoculars on the ship, issue one to each individual man, send the men up on to the monkey island [atop the bridge], divide the sky into sectors and give each man a sector to scan . . .[2]

Bruce Coombes, an aircraft engineer, finally glimpsed a dot against the white of a berg at a distance of ten miles and the bearing was radioed to the aircraft. The ship blustered through the ice to create a pool perhaps forty metres long. Leckie dropped the Auster into it as slowly as he could, but still finished his landing run with the propeller almost touching the ship. Another five minutes and they would have been out of fuel. Once aboard the ship, Law was keen to get ashore that very day. He identified an accessible spot where the ship could moor against fast ice about a mile from the land. The landing party climbed the nearest eminence, Magga Peak, and at its base determined the position by astronomical observation.

On the following day the Auster took off from the ice on skis and flew westwards. Forty minutes later the coastline was seen to veer to the north-west, and Law and Leckie found themselves over a peninsula which extended far out to sea. Its spine appeared to be about 1500 feet high with nunataks 2000–3000 feet high along the western side. Law was eager for a closer look but the Auster began complaining. Apprehensive that a rough engine might suddenly become a dead engine, Leckie turned back. He suspected caburettor icing and sacrificed height but, even with more carburettor heat, the roughness persisted. From 800 feet they had all too close a view of the jumbled ice that might have to make do for a landing field. Later examination of the plane revealed a faulty fuel pump which had been bypassed when they switched from one fuel tank to the other, but they were not to know it, and until Leckie decided that the carburettor was not at fault and reduced the heating there was no comfort in the engine's sound, and no less anxiety until they were safely down at the ship. Law named the peninsula for Mawson.

As usual, at the conclusion of the resupply season all of the geographical data were handed over to the government's Division of National Mapping for charting. The division's Director, Bruce Lambert, was a member of the ANARE Planning Committee. He had long taken a keen interest in the difficulties that Antarctic conditions created for cartographers, and as he stared at the outline of the Mawson Peninsula an idea grew in his mind. He compared his division's sketch map with Wilkes's chart. They did not agree in either latitude or longitude in this sector, nor in the bearing along which features were recorded, but still there was something . . .

He looked at Law's photographs of the peninsula's nunataks and saw in them a shape 'not unlike' the hills west of Wilkes's Cape Hudson. Hadn't High-jump photographed along here? The Magga Peak astrofix could be used as a ground reference point. The US State Department was asked for photographs, flight logs etc. and promptly obliged. After extracting all the information he could from available data, Lambert believed that the relative positions of the features on his provisional map were 'reasonably correct' and that the absolute positions were unlikely to be out by more than 5–10 miles. Then he turned to Wilkes.

Lambert converted the American's chart to the scale and projection of his provisional map and superimposed one on the other, making Wilkes's hills west of Cape Hudson overlie Law's nunataks. He observed that with the maps in this alignment, Wilkes's Point Emmons agreed well with Mawson's Cape Wild-Horn Bluff-Cape Freshfield features, and Peacock Bay coincided with Cook Bay. Moreover, there were hills west of the Pennell Glacier 'very close' to the direction in which Reynolds Peak and Eld's Peak had been seen from USS *Peacock* on 16 January 1840, although the American chart distances were still short. Law's photographs agreed with the descriptions given by Reynolds and Eld. Lines drawn from the ships' positions through Ringgold's Knoll gave mixed results: that from the *Vincennes* passed near the Wilson Hills, but that from the *Porpoise* on the same date did not run to any newly mapped feature.

Lambert suggested that the point at the end of the Mawson Peninsula was Cape Hudson, that Eld and Reynolds had seen the hills west of the Pennell Glacier – although it was not possible to say which – and that Wilkes himself may have seen a peak in the Wilson Hills. It was a masterly reconciliation but it required enormous assumptions. To align Cape Hudson with the tip of the Mawson Peninsula, Lambert had to shift the former 1°40' to the south and 42' to the east, 116 and 18 statute miles respectively. He considered that differences in latitude and underestimates of distance could be accounted for by the old standby, abnormal refraction, but he offered no explanation for the differences in longitude, remarking only that they were 'understandable'.[3]

In the absence of an explanation, an omission remarkable in itself, one can only assume that Lambert was thinking that the *Vincennes* chronometers, which were used to determine longitude, could have been in error. As it happens there was evidence to this effect, although he appears to have been unaware of it. Had he re-read the cartographic report of Mawson's 1911–14 expedition, Lambert would have found that a longitude correction had been made to Wilkes's work further west, beyond the area of his new map. It will be recalled that for three-quarters of a century the credibility of Wilkes had ultimately rested on the rocks of Piner's Bay because they were in the same longitude as those seen by d'Urville, even though the two navigators' descriptions of that coast did not agree. Mawson had expressed difficulty in identifying their named features, with the exception of Point Geology, and commented that Wilkes's map appeared intended to give no more than a 'rough approximation' of the coast.

> Consequently, the identification of his Piner Bay [sic] has been a matter for decision. The longitude given by Wilkes for this feature would place it just to the west of Point Geology, but nothing at that spot answers to his description. Consequently, we must conclude that his longitude is at fault, and that Piner Bay is a few miles further to the east, as shown on our map, where agreement with Wilkes's description of the bay is satisfactorily met.[4]

How much further east? According to Mawson's map, 36', only 6' less than Lambert's correction, a very close agreement. So were the *Vincennes* chronometers at fault? Paradoxically enough, probably not. In the chart Wilkes sent to Ross, drawn up on the *Vincennes*, the longitudes for Cape Hudson and Piner's Bay agree with those assigned by Lambert and Mawson respectively. But in his published map Wilkes moved the features westwards, which placed Piner's Bay on the other side of Point Geology, a feature shown on both map and chart. This is a conscious and serious correction, but for who knows what reason. If the purpose was to incorporate observations made by *Peacock* and *Porpoise*, Wilkes would have done better to trust his own timepieces, the more so as neither of the other ships saw Piner's Bay.

Lambert and Law took their *New Map of the Coastline of Oates Land and Eastern King George V Land* to the Antarctic Symposium held in Buenos Aires in late 1959. It was just prior to the signing of the Antarctic Treaty, and in that era of good feelings the effort by foreigners to vindicate Wilkes was warmly welcomed in the United States. It was front-page news in the *New York Times* under the headline 'Wilkes Is Upheld on 1840 Antarctica Find'.

> Until now . . . the Wilkes discoveries in the sector newly explored by the Australians were largely discredited. Even American maps omit the features that he charted, such as Cape Hudson, Ringgold Knoll and Eld Peak. The new Australian map shows them.[5]

Well, yes and no. The features named for Ringgold, Eld and Reynolds on either side of the Pennell Glacier were arbitrarily chosen from several nearby candidates among the Wilson Hills and Burnside Ridges, which begs the

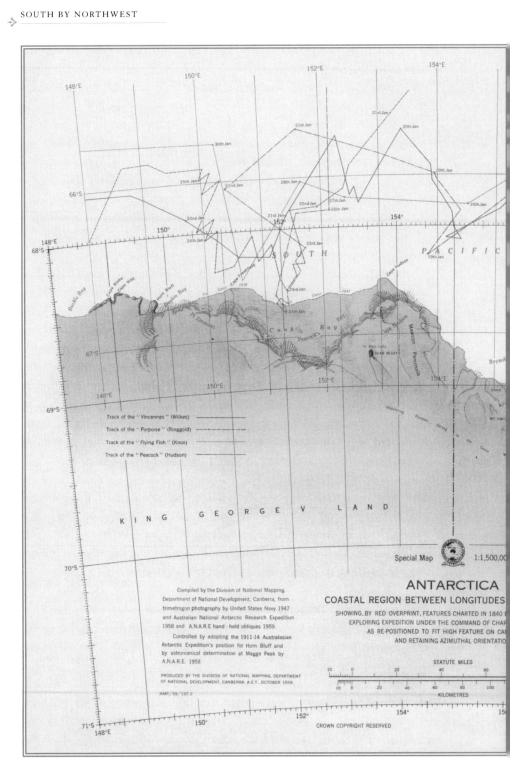

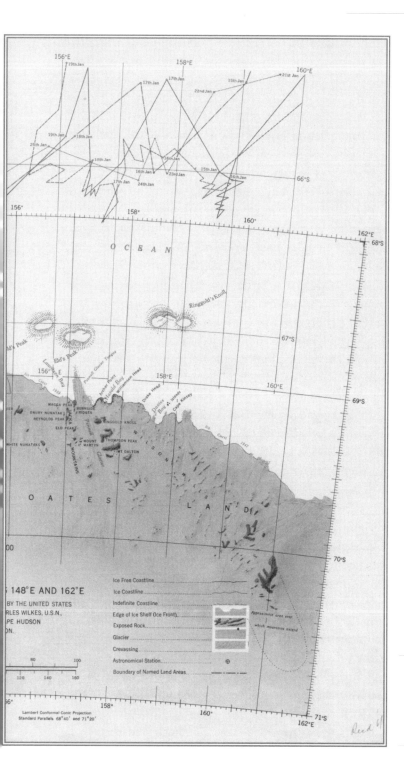

In 1959 Lambert and Law attempted to reconcile Wilkes's eastern discoveries with subsequent exploration.

question why some of the others were not also seen from *Peacock* and *Porpoise*. The Lambert and Law paper concluded by suggesting that perhaps it was time that 'the whole question of the reliability of Wilkes's observations' in the sector should be reviewed, but the men who would have seized the opportunity, Hobbs and Mawson, were not there to resume the debate. Hobbs had died in 1953 and Mawson during IGY. To the best of Phillip Law's knowledge the challenge was not taken up, probably because events in Washington were about to consign the controversy to the dustbin of history, or at least to its recycle bin.[6]

From the first intimation of Soviet interest in the Antarctic the Americans had worried that the Hughes Doctrine might not be sustainable. The United States had never endorsed the Antarctic claims it had sometimes encouraged citizens to make on its behalf. In the absence of other claims, therefore, the area where American exploration and involvement had been strongest, east of the Ross Sea, was still no man's land. Under the doctrine's own terms, the area was open to claim by any power which might follow up 'discovery' (by, say, a Russian navigator called Bellingshausen) with 'actual settlement' (a permanent station?), and the Soviet Union was more than just any power. As early as 1948, the Americans had attempted to persuade the claimant states of the advantages of internationalisation, specifically by proposing a condominium that would include the United States, but exclude both the Soviet Union and the United Nations. Britain, long in dispute with Argentina and Chile over the Falklands Dependencies, and New Zealand, balking at the cost of keeping up appearances in the Ross Sea sector, could see merit in the proposal but they were alone. Australia and the other powers were not prepared to contemplate any diminution of their sovereign rights. All agreed, however, that Antarctica should be reserved for peaceful purposes and for cooperative scientific research.

These were, of course, the cornerstones of IGY, and the Americans, gratified at Russian willingness to put the Cold War into cold storage for the duration, at least in Antarctica, revived the concept of internationalisation in 1958. This time the Russians were invited, as were other non-claimant IGY participants – Japan, South Africa and Belgium. Surprisingly, the discussions in Washington in late 1959 came closest to foundering when the claimant state with the smallest Antarctic stake, France, stood on its dignity. Equally surprisingly, it was talked around by the largest claimant – Australia – which had noted the vast resources Russia had poured into its IGY stations. Some of those, it was clear, were there to stay. The only safety on offer was the safety of numbers, and Richard Casey's brief was to secure it. In what was to be his last major personal initiative as Australia's foreign minister, he intervened with his opposite number, Couve de Murville, over the head of the French delegation: the freezing of existing territorial claims as provided for in Article IV, he cabled privately, was the best guarantee against Soviet ambitions, which might include France's Adelie Land. Publicly, in conference session:

> I finished up by appealing to the French to reconsider their position. I said that Australia was far from happy about the situation in the Antarctic or the situation that would obtain [even] if and when this Treaty was consummated. France, I imagined, would not relish being isolated in a minority of one and so jeopardizing the Treaty.[7]

The French wavered, and then gave way. What Casey liked to refer to as the *Pax Antarctica* was signed by the contracting parties on 1 December 1959.

CHAPTER 17

Vainglory

The Lambert and Law *New Map* of 1959 manifests the spirit of the Antarctic Treaty, a setting-aside of territorial differences in the interests of cooperation, but like the treaty it is not a final resolution. Should the treaty ever be allowed to lapse and territorial claims be reactivated, the limitations of the map would quickly become apparent.

Lambert's adjustment of the longitude extends Wilkes's Point Emmons, as it appears in the American's published map, from Horn Bluff to Cape Freshfield. This is a bad fit. Worse, the shift eastwards undoes a better fit with Cape Wild and places Wilkes's Disappointment Bay inland of the coastline. Lambert did not apply his assumptions west of Cape Wild, where the ever-changing profiles of the Ninnis and Mertz glacier tongues defied certainty about how they would have appeared in 1840. What can be said is that the latitude and longitude of Wilkes's Disappointment Bay, unadjusted, locate it between the two tongues as they have appeared in more recent times. On the other hand, the Wilkes map shows the bay's eastern point, Point Emmons, bearing distinctly north of east from the position of *Vincennes* near the head of the bay. There is no land in that direction short of the Balleny Islands, more than 400 miles away. The adjusted longitude of the western point, Point Case, aligns it with the Mertz Glacier Tongue, but adjusted latitude places it inland. Wilkes's unadjusted latitude could be correct, but only if the tongue then terminated well to the south of where it does today.

Lambert knew that latitude adjustment would be invalid further west. Beyond Cape Denison the *Vincennes* would be sailing over more of Wilkes's land than James Clark Ross ever had. Put another way, beyond Cape Denison, refraction is no longer needed to explain some sightings of land: Wilkes's westerly course had converged with a coastline trending west-north-west. Some of what he subsequently saw would have been directly visible from the masthead. The question therefore changes from 'what could he have seen?' to 'what did he see?' Importantly, the longitude adjustment, despite its failure at Cape Wild, remains otherwise valid as far as Piner's Bay.

Historical analysis of Wilkes's work has naturally focused on his published map, which has to be regarded as his own definitive statement of where he went. The chart he sent to Ross from New Zealand seemed of interest to Hobbs and others only for the disputed land at its eastern end, but a close comparison with the whole of Wilkes's map reveals another interesting discrepancy.[1] Making allowance for the difference of scale in the two documents, the track of the *Vincennes* and the line and detail of the ice barrier are identical in both. The hatching used to indicate land, however, is rather different. It will be recalled that Alden testified to drawing the track and barrier, but attributed the hatching to Wilkes. It is obvious that, in the interval between chart and map, Wilkes must have changed his mind about more than 'Bellamy's Islands'. The Ringgold-Eld-Reynolds hatching on the chart becomes three separate features on the map and, conversely, Cape Hudson becomes continuous with Point Emmons.

What is not so obvious is that Wilkes has shifted the western ends of most of his hatched landforms further west by between one-half and two degrees. The exceptions are Totten's High Land, the western end of which remains unchanged, and the Ringgold-Eld-Reynolds complex, which is moved half a degree east but reduced in longitude to three-fifths of its former extent. This reduction is also anomalous in that all of the other hatched landforms have been extended in length by between one-half and two-and-a-half degrees.

Too much should not be made of these changes. The scales of map and chart make distinctions of less than half a degree problematical and hatching is usually impressionistic (creating another problem, of which more later). But for all that, it can be argued that Wilkes himself, in his chart, gives sufficient warrant for Lambert's readjustment eastward, indeed rather more consistently in relation to the western landfalls than the eastern. It remains, therefore, to compare the longitude of Wilkes's western landfalls, as recorded on his chart rather than on his map, with current knowledge of that coast.

Comparison of Wilkes's Chart and Map of Antarctic Landfalls

Landfall	Charted Position*		Mapped Position*		Shift*
	°East Long.	Extent	°East Long.	Extent	(W end)
'Bellamy's Islands'	163–166	3°	none	none	n/a
Ringgold's Knoll–	154–159	5°	155¹/₂–158¹/₂	3°	1¹/₂°E
Eld's Peak–					
Reynolds Peak					
Point Emmons–	149–153	4°	148¹/₂–154	5¹/₂°	¹/₂°W
Cape Hudson					
Point Case	145–146¹/₂	1¹/₂°	144¹/₂–146¹/₂	2°	¹/₂°W
Point Alden–	132–142¹/₂	10¹/₂°	131–143	12°	1°W
Cape Carr					
North's High Land	125–129¹/₂	4¹/₂°	123–129¹/₂	6¹/₂°	2°W
Totten's High Land	117–120¹/₂	3¹/₂°	117–122	5°	0°
Budd's High Land	111¹/₂–113	1¹/₂°	110–114	4°	1¹/₂°W
Knox's High Land	104¹/₂–108¹/₂	4°	103¹/₂–109	5¹/₂°	1°W
Termination Land	95¹/₂–96¹/₂	1°	94¹/₂–97	2¹/₂°	1°W

*to nearest half degree

Wilkes's Cape Carr of 132–133°E is d'Urville's Clarie Coast, and no adjustment of longitude can make either of them land. Both explorers were looking at an immense ice structure of which the present-day Dibble Ice Tongue, in 134–135°E, is but the echo.

Next west is North's High Land. Mawson was prepared to allow that one of its features, shown in 124–125°E on Wilkes's map, could be Cape Goodenough in 126°30'E. The feature is much more convincing on the chart, where it is the western extremity of North's High Land and located in 125–126°E. Wilkes places the *Vincennes* 32 statute miles north of the feature, which is 56 miles short of the actual distance to Cape Goodenough. The cape is not high enough to be seen from 88 miles away without the aid of refraction.

Totten's High Land is the easternmost of those of Wilkes's lands whose names are accepted by modern geographers as affixed by right of discovery. Wilkes charted its western extremity on both chart and map at 117°E. This is the longitude of what today is called the Totten Glacier. The latitude given by Wilkes, just north of the Antarctic Circle, agrees with the seaward position the glacier's ice tongue is known to have reached during the twentieth century. There was no misjudgement of distance: the feature was charted as being 80 miles due south of the ship's position, and that is where it is. Again however, the feature is not high enough to have been seen at that distance without refraction.

Budd's High Land, 111½–113°E, is most probably today's Law Dome behind Cape Poinsett. Its resemblance to Wilkes's description of 'high, rounded' land seen on 13 February has made some geographers too confident in identifying the land with the dome. A careful reading of the *Narrative* reveals that Wilkes was describing his next landfall, Knox's High Land. The misreading was reinforced by the hatching Wilkes used for Budd's High Land, a dome shape pointing north. This was smoothed into a more gradual arc for the published map and extended another degree to the west, both changes for the worse. Wilkes placed Budd's High Land in about 65°30'S, half a degree too far north. His estimate of the distance from the ship was 35 miles; in fact, it was more like 95, but the significance of the error lies in its remarkable similarity to that made off North's High Land, where 88 miles masqueraded as 32. Refraction would have been needed to bring it into view.

Knox's High Land was considered by Mawson to be the most credible of all the western landfalls. Wilkes's chart hatches between 104½° and 108½°E in about 66°15'S, running east-west with a slight curve to the south. In fact the coast here runs ESE–WNW, nearer to the SE–NW line of the ice barrier shown on the chart. Although the hatching on Wilkes's map is more extensive than that on his chart, and has been shifted westwards, the changes are irrelevant here because, in both documents, the *Vincennes* is closest to the hatching in the same longitude, 106°30'E. Indeed, for once the map is more accurate. It places the *Vincennes* 14 miles from Knox's High Land. In the two sketches of this landfall which Wilkes published, one illustrating his map and the other his narrative, he locates the ship eight miles off the ice barrier, and the position he gives for the barrier tallies with that of the shore as now known to within 5' of latitude, or about six statute miles. The chart's hatching, on the other hand, places the land further south.

Termination Land is the most definitely discredited of all the Wilkes landfalls. On both chart and map the hatching has it running north-south from 64° to 65°S in the longitude of the Termination Ice Tongue. When the *Aurora* sailed around the seaward extremity of the tongue in 1912, it extended north beyond the point at which Wilkes was turned back towards the north-east by the line of the ice barrier. Wilkes saw his Termination Land extending north-east to south-west across the bows: westwards of the ice tongue there is no land except tiny Drygalski Island until Enderby Land is seen, a feat beyond even miracles of refraction. To the south-west lies the Gaussberg, but it is 250 miles distant. One would sail a thousand miles to the west-north-west before encountering land, and then it would be only Heard Island.

So emphatically was Wilkes wrong in this particular mistaking of ice or cloud for land, that the same error must be considered a possibility in relation to his other landfalls. Wilkes himself was not totally convinced about what he saw in every case, but we know the three western landfalls of which he was most confident because he published his sketches of them as illustrations, and they happen to coincide with what we know to be his nearest approaches to land. Furthermore, the *Vincennes* sketches are more convincing than those attributed to the *Peacock*. In all of the former – off Piner's Bay on 30 January 1840, off Cape Robert on 1 February and off Knox's High Land on 14 February – the horizon line might reasonably be described as low and undulating once allowance has been made for a common sketching weakness, the exaggeration of differences in height. It must be said, however, that Wilkes does not serve his own cause by occasionally describing the land as mountainous. The sketches accord with the known profile of this coast – ice cliff backed by a snow ramp rising to an almost flat horizon. They show clouds above, emphasising Wilkes's conviction that the line he could see on the horizon was snow-covered land and not cloud. The *Peacock* sketches, on the other hand, show distinct peaks.[2]

Interpretation of both map and chart is complicated by the absence of any statement from Wilkes about what his hatching represents. Is it coastline or does it show higher features further inland? Ross took it to be the former on the grounds that, if the ice barrier was not land, then the first feature shown beyond it must be the seaward edge of the claimed discovery. The German Antarctic historian, Karl Fricker, when he mapped Wilkes's discoveries sixty years later, made the same assumption.[3] It is easy to understand how Ross might have come to this view in the light of his experience with 'Bellamy's Islands' but it is too crude a test. In the case of the landfalls sketched from the *Vincennes*, which are the three charted closest to the ice barrier, the features could be coastline but are hatched as elevated land without a defined boundary. According to mapping convention a coastline should have a boundary, even if only the uncertainty of a dotted line. Wilkes's difficulty, of course, was that the only *terra firma* he saw in the Antarctic was offshore rock in Piner's Bay. How could he be sure where the coastline lay between the ice barrier and the features he could see beyond it? The best that can be said is that Wilkes's hatching always indicates elevated land, which in some cases is close enough to the line of the ice barrier to raise the possibility that it is a coastal feature.

In the end, after discounting refraction, we are left with Piner's Bay, Cape Robert and Knox's High Land as the only Wilkes landfalls beyond question. With refraction, North's, Totten's, and Budd's high lands become possible, the claims of the last two having been improved by adjustment of their longitude. From North's to Knox's they span, with the gaps between, 25 degrees of longitude or more than 600 statute miles of coast. Mindful of Ross's objections to the gaps, and having regard to the fact that this is about the length of the east coast of Greenland, was Wilkes justified in declaring Antarctica to be a continent? By most objective tests he had insufficient evidence to prove the fact but more than enough to justify the suspicion. Had he announced the 'appearance' of a continent, his reputation would stand higher in our day and have been better insulated from attack in his own.

Wilkes has probably had more doubters in his own time and since than any other major explorer, but in the history of the First Magnetic Crusade he was not the only one to feel that an enigmatic and intractable place had deprived him of a full measure of glory. On the other hand, none of those explorers left Antarctica without a degree of success and some claim to fame. The Economist of Life seemed always to be watching, benignly allowing ambition its reward, but not so much as to let pride to go unchallenged or to deprive others of opportunity. The human agents of this monitor, regrettably, were vanity, rivalry and envy. It is difficult therefore to feel that anyone was particularly hard done by.

Dumont d'Urville was first in 1840, but on a coast already discovered further west by Biscoe in 1831 and near islands found by Balleny in 1839. It was not the discovery he intended, but the South Magnetic Pole was beyond his reach and this would do. Most of his countrymen were determined to make the most of his achievement (without the discovery of Adelie Land it is unlikely that he would have been hailed as France's Cook), but he did not live to enjoy it, nor to defend his reputation against his surgeon-critic.

Wilkes sought the South Magnetic Pole but was easily seduced by the prospect of geographical discovery. By claiming more than he could sustain with evidence, he diminished rather than enhanced his reputation. Meanness of spirit characterised his relations with subordinates and rivals, illustrated most vividly by his reference to Ross's more extensive and definite discoveries of 1841 as a southerly extension of 'our Antarctic Continent'. Ironically, his greatest service to Antarctic exploration was the controversy he generated. While it is true, as Hugh Mill said, that every Antarctic explorer discovered mistakes in his predecessors' work[4], Wilkes had the distinction of inspiring more determination to prove him wrong than almost any explorer before or since.

Ross sought the glory of reaching both magnetic poles. He failed, but in failing he discovered what was arguably a continent, the existence of which he denied in the greater causes of denying Wilkes and of keeping alive his own hopes of being able to sail to the South Magnetic Pole. His behaviour towards Wilkes deserved censure, but he escaped it because Wilkes's behaviour was even worse. His special punishment was to win the debate with Wilkes, but then be denied the satisfaction of having the American admit it.

Drygalski failed even to get properly ashore on the mainland, much less sledge to the magnetic pole, but his discovery of the Gaussberg proved that there was land between the American discoveries and Enderby Land, as Wilkes had predicted. His carefully planned program deserved better luck, but perhaps that had been reserved for old Neumayer, its originator.

The Australian landing parties of the Second Crusade fared little better in the glory stakes, not least because their chief, Mawson, entangled himself in the Wilkes controversy. It will be recalled that it was against his better judgment that he agreed to try for the South Magnetic Pole in 1908–09. His apparently successful journey with David and Mackay was hailed as one of the triumphs of the Shackleton expedition. When it was later demonstrated that they had fallen short of their goal, Mawson was careful to correct the formal record, but by then the mistake had taken on a life of its own: it is widely believed even today that the David party did reach the pole. Part of his motivation in again seeking the pole in 1911–14 was a desire to complete the larger task of multiple observations, but it was subordinated to a greater ambition, the desire to prove that the discoveries of Wilkes and Ross were part of the same continental landmass. In doing so he proved that in a general sense Wilkes was right and Ross was wrong, but it earned him little credit with American geographers because he demolished so many of the Wilkes landfalls in the process. This inspired gleefully malicious comparisons with uncertainties in his own discoveries. It was an exact parallel with Ross and the Parry Mountains. The Economist was still at work.

Mawson's magnetician, Eric Webb, will never figure among the giants of Antarctic exploration, but as far as the South Magnetic Pole is concerned, and indeed in the annals of scientific exploration generally, he stands tall. The quantity and quality of his magnetic observations on the trek south with Bage and Hurley are a model of scientific exactitude in the face of the most adverse of field conditions. His secret ambition to be leader of the first party to reach the pole was unachieved, as was the pole itself, and so public fame eluded him. But the position he assigned to the South Magnetic Pole for epoch 1913 was the magnetician's benchmark for nearly half a century, and is still the best fix from the era of the Magnetic Crusades.

EPILOGUE

Out of Nowhere

Sometime around 1957 the Antarctic gave up one of its secrets. Unseen and unremarked, the South Magnetic Pole wandered out of nowhere, across the coast somewhere between station Dumont d'Urville and Port Martin and into the Southern Ocean. Wilkes and d'Urville had been in the right place at the wrong time.

In 1977 a very old man was invited to revisit Australia after a lifetime working abroad. One of the people he met was a doctoral student in geophysics from the Australian National University. Young Charlie Barton was surprised to learn that the visitor was familiar with a paper he had written on the history of magnetic exploration. He was even more surprised to hear his paper subjected to a vigorous critique. He was discovering what Mawson had learnt over half a century earlier: when you were dealing with Eric Webb you had better know exactly what you were talking about. Two years earlier Webb himself had written a brief history of the Cape Denison magnetograph hut, a structure built to his own design, and had recorded with pride that several of the nine visits made to it since the Australasian Antarctic Expedition had been for the primary purpose of precisely reoccupying his magnetic station:

> In 1914 directions had been left for future scientists who might wish to record magnetic measurements and these were reported by the 1974 Australian

expedition to be in the same biscuit tin in which they were originally placed. Each party in turn reported the hut to be in good to excellent condition and tight against ingress of snow, which is a tribute to the care taken by each party in turn to close the doors securely.[1]

Webb noted that, at his date of writing, the station was within the South Magnetic Polar area, but of more interest to Charlie Barton was the fact that the South Magnetic Pole itself was offshore and in theory could be reached by ship, as Ross had hoped to do. In the meantime he participated in the 1977 overflight of the South Magnetic Pole organised by Australian entrepreneur Dick Smith. This all-too-brief glimpse of the Antarctic firmed his resolve: one day he would take observations on the spot. After leaving university Dr Charles Barton went to work in the Geomagnetism Section of the Australian Bureau of Mineral Resources (BMR), and for years schemed to get ship time on the annual Antarctic base resupply voyage. In 1985 he was told that MV *Icebird* would pause briefly, conditions permitting, to locate the pole.

Barton's biggest challenge was to compensate for the ship's own magnetic field, a far larger problem with steel than it had been with the wooden ships of the heroic age, but at least magneticians were no longer dependent on the needle when observing dip and intensity in the field. His device squatted on a wooden structure which projected two metres over the ship's stern, like the 'bird' used to house an anti-submarine aircraft's magnetic anomaly detector. Like the detector, it was a fluxgate magnetometer, but one designed to detect the direction of the earth's field. It was mounted on gimbals to compensate for the motion of the ship and encompassed by electric coils which partly neutralised the ship's own magnetic field.[2]

Barton was on the verge of achieving an ambition that had been drawing explorers south for a century and a half. Mawson and Webb had come close but, in the end, the magnetic pole had been just a few miles beyond their reach. The French at Charcot and Dumont d'Urville had observed it swirling nearby but, sensibly, had usually been content to record at their fixed stations rather than chase it. Only Pierre-Noel Mayaud, magnetician with the French expedition in 1952, had approached the magnetic pole directly, but he got no closer than 116 kilometres. It was still unvisited by 1986, and when Barton presented himself for the ANARE expeditioners' checks he was conscious that he could be about to make history.

Like so many of his predecessors, he was disappointed. He failed the Antarctic medical. No exemption was possible and he had to brief one of his fellow geophysicists from BMR, Rodney Hutchinson, to take his place. Barton could at least be sure that, ice permitting, the ship would not have to spend much time searching for the pole. Since 1965 the earth's geomagnetic field had been modelled every five years using Gaussian spherical harmonic analysis. Although the observations from which the International Geomagnetic Reference Field (IGRF) were derived were, as they had been in Gauss's day, deficient in distribution for the Southern Hemisphere, the indicated position for the South Magnetic Pole was more than adequate as a starting point for refinement by observation on the spot. The ship's satellite navigation system provided hourly fixes accurate to 100 metres, and even accumulated error in ship speed would leave it accurate to within one statute mile two hours after the last fix.

Icebird made her first spins in the ice-covered sea on 2–3 January 1986, circling within a diameter of about 100 metres. After 16 hours the ship had to continue the resupply voyage, but she returned to the vicinity of the pole on 5–6 January. With the ship in 65°16'S and 139°31'E, about 150 kilometres north-north-west of Dumont d'Urville station, a small crowd of scientists and ship's personnel gathered, not around the structure at the stern, but around an electronic equipment rack on the bridge. Its displays flickered with the output from the magnetometer. When digested by a small computer, the figures resolved themselves into two digits. The horizontal component of the geomagnetic field was 86 nanoTesla, practically non-existent on a scale with terrestrial maxima of 25,000–65,000. No amount of tapping would have budged a compass needle. It was 12.24 pm local meridian time, 6 January 1986, and the South Magnetic Pole appeared to be 11.3 kilometres distant, the ship's closest observed approach. More precision was scarcely possible: in the 2½ hours that had elapsed between two observations made earlier that day the pole had moved 33.8 kilometres, indicating an average speed of 13.9 kph.

The position assigned to the pole for 12.24 pm was 65°19.0'S and 139°18.2'E. Without observations from all directions, a goal that now eluded Hutchinson as it had Ross, Mawson and Webb, it was not possible to give a mean position for the pole. When he later reduced the observations, Barton estimated that the expected diurnal motion of a moderately disturbed day like 6 January would have made the mean position about 65°20'S and 139°10'E.[3]

Barton did not allow personal disappointment to discourage him. In 1994 he talked his friend, Larry Newitt of the Canadian Geological Survey, into allowing him to participate in a survey of the North Magnetic Pole. From a temporary observatory on Lougheed Island, north-east of Melville Island and close by the position predicted for the pole by the IGRF, they monitored its daily motion. They also measured the strength and direction of the field from eight sites to establish the point at which the average dip was 90°. This, they determined, was 78.3°N and 104.0°W, on the Noice Peninsula of Ellef Ringnes Island. The pole was moving north at 15 kilometres per year.

The motion of the magnetic poles continues to stimulate speculation about their respective destinations. The North Magnetic Pole appears to be more or less headed towards the north geographic, while the South Magnetic Pole is moving in the same direction, north, away from its geographical twin. In 1986 Barton noted that, if the South Magnetic Pole maintained its current direction and rate of progress, it would reach Adelaide in about 300 years. Mawson's home town should just about then be celebrating the quadricentenary of his birth. Larry Newitt has threatened to spoil the party by predicting that, if the energy of the dipole continues to decrease as it has in recent times, then sometime between 2370 and 2950 CE the dipole may become so unstable as to trigger a reversal of the Earth's magnetic field.[4] This may not be a sudden caber toss of the dipole but more like the Cheshire Cat's smile, in which the poles fade away to nothing in two places and materialise from nowhere in two others.

In the 1990s both magnetic poles were sought by expeditions organised by a private adventurer. His was one of the more esoteric achievements of our age of meaningless records. He used maps and satellite navigation to identify the positions of the poles and had no reliable means of observing their presence, or absence, when he got to the places indicated. In the meantime Dr Barton continued to negotiate for ship time to conduct magnetic research at the South Magnetic Pole. There was still a need. Science apart, the ever-changing positions of the dip poles continue to be of everyday importance in the charting of magnetic variation, particularly in the high latitudes. Mathematical models can be and are used to update the charts but, as changes in the field are still less than fully predictable, a regular program of physical measurement is a necessary check. So until navigators agree that they can do without the magnetic compass – still the simplest and most reliable of direction-finding instruments – or until the dip poles can be satisfactorily observed using remote sensors, it will be prudent to have someone visit from time to time. Fifteen years after failing the ANARE medical, that someone, finally, was Charlie Barton. In December 2000 he went south with a private expedition. Its 600-tonne ship, MV *Sir Hubert Wilkins* was just large and stable enough to accommodate Barton's Bird.

The few icebergs and bergy bits presented no real problems for the ship, captained by Craig Rogers, as she headed towards the IGRF-indicated position for the South Magnetic Pole. Her aluminium helipad made an admirable magnetometer mount. Although Finnish-built, steel-hulled and diesel-driven, the *Sir Hubert Wilkins* nonetheless had much in common with *Erebus* and *Terror*. Like them, she was small, ice-hardened and, with a cruising speed of ten knots, not much faster. This became a problem when Barton began taking measurements. The pole was 390 kilometres away and moving faster than the ship, across their front. A fax from Dumont d'Urville station confirmed his fears: it was a magnetically disturbed day. Barton plotted an interception but the pole was early for the appointment and, contrarily, then proceeded towards the mean position predicted for it by the IRGF model. The intended interception became a chase as the *Wilkins* was swung in behind her quarry, but the gap did not close and it appeared that the goal of actually catching the pole might elude yet another magnetician.

Then, for possibly the first time in Antarctic magnetic history, the forces of nature relented. The pole slowed and the ship began to overhaul it rapidly. At the same time, snow fell and the sea state quietened to within the tolerance of the gimbal mounts of the magnetic sensors. Barton was hugely relieved. He

Barton's Bird perches on the helipad of MV *Sir Hubert Wilkins*.

had considered that to get within five kilometres would be to 'reach' the pole. The ship closed to four. Congratulations and champagne all round, but the pole had one last surprise. By the light of midsummer's midnight sun Barton returned to his instruments for a few more measurements. At 0045 Australian Eastern Summer Time on 23 December 2000, the South Magnetic Pole was observed to be only 1.6 kilometres from the ship. The pole was then in 64°40' south and 138°00' east, 16 kilometres approximately west-south-west of the IGRF prediction. Theory had assisted observation, which in turn could refine theory. Gauss and Sabine could both rest easy.

No magnetician has made closer spot observations of either magnetic pole than Charles Barton (3 kilometres from the NMP, with Larry Newitt, on 4 May 1994, and 1.6 kilometres from the SMP on 23 December 2000). One hundred and sixty years on, Ross's ambition has been achieved. It is one more step on a long march. The scientific crusade to understand the movement of the poles as an interaction of magnetic forces continues. It will end only when the positions of the poles can be predicted with precision, for only then will the 'great and dark power' that makes them so restless be fully understood.

Appendix

Facsimile of South Polar Times *Article by Bernacchi*

The ESCHENHAGEN MAGNETIC INSTRUMENTS and the MAGNETIC VARIATIONS and DISTURBANCES they record.

It is known that the Earth acts in some respects like a magnet; indeed, it is on the attraction of this great terrestrial magnet on the needles of the mariner's compass that the utility of that instrument depends.

Although the study of Terrestrial Magnetism has been carried to such refinement and perfection we are, as yet, in ignorance of its origin. The mystery therefore which surrounds this branch of science is of a fascinating nature; more especially is this so in high latitudes near the so-called Magnetic Poles, by which we generally mean, the <u>poles</u> <u>of</u> <u>verticity</u> which are the points, one is in the Arctic and one is in the Antarctic regions, coincident with a magnetic dip of ninety degrees, and where the lines of equal magnetic variation converge to a point. We cannot hope in a short paper to give anything like a comprehensive view of the science and its various branches, but will endeavour to give some slight idea of the methods employed to measure changes that are taking place in terrestrial magnetism and the nature of these changes, omitting, as much as possible, technical terms and any mathematical formulae.

To begin with, for purposes of convenience we suppose the Earth's field to be resolved into two components, one of which is horizontal and the other vertical. In order to define each of these components, we require of course to know its <u>direction</u> and its <u>strength.</u>

In the case of the horizontal component its <u>strength</u> is called the <u>horizontal Force</u> and is generally indicated by the letter H, and its <u>direction</u> is what is called the <u>declination</u>, or in nautical cicles, the <u>variation,</u> which is simply the angle that the horizontal Force makes with the geographical meridian. This angle is usually indicated by the letter D.

The vertical component of the Earth's field is called the <u>vertical Force,</u> and is generally indicated by the letter V; its direction is along the vertical: i.e. the radius of the Earth at the point considered.

The actual strength of the Earth's field which of course is the resultant of H and V, is called the <u>Total Force.</u> The <u>dip</u> or <u>inclination</u> is the angle between the direction of the horizontal component and that of the Total Force. Hence it is evident that if we know the declination, horizontal component, and the dip we can by simple mathematical formulae deduce the

strength and direction of the Earth's field. The compass of
the navigator is but a coarse apparatus for the purpose of
scientific measurement. It has to be constructed in such a
robust fashion so as to stand the exigencies attendant on its
position on shipboard. When we desire to measure the magnetism
of the Earth with the delicacy and precision which is demanded
by the needs of science, the rough and ready compass so invaluable
to the navigator, has to be replaced by an instrument of
precision.

In most magnetic observatories, magnetised bars are
suspended so as to record with the utmost delicacy, the precise
state of terrestrial magnetism at the moment. Every precaution
is taken to render the slightest oscillations of the bar
perceptible. The details of the suspension are arranged with
great care, and in order to render movements visible, even
though they are little more than microscopic in magnitude,
a mirror is attached to the magnet, and on this mirror a
slender beam of light is projected from a lantern and the
bright spot is reflected thus to a screen. In order to
preserve a continuous exhibition of the indications of the
needle, the screen is of photographic paper and by this means
the state of the Earth's magnetism at any hour is recorded in
a form which can be preserved for subsequent reference and
comparison.

The beautiful and extremely delicate self recording
instruments or magnetographs now working at our Winter
Quarters, and which are the first photographic recording
instruments ever erected in a high polar latitude, are
a new type, recently designed by Professor Eschenhagen, the
head of the magnetic observatory at Potsdam, in Germany, these
instruments besides being extremely portable, are highly
sensitive, take up infinitely less room than the old Kew form
of magnetograph invented in 1857, are more easily adjusted and
repaired if damaged, and there is the advantage and economy of
having all three curves, D, H, and V, together with a curve
of temperature, on the same magnetogram, whilst in the old
form, three sheets on three separate drums are employed and
there is no temperature curve, the instruments therefore have
to be erected in cellars where a practically constant temp-
-erature can be kept. There is also the advantage of a quartz
fibre suspension, which is the only satisfactory unifilar
suspension yet employed.

The following is a sketch of the instruments as they are erected within the hut on shore. A is the photographic registration apparatus which previously had not been utilized outside of magnetic observatories because of the comparatively elaborate appliance required. This apparatus possesses a convenient easily transportable form; its drum revolves once either in two hours or in twenty four hours so that an hour represents a length on the curves of either twenty four cms or twenty mm. B is the declination instrument, C the horizontal force instrument, and D the vertical force instrument. They are fixed at certain focal distances from the cylindrical lens in front of the drum, and so arranged that the light from a narrow slit in the lantern E falls on the lenses of all three instruments.

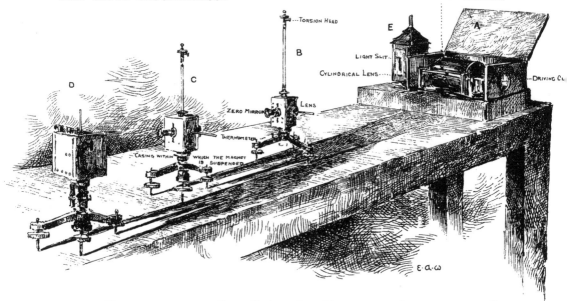

The magnets employed in the first two instruments B and C consist of well hardened laminar pieces of watch-spring steel twenty five mm long and weighing about 1.5 grammes and are attached to slender aluminium frames which also support two tiny mirrors inclined at a certain angle to each other so that the range of registration is increased twofold (magnet and frame marked F in sketch).

The frame with its magnet is then hung by means of a
double hook on a small cross piece attached to the bottom of
the exceedingly fine and fragile quartz fibre suspension. In the
case of the D instrument the magnet is of course freely suspended in the magnetic meridian, but in the H instrument
the upper end of the fibre is twisted until the magnet lies
perpendicular to the magnetic meridian (under which circumstances the Earth's field exerts a turning couple on the
magnet. If the value of the horizontal force alters, the couple
due to the magnetic forces alters also in the same proportion).
Changes in the declination will not affect the position of
the magnet since it is at right angles to the meridian.
The thinner the fibre and the greater therefore the torsion-
angle, the more sensitive is the instrument. In the V instrument
a comparatively large dipping needle or magnet is balanced
in a horizontal position and at right angles to the magnetic
meridian by means of steel pivots resting on agate planes.

If, say, the vertical force decreases, then the
downward force acting on the north pole and the upward
force acting on the south pole both decrease and hence the
north pole of the balanced magnet rises and the south pole
falls, just as when in a balance, the load of one pan is
increased and that of the other is decreased. The motions of
such a balanced magnet will therefore indicate the changes
that take place in the vertical force.

The movements of this magnet are caught by a mirror
arrangement attached to it. All three instruments have a
fixed mirror at the back, the light from which makes a straight
line on the photographic paper and from which the variations
in the curves are measured. These are therefore the base lines.

Small shutters placed in front of the light spots
tracing the base line rise at certain intervals of time and
eclipse them for a few moments, so that the accurate time of
any disturbance or variation of the curve can be immediately
seen; granted, of course, that the clock which causes these
shutters to rise, is keeping correct time.

Having once set up and adjusted the instruments and start-
-ed them recording satisfactorily, the next step is to
determine the sensitiveness of the magnets which is done by
deflecting them with another magnet of known strength placed
at various distances; then the scale values or values of
certain distances of the curve from the base line are ascertained

by taking simultaneous observations in the second hut with
instruments which give the absolute values.

As the H and V magnets are greatly affected by temper-
-ature the temperature coefficients for these magnets have
also to be determined. Any fluctuations in temperature are
recorded in the form of a curve on the photographic paper
traced by a light spot from a mirror attached to a sensitive
thermograph in the V instrument.

The value of the above three elements viz: D, H, and V
varies not alone at different points of the Earth but even at
any stated locality it undergoes continuous changes with
lapse of time. Indeed, these fluctuations are sufficiently
important to engage the attention of the mariner, who has
to observe that the difference between the magnetic pole and
the true pole must be continually corrected up to date.

Since the days of Sir James Ross the values of the
magnetic elements he observed in the Antarctic regions have
entirely changed. These values are now being determined afresh
and the self recording instruments will throw some light
upon the changes that are taking place from year to year so
that magnetic charts may be corrected up to date.

Some of these changes in the magnetic elements are regular
and others are irregular. Of the former the principal is the
(solar) diurnal variation. The amplitude of this variation
(whether in D, H, or V) alters a great deal with the season
of the year. In temperate regions the amplitude is much greater
in the summer months than it is near midwinter. This diurnal
range, depending apparently on the position of the sun, is
greater here in a high latitude than in a low latitude. In
England a freely suspended magnetic needle reaches the easterly
extreme of its range about eight in the morning and the
westerly about two in the afternoon, the total range being
about nine minutes of arc.

Here the times are nearly the same, that is, it reaches
its easterly extreme between eight and nine in the morning
and its westerly between two and three in the afternoon, but
the total range is much greater being at one time nearly
two degrees; since the sun has sunk below the horizon it is
very much less.

A second variation usually met with is termed secular. The
secular variation means the difference between the mean
values of an element for two successive years. If we look
below at the sketch of magnetic curves we see immediately
what an amazing difference exists between them. No.1 represents
typical curves taken here and No.2 typical curves of a
temperate climate, taken with the same set of instruments at
the Astronomical Observatory of Melbourne.

The diurnal variation is seen at a glance between the
points marked 2 P.M. and 8 A.M.; in the first case it is about
forty two minutes of arc and in the second about ten minutes
of arc.

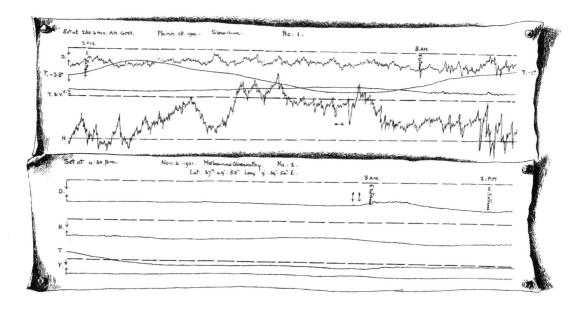

But besides the larger and more important changes the
refined observations of our delicate instruments render minute
angular displacements perceptible. The magnetic needles are
in an incessant movement of one kind or another and the
study of their minute changes or pulsations have opened up
a field of instructive information. From this point of view
the curves taken here (No.1) are perhaps unique.

It has been proved only as recently as 1900 that not only are large perturbations in the curves of a comparatively high latitude traced simultaneously on the curves in lower latitudes but even the most minute ones are shewn if the instruments are highly sensitive.

A perturbation of the nature marked by the arrow in No.1 will be shewn simultaneously at Melbourne in the form marked by arrows in No.2. There is little doubt that all the large pulsations or waves visible on the curves taken here from day to day will also be visible at the same time on curves traced at Christchurch, Melbourne, Capetown, etc. It is for the purpose of establishing these kinds of relations that an International Term Day has been agreed upon.

So called magnetic storms frequently occur in which the magnet is thrown into a state of violent oscillation by contrast with the very deliberate movements by which it is usually affected. It generally happens on the occurrence of a magnetic storm that the three elements are simultaneously affected. This proves that occasional disturbances arise from some cause or other by which the magnetic state of the Earth is thrown into a tremor. Such a magnetic storm is not merely a local phenomenon but the whole Earth is affected by its occurrence.

The same influence which makes the magnetic instruments tremble here may also affect the instruments as far away as England and Germany. So that it is plain the agent, whatever it may be, by which magnetic storms are produced, stirs our globe as a whole. The Aurora Polaris, so frequently seen in high latitudes, is seldom seen in middle latitudes, and when seen, it is the invariable accompaniment of considerable magnetic storms. Time after time a distinct connection between magnetic storms and the appearance of sun spots on the solar surface has been established. Investigations have been carried on for many years and there can be no doubt about the coincidence. Lord Kelvin, however, in 1892, when President of the Royal Society, adversely criticised the theory that terrestrial magnetic storms were directly due to magnetic waves emanating from the sun, and he shewed that, for the changes which take place during an ordinary magnetic storm to have arisen from any action within the sun, the agent must have exerted a horsepower about three hundred and sixty four times as great as that of the entire solar radiation. "Thus", says Lord Kelvin, "In about eight hours of a not very severe magnetic storm, as much work must have been done by the sun in sending magnetic waves out in all directions through space as he actually does in four months of his regular heat and light. There is a very strong resemblance between earth currents, that is, electrical currents which take place in the moist crust of the Earth, and certain movements of the magnetic needle. Earth currents are particularly strong during magnetic disturbances, and it is almost impossible to avoid the conclusion that magnetic disturbances are partly produced by terrestrial galvanic currents below the magnets.

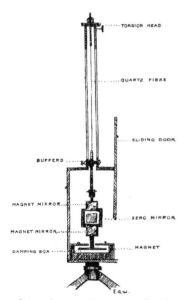

The likeness between the two systems of graphical representation is unquestionably very striking. During the few days that the Eschenhagen instruments were at the Kew Observatory some very fine photograms of earth currents were procured by winding a thin coil of wire around one of the legs of the sensitive declination instrument and connecting it with two copper plates in the earth; thus turn--ing the delicate magnet into a galvanometer. The pulsations thus pro--cured had some resemblance to the pulsations in the magnetic curves of No.1.

The magnetic needles are also subjected to a small lunar influence, and there is also what is called magnetic weather, which interferes with the regular progress of the systematic fluctuations of the magnet. There are many other interesting and little understood phenomena in connection with terrestrial magnetism and magnets.

A highly interesting phenomenon which, however, scarcely comes within the province of this paper, is the power that a magnet has to deflect cathode rays. Cathode rays are produced by sending an electrical spark through a vacuum tube of a very high degree of exhaustion.

Perhaps the study of cathode rays and kindred phenomena may some day throw light upon the origin of terrestrial magnetism and its connection with the Aurora Polaris.

LOADSTONE.

Sources

Manuscripts

David family papers, National Library of Australia Ms. 8809

Lambert, B. P., and Law, P. G., *A New Map of the Coastline of Oates Land and Eastern King George V Land*, 1959 (Law personal records)

Ross papers, Public Record Office, London (BJ 2, Australian Joint Copy Project reel 6795)

Sabine papers, Public Record Office, London (BJ 3, Australian Joint Copy Project reel 6796)

U.S. Exploring Expedition journals, Pacific Manuscripts Bureau, Canberra (New England Microfilming Project reels 146, 773, 774)

U.S. Exploring Expedition records, National Archives and Record Administration, Washington (Microfilm publication M 75)

Webb, E.N., *Magnetic Polar Journey 1912*, 1965 (Australian Antarctic Division library no. 91(*7)(08))

Books and Articles

anon., *Nouveau Voyage autour du Monde en 1838, 1839 et 1840*, Matray, Toulon, 1841

Arago, J., *Narrative of a Voyage around the World*, Treutell, London, 1823

Ayres, P. J., *Mawson: A Life*, Miegunyah Press, South Carlton, 1999

Balch, E. S., *Antarctica*, Allen, Lane & Scott, Philadelphia, 1902

Balch, E. S., Why America Should Re-Explore Wilkes Land, *Proceedings of the American Philosophical Society*, vol. 48, 1909

Barton, C. E., *et al*, Relocation of the South Magnetic Pole at Sea, 1986, *B.M.R. Record*, 1987/3

Bayliss, E. P., and Cumpston, G. S., *Handbook and Index to Accompany A Map of Antarctica*, Government Printer, Canberra, 1939

Beck, P. J., *The International Politics of Antarctica*, Croom Helm, London, 1986

Bernacchi, L. C., Preliminary Report on the Physical Observations Conducted on the National Antarctic Expedition, *Geographical Journal*, vol. 26, no. 6, December 1905

Bernacchi, L. C., *Saga of the* Discovery, Blackie & Son, London, 1938

Bernacchi, L. C., *To the South Polar Regions*, Hurst & Blackett, London, 1901

Bertrand, K. J., *Americans in Antarctica 1775–1948*, American Geographical Society, New York, 1971

Bickel, L., *This Accursed Land*, Macmillan, South Melbourne, 1977

Bixby, W., *The Forgotten Voyage of Charles Wilkes*, D. McKay, New York, 1966

Borchgrevink, C. E., *First on the Antarctic Continent*, George Newnes, London, 1901

Borthwick, D. E., Outfitting the U.S. Ex Ex, *Proceedings of the American Philosophical Society*, vol. 109, 1965

Bowden, T., *The Silence Calling*, Allen & Unwin, St. Leonards, 1997

Bruce, W. S., *Polar Exploration*, Williams & Norgate, London, 1911

Bud, R. & Warner, E. J., (ed.), *Instruments of Science*, Garland, New York, 1998

Buhler, W. K., *Gauss: A Biographical Study*, Springer-Verlag, Berlin, 1981

Bull, H. J., *The Cruise of the* Antarctic, Edward Arnold, London, 1896

Burrows, A. L., Location of the South Magnetic Pole, *N.Z. Journal of Geology and Geophysics*, vol. 6, June 1963

Bush, W. M., *Antarctica and International Law*, Oceana, London, 1982

Casey, R. G., *My Dear PM*, Australian Government Publishing Service, Canberra, 1980

Cawood, J., Terrestrial Magnetism and the Development of International Collaboration in the Early Nineteenth Century, *Annals of Science*, vol. 34, no. 6, November 1977

Cawood, J., The Magnetic Crusade: Science and Politics in Early Victorian Britain, *Isis*, vol. 70, no. 254, December 1979

Chapelle, H. I., *History of the American Sailing Navy*, Bonanza Books, New York, 1949

Clark, J. G., *Lights and Shadows of Sailor Life*, B. B. Mussey, Boston, 1848

Christie, E. W. H., *The Antarctic Problem*, Allen & Unwin, London, 1951

Christie, S. H., *Report on the State of our Knowledge respecting the Magnetism of the Earth*, Report of the 3rd Meeting of the British Association for the Advancement of Science, John Murray, London, 1834

Colvocoresses, G. M., *Four Years in the Government Exploring Expedition*, J. M. Fairchild, New York, 1855

Conklin, E. G., Connection of the American Philosophical Society with our first National Exploring Expedition, *Proceedings of the American Philosophical Society*, vol. 82, no. 5, June 1940

Cook, J., *A Voyage Towards the South Pole and Round the World*, Strahan & Cadell, London, 1777

Cook, J., *Variation of the Compass*, Royal Society, London, 1771

Cyriax, R. J., Sir James Clark Ross and the Franklin Expedition, *Polar Record*, vol. 3, no. 24, July 1942

Davenport, J., & Fogg, G. E., The invertebrate collections of the *Erebus* and *Terror* Antarctic expedition; a missed opportunity, *Polar Record*, vol. 25, no. 155, 1989

David, M. E., *Professor David*, Edward Arnold, London, 1937

Davis, J. K., *With the* Aurora *in the Antarctic*, A. Melrose, London, 1919

Dawson, E. & Newitt, L. R., The Magnetic Poles of the Earth, *Journal of Geomagnetism and Geoelectricity*, vol. 34, no. 4, 1982

Debenham, F., The *Erebus* and *Terror* at Hobart, *Polar Record*, vol. 3, no. 23, January 1942

Debenham, F., Names on the Antarctic Continent, *Geographical Journal*, vol. 81, no. 2, February 1933

de Clercq, P. R., (ed.), *Nineteenth Century Scientific Instruments*, Museum Boerhaave, Leiden, 1985

Dennett, J. F., *The Voyages and Travels of Captains Ross, Parry, Franklin and Mr Belzoni*, W. Wright, London, 1835

Drygalski, E., *The Southern Ice Continent*, Bluntisham Books, Cambridgeshire, 1989

Dumont d'Urville, J. S. C., *Voyage de la Corvette l'*Astrolabe, J.Tastu, Paris, 1830–5

Dumont d'Urville, J. S. C., *Voyage au Pole Sud et dans l'Oceanie*, Gide, Paris, 1842–54

Dunnington, G. W., *Carl Friedrich Gauss, Titan of Science*, Hafner, New York, 1955

Duperrey, L. I., *Voyage autour du Monde*, Arthur Bertrand, Paris, 1827

Enderby, C., Note on Sabrina Land &c., *Proceedings of the Royal Geographical Society*, vol. 2, 1857–8

Ennis, C. C., Magnetic Results of the United States Exploring Expedition, *Terrestrial Magnetism and Atmospheric Electricity*, vol. 39, no. 2, June 1934

Erskine, C., *Twenty Years before the Mast*, Jacobs, Philadelphia, 1896

Farr, C. C., Terrestrial Magnetism, *British, Australian & New Zealand Antarctic Expedition Reports series A, vol. 4, pt. 1*, Government Printer, Adelaide, 1944

Feipel, L. N., The Wikes Exploring Expedition: Its Progress through Half a Century 1826–76, *Proceedings of the U.S. Naval Institute*, vol. 40, no. 5, September–October 1914

Findlay, A. G., *Directory for the Pacific Ocean*, R. H. Laurie, London, 1851

Fogg, G. E., *A History of Antarctic Science*, Cambridge University Press, Cambridge, 1992

Fricker, K., *The Antarctic Regions*, Swan Sonnenschein, London, 1904

Friis, H. R., (ed.), *The Pacific Basin*, American Geographical Society, New York, 1967

Friis, H. R. & Bale, S. G., (eds.), *United States Polar Exploration*, Ohio University Press, Athens, 1970

Gilman, D. C., *The Life of James Dwight Dana*, Harper & Brothers, New York, 1899

Greely, A. W., American Discoverers of the Antarctic Continent, *National Geographic Magazine*, vol. 23, no. 3, March 1912

Gurney, A., *Below the Convergence*, Pimlico, London, 1998

Gurney, A., *The Race to the White Continent*, W. W. Norton, New York, 2000

Hall, H. R., The 'Open Door' into Antarctica: An Explanation of the Hughes Doctrine, *Polar Record*, vol. 25, no. 153, 1989

Hall, T., *Carl Friedrich Gauss*, M.I.T. Press, Cambridge, 1970

Haskell, D. C., *The United States Exploring Expedition and its Publications . . . A Bibliography*, New York Public Library, New York, 1942

Hatherton, T., (ed.), *Antarctica*, Methuen, London, 1965

Hayes, J. G., *Antarctica*, Richards Press, London, 1928

Hayes, J. G., *The Conquest of the South Pole*, T. Butterworth, London, 1932

Hayton, R. D., The Antarctic Settlement of 1959, *American Journal of International Law*, vol. 54, no. 2, April 1960

Henderson, D., *The Hidden Coasts*, Sloane, New York, 1953

Herschel, J. F. W., (ed.), *A Manual of Scientific Enquiry*, J. Murray, London, 1849

Hewson, J. B., *A History of the Practice of Navigation*, Brown, Son & Ferguson, Glasgow, 1951

Hine, A., *Magnetic Compasses and Magnetometers*, Adam Hilger, London, 1968

Hobbs, W. H., Discovery of a New Sketch of Cape Hudson in the Antarctic, *Geographical Review*, vol. 24, no. 1, January 1934

Hobbs, W. H., The Discovery of Wilkes Land, Antarctica, *Proceedings of the American Philosophical Society*, vol. 82, no. 5, June 1940

Hobbs, W. H., The Eastern Landfalls of Wilkes within the Australian Sector of the Antarctic, *Geographical Journal*, vol. 81, no. 6, June 1933

Hobbs, W. H., *An Explorer-Scientist's Pilgrimage*, J. W. Edwards, Ann Arbor, 1952

Hobbs, W. H., *Explorers of the Antarctic*, House of Field, New York, 1941

Hobbs, W. H., Wilkes Land Rediscovered, *Geographical Review*, vol. 22, no. 4, October 1932

Hudson, W. J., *Casey*, Oxford University Press, Melbourne, 1986

Humboldt, A., *Cosmos*, Henry G. Boh, London, 1849–52

Huxley, L., *Life and Letters of Sir Joseph Dalton Hooker*, John Murray, London, 1918

Hydrographic Department, *Antarctic Pilot*, H.M.S.O., London, 1930

Jacka, F. & E., *Mawson's Antarctic Diaries*, Allen & Unwin, St. Leonards, 1988

James, D. E., (ed.), *Encyclopedia of Solid Earth Geophysics*, Van Nostrand Reinhold, New York, 1989

Jenkins, J. S., *Recent Exploring Expeditions to the Pacific and the South Seas*, T. Nelson & Sons, London, 1853

Jerdan, W., *Men I Have Known*, George Routledge & Sons, London, 1866

Jones, A. G. E., John Biscoe (1794–1843), *Mariner's Mirror*, vol. 50, no. 3, August 1964

Jones, B. T., *Elements of Practical Navigation*, E. & F. N. Spon, London, 1950

Joyner, C. C., *Eagle over the Ice*, University Press of New England, Hanover, 1997

Kirwan, L. P., *A History of Polar Exploration*, W. W. Norton, New York, 1960

Knight, R. W., *Australian Antarctic Bibliography*, University of Tasmania, Hobart, 1957

Law, P. G., *Antarctic Odyssey*, Heinemann, Melbourne, 1983

Law, P. G., The Exploration of Oates Land, Antarctica, *A.N.A.R.E. Reports, series A, vol. 1*, Department of External Affairs, Melbourne, 1964

Law, P. G., The I. G. Y. in Antarctica, *Australian Journal of Science*, vol. 21, no. 9, June 1959

Law, P. G., *You Have To Be Lucky*, Kangaroo Press, Kenthurst, 1995

Le Guillou, E., *Voyage autour du Monde*, Berquet et Petion, Paris, 1843

Ley, W., *The Poles*, Time, New York, 1962

Liotard, A.-F., and Barré, M., French Antarctic Expedition 1949–52, *Polar Record*, vol. 6, no. 46, July 1953

Magill, F. N., (ed.), *Magill's Survey of Science*, Salem Press, Pasadena, 1990

Markham, A. H., *The Life of Sir Clements R. Markham*, J. Murray, London, 1917

Markham, C., The Antarctic Expeditions, *Geographical Journal*, vol. 14, no. 5, November 1899

Markham, C., *Antarctic Exploration: A Plea for a National Expedition*, Royal Geographical Society, London, 1898

Markham, C., *Antarctic Obsession*, Bluntisham Books, Aldburgh, 1986

Markham, C., *The Lands of Silence*, The University Press, Cambridge, 1921

Mawson, D., Australasian Antarctic Expedition 1911–14, *Geographical Journal*, vol. 44, no. 3, September 1914

Mawson, D., The Antarctic Cruise of the *Discovery*, *Geographical Review*, vol. 20, no. 4, October 1930

Mawson, D., The B.A.N.Z. Antarctic Research Expedition, *Geographical Journal*, vol. 80, no. 2, August 1932

Mawson, D., Geographical Narrative and Cartography, *Australasian Antarctic Expedition Scientific Reports series A, vol.1*, Government Printer, Sydney, 1942

Mawson, D., *The Home of the Blizzard*, Heinemann, London, 1915

Mawson, D., *The New Polar Province*, Royal Institution of Great Britain, London, 1933

Mawson, D., The Unveiling of Antarctica, *22nd Meeting of the Australian and NewZealand Association for the Advancement of Science*, Melbourne, 1935

Mawson, P., *Mawson of the Antarctic*, Longmans, London, 1964

Maxwell, J. C., *The Scientific Papers of J. C. Maxwell*, Cambridge University Press, Cambridge, 1890

Maxwell, J. C., *A Treatise on Electricity and Magnetism* (1891), Dover, New York, 1954

McCormick, R., *Voyages of Discovery in the Arctic and Antarctic Seas*, S. Low, Marston, Searle, & Rivington, London, 1884

McWhinnie, M. A., (ed.), *Polar Research: To the Present, and the Future*, Westview Press, Boulder, 1978

Merrill, R. T., et al, *The Magnetic Field of the Earth*, Academic Press, San Diego, 1996

Mill, H. R., A Relic of Ross, *Polar Record*, vol. 3, no. 21, January 1941

Mill, H. R., *The Siege of the South Pole*, Alston Rivers, London, 1905

Millar, T. B., (ed.), *Australian Foreign Minister: The Diaries of R. G. Casey*, London, 1972

Mitterling, P. I., *America in the Antarctic to 1840*, Univerity of Illinois Press, Urbana, 1959

Morrell, B., *A Narrative of Four Voyages to the South Sea etc.*, Harper, New York, 1832

Murray, G., (ed.), *The Antarctic Manual for the Use of the Expedition of 1901*, Royal Geographical Society, London, 1901

Murray, J., The Renewal of Antarctic Exploration, *Geographical Journal*, vol. 3, no. 1, January 1894

National Antarctic Expedition 1901–4, *Magnetic Observations*, Royal Society, London, 1909

National Antarctic Expedition 1901–4, *Physical Observations*, Royal Society, London, 1908

Neumayer, G., *Auf zum Sudpol*, Vita Deutsches Verlagshaus, Berlin, 1901

Nierenberg, W. A., (ed.), *Encyclopedia of Earth System Science*, Academic Press, San Diego, 1992

Norman, R., *The Newe Attractive* (1581), Theatrum Orbis Terrarum, Amsterdam, 1974

Oliver, R. L. et al, (ed.), *Antarctic Earth Science*, Australian Academy of Science, Canberra, 1983

Owen, R., *The Antarctic Ocean*, Museum Press, London, 1948

Palmer, J. C., *Thulia; A Tale of the Antarctic*, Samuel Colman, New York, 1843

Parasnis, D. S., *Magnetism*, Hutchinson, London, 1961

Parry, W. E., *Journal of a Voyage for the Discovery of a North-West Passage*, John Murray, London, 1821

Pearsall, A. W. H., Bomb Vessels, *Polar Record*, vol. 16, no. 105, 1973

Pillsbury, J. E., Wilkes' and D'Urville's Discoveries in Wilkes Land, *Proceedings of the U.S. Naval Institute*, vol. 36, no. 2, June 1910

Pitman, J., *Manuscripts in the Royal Scottish Museum*, (pt. 2, Diary of A. Forbes Mackay), Royal Scottish Museum, Edinburgh, 1981

Poe, E. A, *The Narrative of Arthur Gordon Pym of Nantucket* (1837), Penguin, Harmondsworth, 1975

Poesch, J., *Titian Ramsey Peale and his Journal of the Wilkes Expedition*, American Philosopical Society, Philadelphia, 1961

Price, A. G., *The Winning of Australian Antarctica*, Angus & Robertson, Sydney, 1962

Rassias, G. M., (ed.), *The Mathematical Heritage of C. F. Gauss*, World Scientific, Singapore, 1991

Rawnsley, W. F., *The Life, Diaries and Correspondence of Jane Franklin*, Erskin Macdonald, London, 1923

Rees, W. G., Polar Mirages, *Polar Record*, vol. 24, no. 50, 1988

Reynolds, J. N., *Address on the Subject of a Surveying and Exploring Expedition to the Pacific Ocean and the South Seas*, Harper & Brothers, New York, 1836

Reynolds, J. N., *Pacific and Indian Oceans*, Harper, New York, 1841

Rosenman, H., (ed), *An Account of Two Voyages to the South Seas*, Melbourne University Press, Carlton, 1987

Ross, J., *Narrative of a Second Voyage in Search of a North-West Passage*, A. W. Webster, London, 1835

Ross, J. C., *Extracts of a Despatch from . . . Van Diemen's Land, 7 April 1841*, House of Commons Accounts and Papers 1841, session 2, no. 7

Ross, J. C., *A Voyage of Discovery and Research in the Southern and Antarctic Regions*, John Murray, London, 1847

Ross, M. J., *Polar Pioneers*, McGill-Queen's University Press, Montreal, 1994

Ross, M. J., *Ross in the Antarctic*, Caedmon, Whitby, 1982

Royal Society, *Report of the Committee of Physics and Meteorology . . . relative to Observations to be made in the Antarctic Expedition and in the Magnetic Observatories*, Richard & John E. Taylor, London, 1840

Sabine, E., Contributions to Terrestrial Magnetism No. 11, *Philosophical Proceedings of the Royal Society*, vol. 158, 1868

Sabine, E., On the Phaenomena of Terrestrial Magnetism: being an Abstract of the *Magnetismus der Erde* of Professor Hansteen, *Report of the 5th Meeting of the British Association for the Advancement of Science*, John Murray, London, 1835

Sabine, E., Report on the Variations of the Magnetic Intensity observed at different Points of the Earth's Surface, *Report of the 7th Meeting of the British Association for the Advancement of Science*, John Murray, London, 1838

Savours, A., John Biscoe, Master Mariner 1794–1843, *Polar Record*, vol. 21, no. 134, 1983

Savours, A., Sir James Clark Ross 1800–1862, *Geographical Journal*, vol. 128, pt. 3, September 1962

Scott, R. F., *Scott's Last Expedition*, Smith Elder, London, 1913

Scott, R. F., *The Voyage of the* Discovery, Macmillan, London, 1905

Seureau, J., *Dumont d'Urville en Antarctique*, Publisud, Paris, 1995

Shackleton, E., *The Heart of the Antarctic*, Heinemann, London, 1909

Shackleton, E., *South*, Heinemann, London, 1919

Simpson-Housley, P., *Antarctica: Exploration, Perception and Metaphor*, Routledge, London, 1992

Smith, D. G., (ed.), *The Cambridge Encyclopedia of Earth Sciences*, Cambridge University Press, Cambridge, 1981

Stanton, W., *American Scientific Exploration 1803–1860*, American Philosophical Society, Philadelphia, 1991

Stanton, W., *The Great United States Exploring Expedition of 1838–1842*, University of California Press, Berkeley, 1975

Sullivan, W., *Assault on the Unknown*, McGraw-Hill, New York, 1961

Sullivan, W., *Quest for a Continent*, McGraw-Hill, New York, 1957

Swan, R. A., *Australia in the Antarctic*, Melbourne University Press, Parkville, 1961

Taylor, E. G. R., *The Haven-Finding Art*, Hollis & Carter, London, 1971

Thomas, D., & Jackson, D. K., *The Poe Log*, G. K. Hall, Boston, 1987

Tomlinson, C., *Winter in the Arctic Regions and Summer in the Antarctic Regions*, Society for Promoting Christian Knowledge, London, 1872

Triggs, G., *International Law and Australian Sovereignty in Antarctica*, Legal Books, Sydney, 1986

Tyler, D. B., *The Wilkes Expedition*, American Philosophical Society, Philadelphia, 1968

Verne, J., *The Great Explorers of the Nineteenth Century*, Sampson Low, Marston, Searle & Rivington, London, 1881

Verne, J., *The Exploration of the World*, Sampson Low, Marston, Searle & Rivington, London, 1879

Viola, H. J. & Margolis, C., *Magnificent Voyagers: The U.S. Exploring Expedition 1838–42*, Smithsonian Institution Press, Washington, 1985

Webb, E. N., Location of the South Magnetic Pole, *Polar Record*, vol. 18, no. 117, September 1977

Webb, E. N., The Magnetograph Hut: A Historic Scientific Laboratory of the A.A.E. 1911–14, *Polar Record*, vol. 17, no. 111, September 1975

Webb, E. N. & Chree, C., Terrestrial Magnetism, *Australasian Antarctic Expedition Scientific Reports Series B, vol. 1*, Government Printer, Sydney, 1925

Weigert, H. W., *et al*, *New Compass of the World*, Harrap, London, 1949

Whewell, W., *History of the Inductive Sciences* (1857), Cass, London, 1967

Wilkes, C., *Autobiography*, Naval History Division, Washington, 1978

Wilkes, C., *Narrative of the United States Exploring Expedition*, C. Sherman, Philadelphia, 1844

Wilkes, C., *Synopsis of the Cruise of the United States Exploring Expedition*, Peter Force, Washington, 1842

Woodward, F. J., *Portrait of Jane*, Hodder & Stoughton, London, 1951

Wright, H. S., *The Seventh Continent*, R. G. Badger, Boston, 1918

Newspapers and Journals

American Journal of International Law

A. N. A. R. E. News

Annals of the Association of American Geographers

Annals of Science

Asiatic Journal, London

Athenaeum

Australian, Sydney

Australian Journal of Science

B. M. R. Record

Bulletin de la Société Geographié

Colonial Times, Hobart

Courier, Hobart

Edinburgh Review

Eos

Fraser's Magazine, London

Geographical Journal

Geographical Review

Great Circle

Harper's New Monthly Magazine
Hobart Town Advertiser
Illustrated London News
Isis
Journal of Geomagnetism and Geoelectricity
Journal of the Royal Geographical Society
Journal of the Royal Geographical Society of Australasia
    (South Australian Branch)
Journal des Savants
Literary Gazette, London
Mariner's Mirror
National Geographic Magazine
Nature
Nautical Magazine and Naval Chronicle
New York Times
New Zealand Journal of Geology and Geophysics
North American Review
North British Review
Philosophical Transactions of the Royal Society
Polar Record
Proceedings of the American Philosophical Society
Proceedings of the Royal Geographical Society
Proceedings of the United States Naval Institute
Quarterly Review, London
Revue des Deux Mondes
Science, London
Scottish Geographical Magazine
Southern Literary Messenger, Richmond
South Polar Times
Spectator, Washington
Sydney Herald
Terrestrial Magnetism and Atmospheric Electricity
Union, Washington
Westminster Review

Glossary

absolute magnetometer, instrument for measuring magnetic **intensity** without reference to other magnetic instruments

antipodal, diametrically opposite

astrofix, position located by astronomical observation

azimuth, horizontal angle between observed line and true north

blue ice, solid, transparent ice

bomb, mortar-armed bombardment vessel

bonnet, additional section of canvas laced to the foot of a fore-and-aft sail

box off, to, bring a ship's head off the wind by hauling head sheets to windward and head yards aback

braces, gudgeons or sockets on the stern post from which the rudder hangs by **pintles**

brails, ropes for hauling up gaff sails, to spill their wind

brig, two-masted, square-rigged vessel

cable, one-tenth of a nautical mile

cache, a small, usually temporary, storage point

calamite, a type of hornblende rock, from which magnetic iron is extracted

calve, to, be split off from main body of ice

clew up, to, raise the lower corners of a square sail to prevent it drawing wind

corvette, three-masted, flush-decked warship with a single tier of guns

cruise, voyage in search of an objective the location of which is uncertain

declination, see **variation**

degree, (i) one 360th of the circumference of a circle (ii) the power to which a variable is raised

depot, to, deposit stores

dip, angle, measured vertically, between the horizontal plane and the line of the earth's magnetic field

diurnal, during a day

dolerite, coarse basaltic rock

double, to, sail around to other side

field ice, flat, frozen surface of the sea

fluxgate, detector of the magnitude and direction of the external magnetic field acting along its axis

geodesy, science of mapping and surveying the earth's surface

haul wind, to, bring ship's head nearer to the wind

heading, direction of a ship's course

hypsometer, instrument for measuring height above sea level by observing the boiling point of water, which varies with atmospheric pressure

ice barrier, impenetrable ice, specifically the seaward edge of an ice shelf or glacier, typically 30–60 metres high, presenting a flat-topped, unbroken front

ice blink, white light reflected into the atmosphere above ice

icemaster, pilot with polar experience

inclination, see **dip**

intensity, strength of the earth's magnetic field

isocline, line on a magnetic map that joins points of equal **dip**

isodyne, line on a magnetic map that joins points of equal **intensity**

isogonic, of a line on a magnetic map that joins points of equal **variation**

isomagnetic, of a line on a magnetic map that joins points where a magnetic property is the same

isostatic, of movement in the earth's crust

katabatic, of polar wind, cold air draining down slope under the influence of gravity

land blink, yellowish light reflected into the atmosphere above snow-covered ground

lead, narrow track of water traversing pack or field ice

leeward, downwind

magnetograph, instrument for recording magnetic data

magnetometer, instrument for measuring magnetic **intensity**

magnetopause, boundary of the **magnetosphere**

magnetosphere, region surrounding the earth where the solar wind is controlled by the earth's magnetic field rather than the sun's

maintack, rope attached to the windward lower corner of the mainsail

meridian (magnetic), circle on the earth's surface that passes through the north and south magnetic poles

nunatak, rock peak appearing above ice (Inuit)

order, the number of times a variable is differentiated

oscillation, motion that repeats itself, as with a **pendulum**

pack ice, 'broken floe huddled together' (Smythe's *Sailor's Word Book*)

pendulum, instrument for measuring the force of gravity by observing **oscillation** to rest

pemmican, dried and pounded meat mixed with fat

pintles, hooks on the rudder that slot into **braces** on the stern post

point, one 32nd part of a circle, 11¼ degrees

pulley-hauley, manhaul (early C20 colloquial)

quadrant, a quarter of the (Antarctic) circle's circumference

quarter, the part of a ship abaft the beam on each side

round to, to, bring ship's head to the wind

run the easting down, to, sail east with the great following winds in high southern latitudes

sag, to, drift off to **leeward**

sastrugi, wave-like snow ridges that form parallel to the prevailing wind (Russian)

schooner, two-masted fore-and-aft rigged vessel

secular, over a great period of time

semaphore telegraph, upright post with movable arms for signalling

sloop of war, three-masted warship commanded by an officer below the rank of captain

spanker, fore-and-aft sail set with boom and gaff on the aftermost mast

speak, to, close within hail of a ship for that purpose

stator, stationary electromagnetic structure in a dynamo

stem, foremost timber of a ship, which joins the bows together between keel and bowsprit

strake, single breadth of planking running the length of a ship

sun compass, device for finding true north by the direction of the sun, allowing for the time of day

sun sight, observation of the sun to obtain time or latitude

swing ship, to, take bearings of a distant object for each point of the compass, to which the ship's head is brought in turn

tabular, flat-topped

tesla, unit of magnetic flux density equal to one weber of magnetic flux per square metre

term day, day pre-arranged for simultaneous (magnetic) observations at separate locations

theodolite, instrument combining vertical circle and telescope for astronomical observation. 'By this alone, within three hours of each side of noon, the longitude, latitude and magnetic variation of a position may be determined' (Smythe's *Sailor's Word Book*)

unship, to, remove any detachable item from its normal place of use

variation, deviation of the compass needle east or west of north-south true

warp, to, move a vessel by hauling it up to a fixed object

water sky, dark and leaden appearance of the atmosphere above open water

yard, length of timber suspended horizontally from a mast to support a sail

Notes

Prologue: A Great and Dark Power

1 The dip circle was read twice at each observation, once with its face to the east and once to the west. The recorded dip was the mean of the two readings.

2 J. Ross, *Narrative of a Second Voyage in Search of a North-West Passage*, Webster, London, 1835, p. 557

3 ibid., p. 558

4 R. Norman, *The Newe Attractive*, R. Ballard, London, 1581, pp. 8–9

5 W. S. Gilbert, *The Savoy Operas*, OUP, London, 1962, vol. 1, p. 143

6 *5th Report of the British Association for the Advancement of Science*, John Murray, London, 1835, pp. 83–4

7 J. Ross, op. cit., p. 411

8 ibid., p. 555

9 *Edinburgh Review*, vol. 61, no. 124, July 1835, p.447. Brewster believed, as did many scientists of his day, that the magnetic axis intersected the geographic axis in the center of the Earth at an angle of about 11 degrees: they attributed changes in the variation of the compass to regular long-term rotation of the former around the latter.

10 Report to the Academy of Sciences, quoted in J. Arago, *Voyage Round the World*, Treutell, London, 1823, p. xiii

Chapter 1: Le Roi S'Amuse

1 H. Rosenman, *Two Voyages to the South Seas*, MUP, Carlton, 1987, vol. 1, p. xliii. J. S. C. Dumont d'Urville, *Voyage au Pole Sud et dans l'Oceanie*, Gide, Paris, 1846, vol. 10, p. 80

2 H. Rosenman, ibid., vol. 1, p. xlv

3 H. Rosenman, ibid., vol. 2, p. 323

4 H. Rosenman, ibid., vol. 2, p. 324

5 *Journal of the Royal Geographical Society*, London, 1833, p. 112

Chapter 2: America Ventures Abroad

1 J. Reynolds, *Address on the Subject of a Surveying and Exploring Expedition*, Harpers, New York, 1836, p. 97

2 ibid., p. 99

3 Horatio Hale, *North American Review*, vol. 45, no. 9, October 1837. Hale subsequently sailed with the expedition as its philologist.

4 E. A. Poe, *The Narrative of Arthur Gordon Pym* (1837), Penguin, Harmondsworth, 1975, p. 240. One of the more intriguing might-have-beens of the Ex Ex occurred the very month that *Pym* was published, when the then unemployed Poe wrote to the Secretary of the Navy to solicit 'the most unimportant clerkship in your gift – anything, by sea or land'.

5 *New York Times*, 23 September 1837

6 *New York Times*, 4 January 1838

7 *New York Times*, 31 July 1837

8 Ross papers, PRO BJ 2/5

9 *Journal of the Royal Geographical Society*, 1836, vol. 6, p. 440

10 C. Wilkes, *Autobiography*, Naval History Division, Washington, 1978, pp. 341–2

11 C. Wilkes, *Narrative of the United States Exploring Expedition*, C.Sherman, Philadelphia, 1844, vol. 1, p. xxv

12 ibid., vol. 1, p. xxvi

13 J. Cook, *A Voyage Towards the South Pole and Round the World*, Strahan and Cadell, London, 1777, p. 239

14 in C. Wilkes, *Narrative . . .* , vol. 1, p. 431

15 ibid., vol. 1, p. 434

Chapter 3: Science Conspires

1 Resolutions of the Committee of Magnetism, *Report of the Fifth Meeting of BAAS* (Dublin 1834), John Murray, London, 1835, p. 21

2 *Report of the Seventh Meeting of the BAAS* (Liverpool 1837), John Murray, London, 1838, pp. 83–4

3 W. Whewell, *History of the Inductive Sciences*, third edition, J. W. Parker, London, 1857, pt. 3, p. 48

4 7th Meeting BAAS, op. cit., p. 85

5 Ross papers, PRO BJ 2/5

6 in J. Cawood, The Magnetic Crusade etc, *Isis*, vol. 70, no. 254, December 1979, p. 508

7 ibid., p. 510

8 W. F. Rawnsley, *The Life, Diaries and Correspondence of Jane Franklin*, Erskin Macdonald, London, 1923, p. 186–7

9 W. Whewell, op. cit., p. 53

10 Royal Society, *Report on the Instructions . . . for the Scientific Expedition to the Antarctic Regions*, R. & J. E. Taylor, London, 1840, p. 7

11 quoted by J. C. Ross, *A Voyage of Discovery and Research in the Southern and Antarctic Regions*, vol. 2, appendix 10, p. 446

12 Royal Society, op. cit., p. 7

13 Royal Society, op. cit., p. 3

14 Biscoe was on 'a secret expedition to the South Pole' looking for seals for his Sydney owners. He was reported to have reached 75°S, ie. far into the Ross Sea, after leaving Balleny, but made no such extravagant claim himself. He later told d'Urville that he had reached 63°S.

15 *Journal of the Royal Geographical Society*, 1839, vol. 9, p. 529

16 Ross papers, PRO BJ 2/5

Chapter 4: Terre Adélie

1 Irrelevant – it was the French who had crossed what is now known as the International Date Line.

2 Chief Justice of Tasmania

3 H. Rosenman, *An Account of Two Voyages to the South Seas*, Melbourne University Press, Carlton, 1987, vol. 2, p. 451

4 J. S. C. Dumont d'Urville, *Voyage au Pole Sud et dans l'Oceanie*, Gide, Paris, 1841–55, vol. 10, p. 180

5 H. Rosenman, op. cit., vol. 2, p. 463

6 H. Rosenman, op. cit., vol. 2, pp. 465–6. G. Murray (ed.), *The Antarctic Manual*, Royal Geographical Society, London, 1901, p. 438

7 H. Rosenman, op. cit., vol. 2, p. 468. G. Murray, op. cit., p. 441

8 H. Rosenman, op. cit., vol. 2, p. 470. G. Murray, op. cit., p. 443–4

9 H. Rosenman, op. cit., vol. 2, pp. 471–2

10 H. Rosenman, op. cit., vol. 2, p. 477–8

11 H. Rosenman, op. cit., vol. 2, p. 474. G. Murray, op. cit., p. 448

12 G. Murray, op. cit., p. 453

13 E. Le Guillou, *Voyage Autour du Monde*, Berquet et Pétion, Paris, 1843, vol. 2, p. 198. Anon., *Nouveau Voyage autour du Monde*, Matray, Toulon, 1841, p. 201

14 G. Murray, op. cit., p. 59

15 G. Murray, op. cit., p. 461

Chapter 5: An Antarctic Continent?

1 C. Wilkes, *Narrative of the United States Exploring Expedition*, C. Sherman, Philadelphia, 1844, vol. 2, p. 275

2 ibid., p. 287

3 ibid., p. 295

4 ibid., pp. 295–6

5 NARA M75/7

6 Journal, PMB reel 774

7 Journal, PMB reel 146, f. 413

8 ibid., f. 417

9 Journal, NARA M75/7–8

10 quoted by Wilkes in his *Narrative*, vol. 2, p. 344. It will be noted that Ringgold intended only to pass astern, while d'Urville claimed to be expecting him to round up under the *Astrolabe*'s lee, the customary evolution by the windward vessel when two ships were manoeuvering to speak, and made sail accordingly. It is possible that each commander genuinely mistook the intention of the other.

11 Journal, PMB reel 773, f. 230

12 ibid., f. 239

13 Journal, NARA M75/8

Chapter 6: Marking the Territory

1 *Athenaeum*, 4 July 1840

2 H. Rosenman, *An Account of Two Voyages to the South Seas*, Melbourne University Press, Carlton, 1987, vol. 2, p. 524

3 'a small number of fur seals'

4 *Hobart Town Advertiser*, 21 February 1840. *Hobart Town Courier*, 28 February 1840

5 The distance between Piner's Bay and Termination Land.

6 Wilkes did not give longitudes here, but the Balleny Islands are 70° east of Termination Land.

7 NARA M75/6

8 The latitude was out by two degrees – the Hobart typesetter must have moved to Sydney – but the error was quickly corrected.

9 *Sydney Herald*, 13 March 1840

10 *Australian*, 14 March 1840

11 *Hobart Town Advertiser*, 17 April 1840

12 *Athenaeum*, no. 629, 16 November 1839. J. C. Ross, *Voyage of Discovery and Research*, John Murray, London, 1847, vol. 1, p. 294

13 J. C. Ross, ibid., p. 133

14 H. Rosenman, op. cit., pp. 545–6

15 *Athenaeum*, no. 662, 4 July 1840. *United Service Gazette*, 18 June 1840. Wilkes's effort to be credited with a few hours priority was as unnecessary as it was devious; d'Urville had still not corrected his calendar for the date line – his 19 January was in fact the 20th. Wilkes's calendar, correct for local time, was a day ahead of the Frenchman's.

16 C. Wilkes, *Narrative of the United States Exploring Expedition*, C. Sherman, Philadelphia, 1844, vol. 2, p. 357

17 ibid., p. 481. Wilkes placed the pole two degrees further north than d'Urville did, although their observations were, effectively, simultaneous.

18 ibid., p. 483

19 The 'Icy Barrier', as it appears on his chart, is uniform. Wilkes's *Narrative* and the other American sources indicate that sometimes it was impenetrable pack ice and sometimes ice cliff, which could have been a tabular iceberg or the seaward edge of a glacier. It should not be taken for what Ross called ice barrier, which was unbroken ice cliff.

20 Letter to the editor of the *Spectator* (Washington), 1842. PRO BJ 2/4

Chapter 7: Victoria's Land

1 Ross papers, PRO BJ 2/5

2 J. C. Ross, *Voyage of Discovery and Research*, John Murray, London 1847, vol. 1, p. 22

3 ibid., p. 91

4 ibid., p. 106

5 Ross papers, PRO BJ2/5

6 J. C. Ross, op. cit., vol. 1, p. 117

7 Diary, 20 August 1840, quoted in M. J. Ross, *Ross in the Antarctic*, Caedmon, Whitby, 1982, p. 72

8 J. C. Ross, op. cit., vol. 1, appendix 1, pp. 327–8

9 J. C. Ross, op. cit., pp. 177–8

10 ibid., p. 18

11 L. Huxley, *Life and Letters of Sir J. D. Hooker*, John Murray, London, 1918, pp. 116–7

12 J. C. Ross, op. cit., pp. 187–8

13 ibid., p. 217

14 W. J. Hooker, *Notes of the Botany of the Antarctic Voyage*, H. Bailliere, London, 1843, p. 25

15 J. C. Ross, op. cit., p. 218

16 quoted in M. J. Ross, op. cit., pp. 96–7

17 J. C. Ross, op. cit., p. 246

18 ibid., pp. 246–7

19 ibid., pp. 259–60

20 ibid., p. 265

21 Gauss had been misled by anomalous observations made years before at Hobart. He had so few observations for the Southern Hemisphere that, after having factored the Hobart readings into the calculations as his theory required, he then made a second allowance for them. His original calculation of the position of the South Magnetic Pole was far closer than his Hobart-corrected one.

Chapter 8: The Economy of Life

1 House of Commons Accounts and Papers 1841, session 2, no. 7

2 *The Times*, 12 August 1841

3 Herschel to Sabine, 11 October 1841, PRO BJ 3/26

4 Sabine papers, Royal Society, quoted in M. J. Ross, *Ross in the Antarctic*, Caedmon, Whitby, 1982, p. 111

5 PRO HO P 204

6 quoted in M. J. Ross, op. cit., pp. 111–12

7 Hudson's journal records a visit to the McLeay residence. PMB 146, ff. 451–2

8 J. C. Ross, *A Voyage of Discovery and Research*, John Murray, London, 1847, vol. 2, p. 51

9 quoted in M. J. Ross, op. cit., pp. 148–9

10 J. C. Ross, op. cit., p. 168

11 Ross to Admiralty, letter no. 343 of 4 April 1843, quoted in M. J. Ross, op. cit, p. 199

12 J. C. Ross, op. cit., pp. 217–8

13 R. McCormick, *Voyages of Discovery in the Arctic and Antarctic Seas*, Sampson Low, London, 1884, vol. 1, p. 276

14 quoted in M. J. Ross, op. cit., p. 164

15 J. C. Ross, op. cit., p. 332

16 ibid., p. 357

17 ibid., appendix 10, p. 447

18 ibid., pp. 366–7

19 Hooker to his father, 7 March 1843, quoted in M. J. Ross, op. cit., p. 203

Chapter 9: Paper Warfare

1 *Athenaeum*, no. 633, 14 December 1839, p. 948

2 C. Wilkes, *Synopsis of the Cruise of the United States Exploring Expedition*, Peter Force, Washington, 1842, p. 19

3 ibid., p. 21

4 *Athenaeum*, no. 782, 22 October 1842

5 C. Wilkes, *Defence*, p. 34, NARA M75/28

6 ibid., p. 53

7 *Bulletin de la Société Géographie*, Paris, 2nd series, vol. 19, no. 109, January 1843

8 E. Le Guillou, *Voyage Autour du Monde*, Berquet et Pétion, Paris, 1843, p. 369

9 This note had been read to the Academy of Sciences by François Arago on 13 December 1841

10 It was a common theory of the day. Wilkes believed that an intimate connection between currents and magnetic variation was 'allowed by all navigators' (U.S. Exploring Expedition, vol. XXIII, *Hydrography*, p. 19). Both d'Urville and Wilkes placed the South Magnetic Pole considerably to the west of where Ross more correctly located it. Additionally, the latitude assigned by Wilkes differed from that indicated by Ross by five degrees.

11 C. Wilkes, *Narrative of the United States Exploring Expedition*, C. Sherman, Philadelphia, 1844, vol. 2, pp. 297–8

12 ibid., p. 298. Wilkes misrepresents this as 'd'Urville's Clarie Land'. It was Adelie Land.

13 *North American Review*, vol. 61, no. 128, July 1845, pp. 71–2

14 J. S. C. Dumont d'Urville, *Voyage au Pôle Sud et dans l'Oceanie*, Paris, Gide, 1845, vol. 8, pp. 201, 220

15 ibid., pp. 251–2

16 ibid., p. 255

Chapter 10: Contradictions

1 Ross papers, PRO BJ 2/8

2 J. C. Ross, *Voyage of Discovery and Research*, John Murray, London, 1847, vol. 1, pp. 115–6

3 ibid., pp. 274–5

4 Ross papers, PRO BJ 2/4

5 J. C. Ross, op. cit., pp. 115–6

6 ibid.

7 This was not justified. See the explanation of the McLeays' statement in chapter 8.

8 J. C. Ross, op. cit., pp. 298

9 J. C. Ross, ibid., pp. 298–9

10 ibid., p. 275

11 ibid., pp. 275–6

12 Letter to the Editor, *The Union*, Washington, 12 August 1847

13 ibid.

14 HO SL 25a, quoted in M. J. Ross, *Ross in Antarctica*, Caedmon, Whitby, 1982, pp. 129–30

15 ibid.

16 *Royal Geographical Society Proceedings*, 22 February 1858, pp. 171–2

17 M. J. Ross, op. cit., p. 248

18 quoted in R. Owen, *The Fate of Franklin*, Hutchinson, London, 1978, p. 269

19 W. Jerdan, *Men I Have Known*, George Routledge, London, 1866, p. 390

20   Hooker to J. Scott Keltie, 16 November 1902, quoted in M. J. Ross, op. cit., p. 233

21   Royal Society, *Philosophical Transactions*, vol. 158, p. 384

Interlude: The Sphinx in the Ice

1   quoted in H. R. Mill, *The Siege of the South Pole*, Alston Rivers, London. 1905, p. 341

2   J. Murray, The Renewal of Antarctic Exploration, *Geographical Journal*, vol. 3, no. 1, p. 2

3   E. A. Poe, *The Narrative of Arthur Gordon Pym* (1837), Penguin, Harmondsworth, 1975, pp. 238–9

4   Probably because he had already appropriated it. The figure turns up in *Journey to the Centre of the Earth* (1864) tending a herd of mastodon far underground.

5   Verne does not say so, but its location makes this a southern extension of Victoria Land.

6   Verne appears to have taken for fact Ross's speculation about a possible passage west of the South Magnetic Pole. In his history of 'Great Explorers of the Nineteenth Century' (Sampson Low, Marston, Searle and Rivington, London, 1881) he stated that Ross had circumnavigated the pole (p. 354).

7   It could owe something to d'Urville's Monument.

8   J. Verne, *Le Sphinx des Glaces*, appended in part to Poe's *Narrative* in the Penguin edition of 1975, p. 307

9   ibid., pp. 307–8

10   ibid., p. 308

Chapter 11: Poles Apart

1   H. J. Bull, *The Cruise of the* Antarctic *to the South Polar Regions*, Edward Arnold, London, 1896, p. 233

2   L. C. Bernacchi, *To the South Polar Regions*, Hurst & Blackett, London, 1901, p. 93

3   ibid., pp. 29–31

4   in C. E. Borchgrevink, *First on the Antarctic Continent*, George Newnes, London, 1901, p. 310.

5   ibid., p. 312

6   L. C. Bernacchi, op. cit., p. 283

7   ibid., p. 218

8   ibid., p. 216

9   quoted by M. M. Raraty in his introduction to E. von Drygalski's *The Southern Ice Continent*, Bluntisham Books, Huntingdon, 1989, p. viii

10   ibid., p. 77

11   In the 1890s E. A. Reeves had theorised that the latter view was correct and in 1901 he predicted to the Royal Geographical Society that, if so, the great mass of Antarctic land would be found to lie south of Australia.

12 *Nature*, 23 May 1901

13 L. C. Bernacchi, *Saga of the Discovery*, Blackie & Son, London, 1938, p. 32. This had not been his view thirty years earlier, when he described Wood Bay as backed by 'lofty mountain ranges' which might present 'considerable difficulties'. At that time he favoured Newnes Bay, further north, as an easier route to the plateau. Either would probably have been easier than the route subsequently taken by David, Mawson and Mackay, and Newnes Bay was no further. NAE, *Physical Observations*, Royal Society, London, 1908, p. 132

14 R. F. Scott, *Voyage of the* Discovery, Scribners, New York, 1905, vol. 1, p. 171

15 ibid., pp. 280–1.

16 The antique spelling was probably an expedition pun about Bernacchi's ample girth.

17 see the Appendix, which appeared in the May 1902 issue of the *South Polar Times* (collection published by Smith Elder & Co., London, 1907)

18 ibid., vol. 2, pp. 392–3

19 ibid., vol. 2, pp. 433–4

20 NAE, op. cit., pp. 155–7

Chapter 12: Thereabouts

1 In E. Shackleton, *The Heart of the Antarctic*, Heinemann, London, 1909, vol. 2, p. 96

2 ibid., p. 149

3 ibid., p. 158

4 F. & E. Jacka (ed.), *Mawson's Antarctic Diaries*, Allen & Unwin, North Sydney, 1988, pp. 34–5

5 ibid, p. 40

6 BANZARE Reports, Government Printer, Adelaide, 1944, series A, vol. 4, pt. 1, p. 26

7 in E. Shackleton, op. cit., p. 181

8 ibid., appendix 4, p. 359

9 A. F. Mackay diary transcript, Royal Scottish Museum, Edinburgh, 1982, p. 63

10 in F. & E. Jacka, op. cit., p. 46. This passage has been cited as evidence of brutality on Mackay's part, but the matter-of-fact tone of Mawson's account – the only record – suggests that the contacts were accidental and inevitable as Mackay overran David, who must often have been slack in the traces ahead.

11 ibid., p. 46

12 T. W. E. David, in E. Shackleton, op. cit., p. 211

13 A. F. Mackay, op. cit., p. 65

14 E. Shackleton, op. cit., vol. 1, p. 348

Chapter 13: Jemima's Secret

1   P. Mawson, *Mawson of the Antarctic*, Longman, London, 1964, p. 23

2   *Geographical Journal*, vol. 37, no. 6, June 1911, p. 616. The Colonial Office, which already had oversight of quite enough useless real estate, refused him.

3   *BANZARE Reports*, Government Printer, Adelaide, 1944, series A, vol. 4, pt. 1, p. 27

4   F. & E. Jacka, Mawson's *Antarctic Diaries*, Allen & Unwin, North Sydney, 1988, p. 56

5   At the time, before he named his discovery King George V Land, Mawson described the bay as being part of Adelie Land. He may have been misled by the Hobart typesetter's error of 1840 that had placed Adelie Land's boundary at 147°E. In his subsequent writings he always quoted the (correct) French text of d'Urville's Hobart announcement, which referred to 142°E.

6   D. Mawson, *The Home of the Blizzard*, Heinemann, London, 1915, vol. 1, p. 72

7   *AAE Scientific Reports*, Government Printer, Sydney, 1942, series A, vol. 1, p. 301. Curiously, there is no mention of this event in Mawson's diary, and he nowhere gives a date more precise than March 1912 for his proclamation of the region as British territory. Furthermore, he had no authority for the act. On Christmas Day 1912 Wild performed a similar ceremony at the western base, taking possession for the King and the Commonwealth of Australia.

8   F. & E. Jacka, op. cit., p. 125

9   P. Ayres, *Mawson: A Life*, Miegunyah Press, South Carlton, 1999, p. 70. David could only accept the expertise of the New Zealanders, and later acknowledged in *Nature* 'the uncertainty of our rough determination'.

10 E. N. Webb, *Magnetic Polar Journey 1912*, Australian Antarctic Division library, Hobart, MS 91(*7)(08), 1965, p. 9

11 R. Bage in *AAE Scientific Reports*, op. cit., p. 200

12 The Lloyd-Creak circle was still in use for sea service, and indeed was used as the field instrument at Wild's western base.

13 R. Bage, op. cit., p. 207

14 ibid., pp. 206, 208

15 ibid., p. 211

16 ibid., p. 213

17 E. N. Webb, op. cit., p. 8

18 R. Bage, op. cit., p. 217

19 E. N. Webb, op. cit., p. 13

20 Sledging diary entry, 12 January 1913, in E. N. Webb, op. cit., p. 20

21 F. & E. Jacka, op. cit., p. 185

22 E. N. Webb, op. cit., p. 20

23 F. & E. Jacka, op. cit., p. 186

24 D. Mawson, *The Home of the Blizzard*, Hodder & Stoughton, London, 1930, p. 223

25 *Nature*, no. 2286, vol. 91, 21 August 1913, p. 651

Chapter 14: Frozen Frontiers

1 quoted in P. J. Ayres, *Mawson: A Life*, Miegunyah Press, South Carlton, 1999, p. 108

2 *AAE Scientific Reports*, Government Printer, Sydney, 1925, series B, vol. 1 (*Terrestrial Magnetism*), p. 52

3 ibid., pp. 54–5

4 ibid., p. 4

5 I. Bowman (ed.), *Problems of Polar Research*, American Geographical Society, New York, 1928, pp. 254–5

6 W. M. Bush (ed.), *Antarctica and International Law*, Oceana, London, 1988, vol. 3, p. 430

7 R. G. Casey, *My Dear PM*, AGPS, Canberra, 1980, p. 492

8 A. Grenfell Price, *The Winning of Australian Antarctica*, Angus & Robertson, Sydney, 1962, p. 23

9 D. Mawson, The BANZ Antarctic Research Expedition, *Geographical Journal*, vol. 80. no. 2, August 1932, p. 124

10 F. & E. Jacka, *Mawson's Antarctic Diaries*, Allen & Unwin, North Sydney, 1988, p. 310

11 *Geographical Journal*, op. cit., p. 111. Note that this was 2–7° more than he had claimed at Proclamation Island. Mawson was now overriding the adjustment he had then made to accommodate a Norwegian claim.

12 D. Mawson, *The Home of the Blizzard*, Hodder & Stoughton, London, 1930, p. 47

13 A. Grenfell Price, op. cit., p. 120

14 F. & E. Jacka, op. cit., p. 376

15 ibid., p. 378

16 A. Grenfell Price, op. cit., p. 156

17 *Geographical Journal*, op. cit., p. 122

18 ibid.

Chapter 15: 'Hazy, Indistinct and Movable'

1 W. H. Hobbs, Wilkes Land Rediscovered, *Geographical Review*, vol. 22, no. 4, October 1932, p. 634

2 E. Shackleton, *South*, Heinemann, London, 1919, p. 326

3 *Geographical Journal*, vol. 81, no. 2, February 1933, pp. 144–8

4 Too true. Hobbs himself had condemned as 'quite absurd' Ross's figure of 300 miles for the Adelie Land coast, a mistake that Ross had copied from the ubiquitous Hobart typesetter.

5 *Geographical Journal*, vol. 81, no. 6, June 1933, pp. 538–40

6 ibid.

7 *Geographical Review*, vol. 24, no. 1, January 1934, pp. 115–7

8 *Proceedings of the Royal Geographical Society of Australasia (South Australian Branch)*, vol. 34, 1934, p. 81

9 ibid., p. 93

10 ibid., p. 113

11 D. Mawson, *The New Polar Province*, Address to the Royal Institution, London, 1933, p. 7

12 D. Mawson, *The Unveiling of Antarctica*, 22nd ANZAAS Meeting, Melbourne, 1935, p. 28

13 ibid., p. 24

14 W. H. Hobbs, The Discovery of Wilkes Land, Antarctica, *Proceedings of the American Philosophical Society*, vol. 82, no. 5, June 1940, p. 575

15 Sleight of hand by Hobbs. The only land behind 'Termination Land' when approached from the east, as Wilkes did, is Drygalski Island, of inconsequential extent and 1148 feet high. The land 'behind' the shelf-ice lay far to the south, as Hobbs knew.

Chapter 16: Pax Antarctica

1 P. G. Law, *Antarctic Odyssey*, Heinemann, Melbourne, 1983, p. 14

2 quoted in T. Bowden, *The Silence Calling*, Allen & Unwin, North Sydney, 1997, p. 235

3 B. P. Lambert and P. G. Law, *A New Map of the Coastline of Oates Land and Eastern King George V Land*, 1959. Typescript copy courtesy of Phillip Law.

4 *AAE Scientific Reports*, Government Printer, Sydney, 1942, series A, vol. 1, p. 314

5 *New York Times*, 10 January 1960

6 personal interview with author, 20 March 1999

7 diary entry for 21 October 1959, in *Australian Foreign Minister*, ed. T. B. Millar, Collins, London, 1972, p. 331

Chapter 17: Vainglory

1 Hereafter, when mention is made of map and chart these are the two documents being so distinguished, although strictly the published map is also a chart.

2 One of the missed opportunities of 1840–41 was a photographic record of discoveries, which might have illuminated many a subsequent controversy, not least that over the Parry Mountains. The Ross expedition had a camera and Fox Talbot himself had instructed Surgeon McCormick in its use with sensitised paper, but the device lay undisturbed in its packing case for the entire voyage.

3 K. Fricker, *The Antarctic Regions*, Swan Sonnenschein, London, 1900, p. 211

4 *Geographical Journal*, vol. 80, no. 2, August 1932, p. 129

Epilogue: Out of Nowhere

1 *Polar Record*, vol. 17, no. 111, September 1975, pp. 694–7

2 *ANARE News*, no. 45, March 1986, pp. 5–6

3 C. E. Barton *et al*, Relocation of the South Magnetic Pole at Sea, 1986, *BMR Record*, Canberra, 3/1987

4 Already well overdue after 780,000 years. The average is every 250,000 years.

Acknowledgments

I take this opportunity to record my appreciation for the assistance I have had from many quarters. I especially valued the privilege of an interview with Phillip Law, Douglas Mawson's successor in Australian Antarctic exploration, who also found for me a copy of his 1959 review of Charles Wilkes's eastern landfalls. Dr Charles Barton generously tried to improve my understanding of magnetism only to be dragged into the narrative, for which liberty I hope he will forgive me. My friend Anne Edgeworth, Professor Edgeworth David's granddaughter, kindly arranged for me to have access to those of his papers held by the National Library of Australia. The staff of the Library's Petherick Room were always able to locate obscure texts for me on the rare occasions when their own collections were found wanting, and often went to considerable pains to get them for me. My Petherick colleagues, Dr Michael Pearson and Bernadette Hince, both deeply knowledgeable on matters Antarctic, kindly read the manuscript and made helpful suggestions, as did Pat Quilty, manager of the *Icebird* visit to the South Magnetic Pole. The librarian of the Australian Antarctic Division assisted by providing me with a copy of Eric Webb's unpublished reminiscences. Lastly, my wife Elizabeth has not only cheerfully put up with the moods of authorship but, in the role of in-house reader, has made this a clearer and more concise work than would otherwise have been the case.

Index

Page numbers in bold type indicate detailed discussion of the topics.
Page numbers in italic type indicate illustrations, including maps.

BIRLINN LTD (incorporating John Donald and Polygon) is one of Scotland's leading publishers with over four hundred titles in print. Should you wish to be put on our catalogue mailing list **contact**:

Catalogue Request
Birlinn Ltd
West Newington House
10 Newington Road
Edinburgh EH9 1QS
Scotland, UK

Tel: + 44 (0) 131 668 4371
Fax: + 44 (0) 131 668 4466
e-mail: info@birlinn.co.uk

Postage and packing is free within the UK. For overseas orders, postage and packing (airmail) will be charged at 30% of the total order value.

For more information, or to order online, visit our website at
www.birlinn.co.uk

COMPASS ROSE

The magnetic needle could be used for precise direction-finding by attaching it to a fly, or card, on which was printed a compass rose. The rose gave prominence to the cardinal points – north, south, east and west. Then came the half-cardinals – northeast, southeast, northwest and southwest – with further subdivisions down to 32 points, each named. In the nineteenth century every sailing apprentice quickly learned to 'box the compass', reciting the points in order, clockwise and counter-clockwise, from memory. That, or have his ears boxed.